THE 1998 BRITANNICA CHILDREN'S YEARBOOK

EVENTS OF 1997

Encyclopædia Britannica, Inc.

Budapest, Chicago, London, Seoul, Sydney, Taipei, Tokyo, Warsaw

17 68

Children's Publisher and Editorial Director: Stephen Lustig
Managing Editor: Louise Cameron
Editor: Jennifer Cox
Associate Editor: Barbara Carragher

Assisted by:
Lucy Baker
Andrew Bramwell
Tony Germing
Julie Ottolangui
Lesley Riley
Jim Somerville

Internal Design: Nigel Partridge
Cover Design: Trickett and Webb
Maps: Cartographic department, Encyclopædia Britannica, Inc.; Stratigraphics; John Flower

Encyclopædia Britannica, Inc.
JACOB E. SAFRA, Chairman of the Board
CONSTANTINE S. YANNIAS, Chief Executive Officer
JAMES E. GOULKA, Chief Operating Officer
PAUL HOFFMAN, Publisher

International Standard Book Number: 0 85229 248 1
International Standard Serial Number: 1097-1858
Library of Congress Catalog Card Number: 97-078121

Printed in Great Britain by BPC Wheatons Ltd., Exeter

Recollections of 1997

The pop star Elton John performing a version of his hit song "Candle in the Wind" at the funeral of Diana, Princess of Wales, in Westminster Abbey, London, on 6 September 1997. He rewrote the song as a tribute to the princess, who was a good friend of his.

It was a year of dramatic events that revealed a depth of emotion that people hardly knew they had. The world united in an outpouring of grief at the death of Diana, Princess of Wales. During her lifetime she worked to help the poor, sick, and under-privileged. And as people watched and read about scenes of human suffering all over the world, it was painful to know that they had lost someone who had the power and the personality to help a little.

The year had more than its fair share of natural disasters, from the massive volcano eruption on Montserrat that half-buried much of the island in grey ash, to tornadoes that swept across Texas, in the United States, destroying a small town. Western Europe suffered its worst flooding in 200 years, while torrential rains over northeast Africa brought floods that killed thousands and destroyed the homes and livelihoods of countless more.

Not all the tragedies were caused by the forces of nature; the horrifying massacres in Algeria and the killing of 58 tourists in Egypt sadly demonstrated the continuing horror of human violence.

1997 was the year that Hong Kong became Chinese once more, China lost Deng Xiaoping, its "paramount leader", and a dramatic rescue in Peru released 72 hostages. Scientists made some amazing announcements – one group introduced us to "Dolly", a sheep cloned from her mother, and in the United States, there was exciting news in the race to find a cure for the virus that causes AIDS.

Explorers and adventurers gave us plenty to wonder at too. Norwegian Boerge Ousland became the first man to cross the Antarctic without back-up of any kind, and British sailor Tony Bullimore survived for five days trapped under the capsized hull of his yacht.

1997 was quite a year, and all of it – the tragedy, the wonder, the humour, and the sadness – is captured in the pages of the *Britannica Children's Yearbook*.

Contents

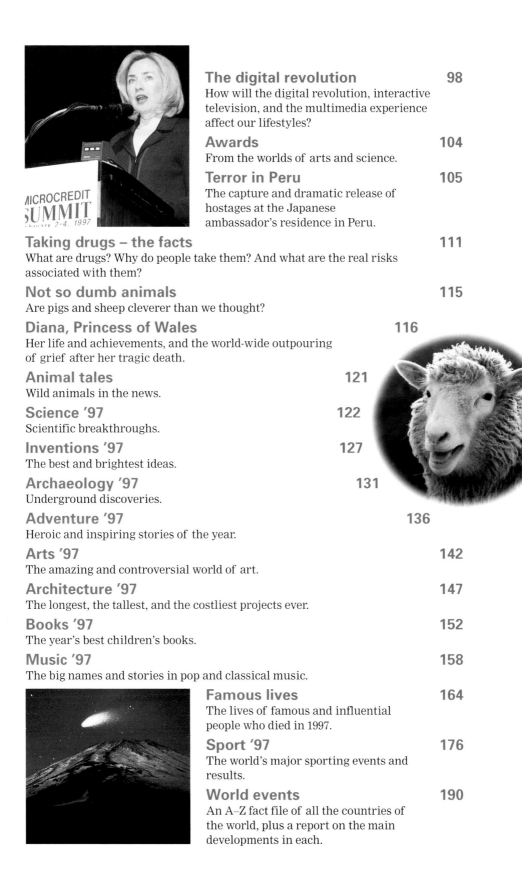

1997 in words and pictures

JANUARY

- Hundreds of thousands of **Albanians** lost their life-savings when a number of fraudulent "pyramid" investment schemes collapsed. Across Albania military police were used to stop riots and demonstrations as people demanded that the government take action to get their money back. *See article on pages 44–50.*
- Thousands of refugees from the **civil war in Sudan** fled into western districts of neighbouring Ethiopia in early January, with 15,000 more waiting to cross the border. All were suffering the effects of starvation.
- **An economic crisis in Bulgaria** reduced the country to chaos as protesters demonstrated in the streets every day, and workers went on strike against the government. With the value of the Bulgarian currency (the lev) falling sharply and inflation surging, people queued outside banks to withdraw their money, hoping to change it to dollars or marks. The lev had lost so much value that many Bulgarians bought goods such as cheap electrical equipment rather than hold on to cash.

▼ **January:** miners from the northwest region of Bulgaria join thousands of protesters demanding early elections in the country.

- **Russian politicians** tried to force President Boris Yeltsin to resign from office, claiming that poor health made him unable to carry out his duties. Yeltsin had made a good recovery from major heart surgery in November 1996, but had to return to hospital suffering from double pneumonia. He had worked for only 11 days since his re-election as president in July 1996.
- Tension grew between the **Greek and Turkish communities** in Cyprus when the Greek Cypriots revealed that they had placed an order for Russian-made anti-aircraft missiles. The government of Turkey warned that it was prepared to take military action if necessary to protect Turkish Cypriots. The United States sent a diplomat to try to ease the situation.
- After months of negotiations, the **Israelis and the Palestinians** signed an agreement over the West Bank city of Hebron. Israel withdrew its troops from much of the city, although 2,500 soldiers remained to protect Jewish settlers there.
- Beaches and harbours along a 95-kilometre stretch of the west coast of **Japan** were contaminated with oil when a Russian tanker broke in two, spilling 23 million litres of oil into the sea. Environmentalists reported that Sado Island, the habitat of the country's last crested ibis (a rare bird) had been affected by the accident.
- In **Austria,** Chancellor Franz Vranitzky resigned after more than 10 years in office, saying that he wanted to make way for a younger generation of politicians. Finance Minister Viktor Klima was appointed to succeed him.
- **Hutu extremists** began a new wave of killings in northwestern Rwanda. At least 60 people were killed, including three Spanish people who were working for the medical charity Médecins Sans Frontières. The Rwandan army retaliated, shooting at least 80 people.
- One of the biggest steel companies in **South Korea,** Hanbo, was declared bankrupt, with debts of about 5,000 billion won (£3.7 billion). Hanbo's founder, Chung Tai Soo, was arrested and charged with embezzlement and fraud.
- Boerge Ousland of Norway became the first person ever to cross **Antarctica** alone and unaided.

Ousland took 64 days to complete the 2,690-kilometre trip across the frozen continent. He used skis and a sail to allow him to take advantage of the wind, and towed a sled carrying 180 kilograms of supplies. In 1994 Ousland became the first person to reach the North Pole alone. *See article on pages 136–141.*

▲ **January:** a woman from the small town of Mikuni, on Japan's western shoreline, helps clear the oil spilled from a sunken Russian tanker in the Sea of Japan. Fishermen feared that the giant oil slick would ruin the seaweed, abalone, and shellfish cultivated in the area.

▶ **January:** Turkish warships dock at the Cypriot port of Famagusta as tensions grow between the Greek and Turkish communities in Cyprus.

• Diana, Princess of Wales, went to **Angola** to meet people who had been injured or disabled by land mines. Angola is one of the countries worst affected by land mines, with up to 15 million buried in its soil. Princess Diana's visit was designed to draw attention to the international campaign to ban these weapons, which kill more than 24,000 innocent people each year. *See article on pages 116–120.*

• The skeleton of a previously unknown species of **dinosaur,** which lived 120 million years ago, was found on the Isle of Wight, off the south coast of Britain. Scientists named the flesh-eating creature *Neovenator salerii;* they estimated that it was 7.8 metres long, with teeth as long as 5 centimetres.

• In **South Africa,** five former policemen admitted to the Truth and Reconciliation Commission that they had killed the black anti-apartheid activist Steve Biko in 1977. Biko's death while in police custody, officially described as an accident, had sparked international outrage at the South African government.

• The Australian navy rescued a British yachtsman, **Tony Bullimore,** from the icy waters of the Southern Ocean five days after his boat capsized in a storm 2,700 kilometres from the coast of Australia. Bullimore survived by lashing himself to a makeshift hammock in an air pocket in the yacht's upturned hull. *See article on pages 58–63.*

FEBRUARY

• Three major **Swiss banks** announced they were setting up a fund to compensate victims of the Holocaust, the Nazis' programme to exterminate Jews during World War II. Many Jewish people had left money in Swiss banks for safe-keeping during the war, but neither they nor their relatives had been able to retrieve it. The decision to establish a fund was taken following claims that Switzerland had profited financially from the war, and continued to hold over £3 billion of assets belonging to Holocaust victims.

• China's "paramount leader", **Deng Xiaoping,** died at the age of 92. Deng had been suffering from Parkinson's disease for some time, and had not been seen in public since early in 1994. *See article on pages 51–56; and* Famous Lives *on pages 164–175.*

• At least 300 people were killed in and around Algiers, capital of **Algeria,** by Islamic extremists trying to overthrow the government. The victims – men, women, and children – died in car bomb explosions or were brutally murdered because they did not support the guerrillas' aims.

• A late-night curfew was imposed on teenagers in Taipei, capital of **Taiwan**. The authorities threatened to close any cinema, karaoke bar, or café that served customers under the age of 18 between midnight and 5 a.m.

• **South Africa** saw its worst rioting for years when police tried to stop a demonstration in Johannesburg. At least four people were killed and

▼ **February:** Michael Hickey, one of the Bridgewater Three wrongly convicted of murdering 13-year-old Carl Bridgewater in 1978, raises his arms in celebration after being released from prison in Britain.

▲ **February:** a policeman watches as protesters dance around some burning tyres in Johannesburg, South Africa. The demonstrators are people of mixed race who feel that they have been unfairly treated by South Africa's government.

more than 200 injured. The protesters were people of mixed race who felt they were being unfairly treated compared with black people.

• At a civil trial in Santa Monica, California, in the United States, the jury found that former football star **O J Simpson** had caused the death of Ronald Goldman, a friend of his former wife Nicole Brown. Goldman's family brought the case against Simpson, and was awarded damages of $33.5 million (£21 million). Simpson had been acquitted of murder in a much-publicized criminal trial in 1996.

• The Pakistan Muslim League won an overwhelming victory in elections in **Pakistan**. President Leghari called the election after sacking Benazir Bhutto's government in November 1996, accusing it of corruption and mismanagement. The election was the fourth in nine years, and only 25 per cent of those eligible to vote actually did so.

• There were renewed calls for more controls on gun ownership in **New Zealand** after six people were killed and five seriously injured by a gunman at a ski resort on North Island. This was the fifth mass killing in the country in the 1990s.

• A huge demonstration took place in Tubize, **Belgium,** against the closure of a major steelworks, which threatened 1,800 jobs. This march took place a week after a massive protest in Brussels against the government's cuts in public spending.

• In **Britain,** three men (known as the Bridgewater

▲ **February:** a young man mourns the death of China's leader Deng Xiaoping at Tian'anmen Gate in Beijing, China.

Three) were released from prison after serving nearly 19 years for a murder they did not commit. New evidence in the case of the murder of 13-year-old Carl Bridgewater in 1978 proved that the police had forged the confessions leading to their convictions.

● Crew members from the **US Space Shuttle** *Discovery* went on a series of five spacewalks to carry out a major overhaul of the *Hubble Space Telescope.* They moved *Hubble* to a higher orbiting position above Earth, repaired tears in the insulation panels, and installed equipment that would make the telescope much more accurate. *See article on pages 40–43.*

● Scientists at the Roslin Institute in Edinburgh, Scotland, announced they had created the **first clone of an adult animal**. The Roslin team grew an embryo from a cell taken from an adult sheep and implanted it in another ewe; a few months later, she gave birth to a lamb, which they named Dolly. The experiment was hailed as a scientific breakthrough, but many people expressed concern that the technique might be used to clone humans. *See article on pages 64–70.*

● Nearly 1,000 people were killed in an earthquake in the mountainous region of **Ardabil, in northwest Iran,** and more than 2,600 were injured. This was the third earthquake to strike Iran in less than a month.

● Three months of angry street protests in **Serbia** came to an end after the government agreed to accept that the opposition coalition Zajedno had won local elections held in November 1996. One of the leaders of Zajedno, Zoran Djindjic, was elected mayor of Belgrade, the first time the city had had a non-communist government in 50 years.

MARCH

- A Jordanian soldier opened fire on a group of **Israeli schoolgirls,** who were on a field trip to the River Jordan, killing seven and wounding six others. He claimed the girls had mocked him while he was praying. After the attack, King Hussein of Jordan travelled to Israel to apologize to the families of the dead girls.
- Eight lorry-loads of food arrived in **northern Iraq,** as part of an agreement with the United Nations allowing Iraq to sell oil in order to raise money for food and medicines. The UN had banned Iraq from selling oil after the Gulf war of 1990–91.
- Voluntary euthanasia (helping people to die without pain when they are incurably ill) was made illegal again in **Australia's Northern Territory** after the federal parliament overruled the law passed by the territorial government in 1996. Although religious leaders were in favour of this change, opinion polls indicated that the public overwhelmingly supported euthanasia.
- **Papua New Guinea's** prime minister Sir Julius Chan was forced to resign when it was discovered that he had hired foreign mercenary soldiers to help defeat rebels on the island of Bougainville. Most of the mercenaries were captured by rebellious government troops, who were angry because they

had not been paid and were short of food and supplies.
- The bodies of 39 men and women were found in a mansion near **San Diego, in southern California,** in the United States. They had all apparently committed suicide. Members of the Heaven's Gate cult, they had timed their deaths to coincide with the arrival of a spaceship they believed was following the comet Hale–Bopp and would carry their souls away from Earth. *To read about Hale–Bopp see article on pages 40–43.*
- Riots, violence, and looting spread throughout **southern Albania** following the collapse of "pyramid" investment schemes earlier in the year.

▲ **March:** a local fisherman takes a closer look at Moby, a 12-metre sperm whale that became trapped in shallow water in the Firth of Forth, northeast Scotland. Despite repeated rescue attempts, the whale died after becoming beached on mud flats in the river's estuary.

◄ **March:** 39 members of the Heaven's Gate cult committed suicide at this Californian mansion (lower right). They had timed their deaths to coincide with the arrival of a spaceship that they believed was following comet Hale–Bopp.

The government declared a state of emergency as protesters took over almost all of the southern region. Tens of thousands of Albanians began to leave the country to escape the crisis. Many crossed the Adriatic Sea to Italy, which itself imposed a national state of emergency in order to cope with the refugees. *See article on pages 44–50.*

• For two weeks, a flotilla of boats and divers tried to guide a **12-metre sperm whale** out to sea after it became trapped in shallow water in the Firth of Forth, northeast Scotland. The whale, nicknamed Moby, had been heading towards breeding grounds in the Azores when it apparently became disoriented. Despite repeated rescue attempts, Moby died after becoming beached on mud flats in the estuary.

• Thousands of **car workers from France, Belgium, Spain, and Portugal** marched to the headquarters of Renault outside Paris, France, after the company announced it was closing one of its factories in Belgium, making more than 3,000 workers redundant. On the same day, in Germany, several thousand miners surrounded the government building in Bonn, objecting to proposed job cuts, while in Berlin, building workers protested that half a million people in the construction industry were without jobs.

• Research into **"human-friendly" robots** was publicized in Japan as part of the government's programme to find new ways to care for the country's increasing ageing population. A number of electronics firms is working to design a robot that can carry out routine tasks in hospitals and old people's homes, to allow nurses to devote more time to patient care.

• There were violent clashes between **Palestinians and Israeli soldiers** as builders began work on a new Jewish settlement in East Jerusalem, on land claimed by the Palestinians. Many foreign governments condemned Israel's decision to go ahead with the settlement, fearing it would damage the fragile negotiations for peace in the Middle East.

• The **Zairean army** fled from the city of Kisangani as rebel forces led by Laurent Kabila marched in. Mercenary soldiers, mostly from Serbia and Croatia and paid by the government to help fight the civil war in the country, had already escaped by plane and helicopter. People in Kisangani said they had

lived in terror of the mercenaries, who had killed and tortured innocent people.

• A French journalist, **Jean-Dominique Bauby,** who had been paralysed and unable to speak following a stroke, wrote a 130-page book using his left eyelid, the only part of his body that he could move. Bauby dictated his novel, *Le Scaphandre et le Papillon* (The Diving Suit and the Butterfly), by blinking his left eye to indicate each letter.

• The wreck of a **Spanish galleon,** with a cargo of gold and silver estimated to be worth as much as £2.5 billion, was found off the coast of Ecuador. The ship had sunk in 1654.

• Two months after being appointed to fight corruption in **Mexico's anti-drug agency,** General Jesus Gutiirrez Rebollo was himself jailed for corruption. He was found taking money from one of the country's major drug dealers.

• An attempt by 95 **IRA (Irish Republican Army)** prisoners to dig their way out of the top-security Maze prison, in Northern Ireland, was foiled when their tunnel started to collapse. A prison officer became suspicious when he noticed that the ground was beginning to subside 30 metres from the perimeter wall.

▼ **March:** residents of Kisangani, Zaire, hoist a member of Laurent Kabila's rebel forces, on to their shoulders, as they celebrate the expulsion of the much-feared Zairean army from the city.

APRIL

- One of the world's most famous horse races, the **Grand National** at Aintree in northwest England, was called off because of fears that the IRA had planted a bomb at the racecourse. Police evacuated 60,000 people and hundreds of horses from the grounds. No bomb was found, and the race went ahead two days later. The IRA carried out several more bomb hoaxes throughout the month, and planted a number of small bombs, in a campaign to disrupt life on the British mainland.
- British scientists helped to stop **Italy's Leaning Tower of Pisa** falling over by suggesting that 900 tonnes of lead should be placed on the ground on one side of its base. The famous monument has been tilting since it was built in the 12th century, because the layers of mud and clay beneath it are sinking. Experts reckoned the tower would fall down by the year 2050 unless something could be done to stop it leaning ever further over.
- Commandos stormed the **Japanese ambassador's residence in Lima, Peru,** freeing 72 people who had been held hostage there for four months by guerrillas of the left-wing Tupac Amaru Revolutionary Movement. One of the hostages died in the raid, and all of the guerrillas were killed. *See article on pages 105–110.*
- Fire swept through a city of tents on the outskirts of **Makkah, Saudi Arabia,** killing more than 200 people and injuring over 1,000 others. There were 70,000 tents at the camp, erected to house some of the two million Muslims taking part in the annual hajj (pilgrimage) to Makkah, Islam's holiest city.
- India's prime minister **H D Deve Gowda** resigned after his United Front coalition government lost a vote of confidence in parliament. Inder Kumar Gujral became the new leader, the fourth person to hold the post in 12 months.
- After walking across **Brazil** for two months, 1,500 members of the Landless People's Movement marched into the capital Brasilia to demand that the government speed up its programme of land reform. More than 25,000 people joined in the demonstration, which was one of the largest protests the government had ever faced.

▲ **April**: orphaned children eat food rations delivered by the Red Cross after an international appeal to send food to North Korea where many thousands of people were suffering from the effects of famine.

◄ **April**: Lord Gyllene ridden by Tony Dobbin passes the finishing post to win the 1997 Grand National horse race at Aintree, Liverpool, England. The race had been called off at the last minute due to an IRA bomb hoax and had to be held two days later under tight police security.

▲ **April:** after marching across Brazil for two months, members of the Landless People's Movement arrive in the capital Brasilia to demand that the Brazilian government speed up its programme of land reform.

● **The United State**s announced it was banning all new investments by US companies in Burma (Myanmar), because of the country's poor record on human rights. It was hoped that the ban would help to persuade Burma's military rulers to adopt a more democratic approach to government.

● A rocket, launched from the Canary Islands, carried the ashes of 24 people into space in the world's first **extra-terrestrial "burial"**. Gene Roddenberry, the creator of the TV series *Star Trek*, was among those who had arranged to be buried in this way. After staying in orbit for 10 years, the rocket will burn up when it re-enters the Earth's atmosphere.

● The **Chemical Weapons Convention** came into effect at the end of April, making it illegal to use, transfer, or stockpile chemical weapons. Cuba, China, and Iran are among those who have agreed to the treaty, although Russia, Libya, and Iraq have not yet signed it.

● There were celebrations in **Angola** as the two sides in the country's long-running civil war joined forces to create a new government of Unity and National Reconciliation. The war had officially ended more than two years before but relations between the two sides had not been easy. Even now, the leader of UNITA, the former rebels, refused to attend the inauguration ceremony.

● Following a fire and an explosion at a nuclear waste reprocessing plant in **Tokai, Japan,** senior officials of the nuclear industry visited every household in the town to present a letter of apology. The officials had earlier lied about the seriousness of the accident, which was the worst ever to have happened in Japan.

● The **World Food Programme** launched an international appeal to send more than one million tonnes of food, agricultural supplies, and medicines to North Korea, where the people were suffering from the effects of famine. In northern regions, villagers were surviving on a diet of straw, grass, and weeds.

MAY

• In **Zaire,** the rebel army led by Laurent Kabila forced President Mobutu to flee into exile. The military campaign to depose the dictator who had ruled the country for 32 years had taken just eight months. Kabila announced that he would be the new president, and that the country would now be known as the Democratic Republic of the Congo.

• More than 50,000 Turkish soldiers crossed the border into **northern Iraq** and attacked camps set up by the Kurdistan Workers Party (PKK). Fighter planes, helicopters, and tanks were also used in the raids, in which over a thousand people were killed. The PKK has been fighting for 13 years to establish an independent Kurdish state in Turkey.

▼ **May:** Tony Blair, Britain's new prime minister, waves to the crowd outside No.10 Downing Street, London, with his wife and three children. The Labour Party won a landslide victory in Britain's general election.

• The **Labour Party in Britain** won a landslide victory in a general election, ending 18 years of government by the Conservative Party. The size of the victory took everyone by surprise, with Labour winning 419 of the 659 seats in the House of Commons. Former prime minister John Major immediately announced he would resign as leader of the defeated Conservatives.

• One of the biggest mining frauds in history was exposed in **Indonesia.** Thousands of people had invested in a small Canadian mining company, Bre-X Minerals, after it announced the discovery of huge gold deposits in Borneo. The company's share price rocketed, then fell sharply when experts revealed that samples from the mine had been tampered with in order to boost the amount of gold they contained. In reality, there was no gold worth mining at the site.

• Voters in **Iran** elected Mohammed Khatami as their new president. The candidate favoured by the country's religious leaders had been expected to win the election, but Khatami's policies were more liberal, promising the people greater freedom in the way they live their lives.

• **New York police** arrested a Danish tourist who left her 14-month-old daughter in a pushchair outside a restaurant while she had a meal inside. Annette Sørensen spent two nights in jail for endangering her child, who was taken into care for four days. In her defence Sørensen explained that in Denmark, where there is relatively little crime, mothers often keep watch on a baby from inside a shop or restaurant.

• For the fourth time in as many months, **northern Iran** was struck by an earthquake. This was the worst quake so far, measuring 7.1 on the Richter scale, and killing at least 1,500 people, injuring 2,000 others, and leaving 50,000 homeless.

• **US-pilot Linda Finch** flew round the world to commemorate the flight attempted by pioneer aviator Amelia Earhart 60 years before. Earhart's plane vanished in the South Pacific, off the coast of Hawaii, and no trace has ever been found. Linda Finch flew the same model plane, a twin-engined Lockheed Electra, built in 1935. *See article on pages 136–141.*

• The authorities in **Vladivostok, eastern Russia,** declared a state of emergency as homes and businesses suffered power cuts lasting up to 20 hours a day. Angry miners had stopped coal being delivered to power stations because they were owed several months' wages.

• There were controversial elections in **Mali, West Africa.** President Konari was re-elected in a vote that was boycotted by virtually all other candidates. A special court annulled parliamentary elections held the previous month because a shortage of ballot papers had stopped some people from voting.

• The Japanese parliament passed a law to preserve the culture of the **Ainu people of Hokkaidu,** the most northerly of the country's four main islands. This law formally acknowledged the Ainu, for the first time, as one of Japan's native peoples.

• There was chaos in **Sierra Leone** after soldiers took power from the elected president, Ahmad Tejan Kabbah, and forced him to leave the country. The leader of the coup, Major Johnny Paul Koroma, declared himself head of state, abolished the country's constitution, and banned all political parties.

• Russia and the 16 members of the **North Atlantic Treaty Organization (NATO)** signed an important agreement to work together to ensure peace in Europe. Russia also agreed that countries with which it shares borders, such as Poland and Hungary, could join the alliance. NATO was set up in 1949 specifically to defend Western Europe against attacks by the Soviet Union.

• **Australia's prime minister, John Howard,**

▼ **May:** a woman in the east of Iran laments the loss of her home after a series of severe earthquakes that killed and injured thousands of people.

▲ **May:** a tornado moves through downtown Miami, Florida, in the United States.

apologized for the controversial policy that had forced Aboriginal families to give up their children. Between 1910 and 1970 about 100,000 children were taken from their parents and placed in orphanages or adopted by white families. Later investigations revealed that many were cruelly treated in their new homes. At the time, the authorities wanted the Aboriginal people to die out.

• A series of tornadoes swept across **Texas, in the United States,** destroying vehicles and reducing buildings to rubble. The small town of Jarrell, north of Austin, was badly hit, with more than 30 people killed. This year's tornado "season" was the worst in several decades.

JUNE

• In the United States, after a trial lasting seven weeks, **Timothy McVeigh** was sentenced to death for bombing the Alfred P Murray building in Oklahoma City in 1995. One hundred and sixty-eight people died as a result of the bomb.

• In **Afghanistan,** enemies of the Taliban, the Muslim fundamentalists in control of much of the country, joined together and forced the Taliban to withdraw from the whole of the region north of the capital Kabul.

• In a general election in **Canada,** the people voted for the Liberal Party to return to power for a second term. This was the first time in 40 years that a Liberal government had won two consecutive elections.

• At a meeting to review the **United Nations Convention on Trade in Endangered Species (CITES),** it was agreed to ease the ban on taking and selling ivory, which had been in force since 1989. Botswana, Namibia, and Zimbabwe had argued that their elephant populations had been growing steadily and the animals no longer belonged on the list of "most endangered" species. The partial lifting of the ban would allow these countries to sell live animals, as well as their stocks of ivory tusks, valued at more than £5.3 billion. Animal rights campaigners condemned the decision, fearing that the existence of Africa's elephants would once again be threatened.

• For the fourth year in a row, **Canada** came top of the Human Development Index, which measures every country's social progress in terms of its people's income, education, and life expectancy. Next on the list were France, Norway, the United States, and The Netherlands. Sierra Leone, Rwanda, and Nigeria were ranked the lowest.

• In a historic settlement, **US tobacco companies** agreed to pay a total of $368.5 billion (£231 billion) over 25 years to settle legal claims against them. The money would be used to help states cover the cost of treating people with smoking-related illnesses. The tobacco companies also agreed to launch major education programmes aimed at discouraging young people from

▲ **June:** the countdown clock in Beijing's Tian'anmen Square shows one remaining day of British rule before Hong Kong is returned to Chinese rule. Soldiers prepare seating for celebrations starting late in the evening on 30 June 1997 before the midnight handback of power.

taking up smoking, and to reduce cigarette advertising.

• **The Russian space station** *Mir* collided with an unmanned supply ship more than 300 kilometres above the Earth, damaging *Mir*'s solar panels and tearing a hole in its hull. Power cables to the space station were also cut in the accident. The three astronauts on board spent several days living in virtual darkness and with very little oxygen, until another supply ship

◀ **June:** Timothy McVeigh was sentenced to death for bombing a federal government office block in Oklahoma, United States, in April 1995 killing 168 people.

arrived with equipment to enable them to carry out repairs. *See article on pages 40–43.*

- Two-thirds of the island of **Montserrat,** in the Caribbean, was buried under ash and rubble after eruptions by the Soufriere Hills and Chance's Peak volcanoes. Over 5,000 people were evacuated to neighbouring islands, and thousands more left their homes for makeshift shelters.
- The longest trial in English legal history ended after 314 days when a judge ordered two environmental campaigners to pay the **hamburger chain McDonald's** £60,000 in damages for libel. The judge dismissed the campaigners' claims that, among other things, McDonald's caused starvation in the developing world and served unhealthy food. McDonald's was believed to have spent £10 million on taking the libel case to court.
- A new left-wing government was elected in

France, headed by the Socialist Party leader Lionel Jospin. He faces a five-year period of sharing power with the right-wing president, Jacques Chirac.

- In **Germany,** the Bundesbank (central bank) forced the government to abandon a controversial plan to increase the value of the country's reserves of gold and foreign currency. The idea was to use the money raised by the revaluation to reduce the government's debts. This would have allowed Germany to meet the terms of joining the single European currency at its planned starting date in 1999.
- After more than 150 years as a British colony, **Hong Kong** was formally handed back to the People's Republic of China. *See article on pages 78–83.*
- The military government in **Algeria** was returned to power in the country's first multiparty elections, although opposition parties claimed the results were false. It was hoped that the vote would end the civil war, in which 60,000 people have been killed since 1992, but the violence continued.

▼ **June:** Plymouth, the former capital of the island of Montserrat, is now a ghost town after eruptions from the Soufriere Hills volcano enveloped it in volcanic debris.

JULY

- **Prince Norodom Ranariddh,** one of Cambodia's joint prime ministers, was removed from power in a military coup led by the country's second prime minister, Hun Sen. Anyone thought to be a threat to the new regime was arrested, including journalists and human rights campaigners, and thousands of tourists and foreign residents fled in fear.
- Sixteen-year-old **Martina Hingis of Switzerland** won the women's lawn tennis championship at Wimbledon, becoming the youngest champion since 15-year-old Lottie Dod took the title in 1887. US-champion Pete Sampras won the men's championship for the fourth time.
- *Pathfinder,* **an unmanned spacecraft** launched by NASA, landed on Mars in the first of a series of missions to search for evidence of life on the planet.

◀ **July:** demonstrators in Barcelona, Spain, raise their hands in protest against the killing of the politician Miguel Angel Blanco by the Basque terrorist group, ETA.

The craft's robot explorer, *Sojourner,* collected new information about the climate, atmosphere, and geology of Mars. *See article on pages 40–43.*

- In elections in **Albania** the Socialist Party won a resounding victory over the ruling Democratic Party. Rexhep Mejdani became the new president. He replaced Sali Berisha, who was widely criticized for the way he handled the crisis over the "pyramid" investment fraud in which many Albanians lost their savings. *See article*

▼ **July:** members of the team controlling *Sojourner,* a robot explorer sent by NASA on board the unmanned spacecraft *Pathfinder,* celebrate as they receive "live" pictures from the planet Mars.

on pages 44–50.

• There was growing violence in **Kenya** as police broke up demonstrations by people demanding democratic reforms before the next elections. Nairobi University was closed after students rioted in protest at the government's behaviour.

• In **Spain,** the Basque terrorist group ETA murdered a young politician, Miguel Angel Blanco, after the government refused to transfer hundreds of ETA prisoners to jails in the Basque region. Hundreds of thousands of people took to the streets in protest at the killing and to demand that the terrorists end their violence.

• Italian fashion designer **Gianni Versace** was shot dead outside the gates of his villa in Miami Beach, Florida, in the United States. After carrying out a nationwide search for the suspected murderer, Andrew Cunanan, who had killed four other men, the police found his body in a houseboat not far from Versace's home. Cunanan had committed suicide as the police surrounded the boat. *See* Famous lives *on pages 164–175.*

• The IRA (Irish Republican Army) announced that it was restoring the **cease-fire in Northern Ireland,** bringing fresh hope that members of Sinn Fein, the organization's political wing, would be invited to join peace talks taking place in Belfast, Northern Ireland. Sinn Fein had been forbidden to join the talks because the IRA refused to end its terrorist activities.

• After nearly 70 years in power, **Mexico's Institutional Revolutionary Party** lost its majority in parliament. More than 70 per cent of registered voters took part in the election, which was the country's first free election in modern times.

• **Central Europe** suffered its worst flooding in 200 years as torrential rain caused the River Oder to burst its banks. Hundreds of thousands of people were evacuated from their homes, crops were ruined, and farm animals were injured. In Poland and the Czech Republic more than 100 people died in the floods. In Germany thousands of soldiers and volunteers worked frantically to repair the walls of centuries-old dykes weakened by the water.

• Two Palestinians set off powerful bombs in a crowded market in **Jerusalem** killing 13 people and injuring more than 150 others. The bombers were members of the militant Islamic organization Hamas; both men died in the explosions.

▲ **July:** a dog tries to swim to safety as flood waters rise in the streets of Uherske Hradiste in the Czech Republic.

• The former warlord Charles Taylor was voted president of **Liberia,** Africa, in the country's first-ever democratic election. Taylor had led Liberia into civil war in 1989, but now urged the people to work together to rebuild the country.

• The world's oldest plant was found in **Tasmania,** Australia's smallest state. Scientists believe the plant, called king's holly, has been growing for at least 43,000 years – 30,000 years longer than the previous record holder, an American huckleberry bush.

• **Pol Pot,** the deposed leader of Cambodia's Khmer Rouge guerrilla movement, was put on trial by his former comrades, charged with stealing party funds and executing his former security chief. Human rights campaigners called the trial a sham and demanded that Pol Pot face an international tribunal for crimes against humanity – he is accused of causing the deaths of two million people between 1975 and 1979 .

AUGUST

• In the **United States,** it was revealed that the air force had lied about the real nature of UFOs reported by members of the public, pilots, and aviation experts in the 1950s and 1960s. During this time there were hundreds of sightings of strange objects in the skies, which were repeatedly explained away as natural phenomena. In fact, the objects were top-secret, newly developed spy planes, flying at high altitudes.

• Asian nations and the International Monetary Fund promised to lend **Thailand** £10 billion to help it through an economic crisis. The Thai economy had been one of the strongest in Southeast Asia since the mid-1980s, and the crisis was affecting other currencies throughout the region.

• In **South Africa,** former president F W de Klerk announced he was resigning as head of the National Party and retiring from politics. De Klerk helped to end apartheid in South Africa, and paved the way for multiracial elections in 1994.

• There were two days of celebrations in **India and Pakistan** to mark 50 years of independence from British rule. Prayers were said in both countries in memory of the million people who were killed in 1947, when British India was divided into India and Pakistan.

• A landslide at the Thredbo ski resort, in the Snowy Mountains of **New South Wales, Australia,** engulfed

▼ **August:** schoolchildren in Bombay, India, wave flags to celebrate 50 years of independence from British colonial rule.

▲ **August:** Jeanne Calment, seen here celebrating her 122nd birthday, was believed to be the oldest person in the world. She died on 4 August 1997, at a nursing home in Arles, France.

two ski lodges, burying 20 people beneath mud and rubble. One ski instructor was found alive three days later; he had been sandwiched between two concrete slabs, which had saved him from being crushed. There were no other survivors.

• Scientists warned that this year's **El Niño,** a periodic warming of the tropical Pacific Ocean that affects weather patterns throughout the world, could be the worst on record. The current El Niño has already caused floods in Chile, Peru, and Argentina, severe drought in Australia and Indonesia, and crop failures in North and South America, as well as Africa.

• Schools in **Burma** were allowed to open for the first time since March, when they were shut because of student demonstrations against the military government. Thirty colleges and universities linked to the protests remained closed.

• The **Turkish parliament** passed a controversial bill to increase compulsory education in non-religious schools from five to eight years. The aim was to reduce the length of time secondary pupils could spend in Islamic schools, which were believed to encourage religious fanaticism. Demonstrations against the new law were held throughout the country.

• One of the biggest scandals in **British football** came to an end when a court cleared three

▲ **August:** police investigators in Paris, France, examine the wreckage of the car in which Diana, Princess of Wales, had been travelling on 31 August 1997. Her companion, Dodi Fayed, and their driver died in the crash. Diana died later in hospital.

professional soccer stars of accepting bribes to deliberately lose matches. Bruce Grobbelaar, John Fashanu, and Hans Segers were accused of conspiring with Malaysian businessman Heng Suan Lim to fix games on behalf of a gambling syndicate in Southeast Asia.

• A **Korean Airlines jumbo jet** crashed during a tropical storm while trying to land on the Pacific island of Guam. All but 32 of the 254 passengers and crew were killed.

• The world's oldest person, 122-year-old Jeanne Calment, died at the retirement home in Arles,

France, where she had lived since the age of 110. Madame Calment believed that laughter had helped her to live so long. The title of oldest living person now passes to a Danish-born American, Christian Mortensen, who is 115.

• The **island of Anjouan** declared its independence from the rest of the Comoros chain, in the Indian Ocean, saying it wanted to return to French rule, which had ended in 1975. The Comoros government sent troops to recapture the island, but the rebels defeated them.

• **Diana, Princess of Wales,** died following a road accident in Paris. Her companion, Dodi Fayed, and their driver were also killed in the crash. More than a million people laid flowers outside the royal palaces in London and queued for hours to sign books of remembrance. *See article on pages 116–120.*

SEPTEMBER

• Smoke from hundreds of **forest fires in Indonesia** spread across Southeast Asia, covering the region in a blanket of smog for several weeks. Air pollution hit record levels and tens of thousands of people were treated for breathing problems. Visibility was so poor that an airliner crashed as it was trying to land at Medan airport in Sumatra, killing all 234 passengers and crew.

• Representatives of 89 countries approved a **treaty to ban land mines,** and to increase efforts to clear mines already laid. The United States, however, refused to accept the treaty, claiming that land mines are needed to protect South Korea – where 37,000 US troops are stationed – from invasion by North Korea. Other major nations that have not yet agreed to the ban include China, India, Iran, and Iraq.

• In **India,** people of all faiths mourned the death of the Roman Catholic nun Mother Teresa, who died at the age of 87. She was given a state funeral, normally reserved for presidents and prime ministers, and was buried in the chapel of the convent she had founded in Calcutta in 1952. *See* Famous lives *on pages 164–175.*

• People in **Scotland** voted overwhelmingly in favour of the British government's plan to set up a Scottish parliament, with the power to raise or lower taxes and to make laws on local issues such as education and health. In Wales, too, the people voted in favour of a Welsh assembly, although this

▲ **September:** firefighters tackle a forest blaze in Bayung Lincir, central Sumatra. Vast areas of Southeast Asia were blanketed for weeks by a thick, choking smog caused by hundreds of raging forest fires in Indonesia.

will be much less powerful than the one planned for Scotland.

• Up to 400 people drowned when a crowded ferry sank 50 metres off the coast of **Haiti.** The ship, the *Pride of Gonave,* capsized when most of the passengers moved to one side in order to transfer to smaller boats that would take them ashore.

• Members of the **Economic Community of West African States (ECOWAS)** imposed a ban on trade with Sierra Leone, in an attempt to persuade the leaders of the military coup, which took place in May, to return power to the civilian government. ECOWAS also agreed to send a peace-keeping force, led by Nigerian troops, to the country to help enforce the sanctions.

• A gang of armed robbers held up a post office in **Zurich, Switzerland,** and stole 53 million Swiss francs (£21 million) in cash. This was believed to be the largest cash robbery in history.

• A series of earthquakes struck central **Italy,** killing ten people and causing widespread damage. The

▼ **September:** two women from the village of Ben Ali, Algeria, mourn the deaths of 64 people believed to have been massacred by Islamic fundamentalists in a dawn attack.

famous Basilica of St Francis was on the verge of collapsing, and some of its treasured frescoes (wall paintings) were destroyed.

• Emma Bonino, the European Commissioner for Humanitarian Affairs, was one of 20 Westerners who were arrested in **Kabul, Afghanistan,** for filming women in a hospital there. Photography and television have been banned in Afghanistan, under the strict Islamic law imposed by the Taliban leaders.

• Islamic fundamentalists in **Algeria** slaughtered 200 people at Bentoumi-Bentalha, a suburb of Algiers, before setting fire to their bodies and their homes. This was the second such massacre in three weeks, and it brought the total number of civilians killed in the past three months to 1,800. The Islamic Salvation Front called for an end to the violence, but this was ignored by their rivals, the Armed Islamic Group.

• **New York's Kennedy Airport** hired 13 peregrine falcons to help prevent gulls, geese, and other birds colliding with aircraft. The airport is built on the seashore and the huge flocks that feed and breed in the area, especially in autumn, present a major safety hazard. Under the scheme, falconers would patrol from dawn till dusk, and release their hawks when necessary to scare off the other birds.

• Over half a million people joined a demonstration in **Manila, capital of the Philippines,** to protest against President Ramos's attempts to remain in power. The constitution restricts a president to one term of office, lasting six years, but Ramos had announced plans to change the law so that he could stand for election again.

• Priceless drawings, including works by **Albrecht Durer and Rembrandt,** stolen from Germany at the end of World War II, were recovered in a New York hotel after a Japanese businessman tried to sell them to pay for a kidney transplant.

• Two British nurses working in **Saudi Arabia** were convicted of the murder of an Australian colleague, Yvonne Gifford. One nurse, Deborah Parry, was expected to have been sentenced to death, although it seemed likely that her life would be spared after the murdered woman's brother agreed to waive the death penalty in return for a payment of £700,000.

▼ **September:** mourners line the streets of Calcutta, India, as Mother Teresa's funeral cortège passes by.

OCTOBER

• Fossilized footprints made by a lizard-like animal 385 million years ago were discovered on **Valentia Island, off County Kerry,** in southwest Ireland. These are the oldest footprints ever found in the northern hemisphere.

• The **Israeli government** pardoned and released Sheikh Ahmed Yassin, spiritual leader of Hamas, the militant Islamic group, from a life sentence imposed eight years earlier for terrorist offences. The sheikh was flown to Jordan, and exchanged for two Israeli undercover agents who had been caught in an attempt to assassinate a senior Hamas leader in Jordan the week before.

▼ **October:** a Parisian cyclist wears a mask as protection from the heavy smog that covered Paris, France, in early October. It was caused partially by exhaust fumes from cars, and the government tried to reduce the pollution by allowing only vehicles with even-numbered plates to be used one day, and only odd-numbered ones the next.

• Smog blanketed **Paris, France,** for a week because of a combination of weather conditions, industrial pollution, and exhaust fumes from cars. The authorities declared public transport would be free, and car traffic was cut by half by banning vehicles with even-numbered licence plates on one day, and those with odd-numbered plates the next.

• **Charlie Nobbs, aged 11,** became the youngest person ever to address a party political conference in the UK. He told Labour delegates how a government-sponsored summer school had dramatically improved his reading skills.

• **Japanese sumo wrestlers,** renowned for their size, were told to start slimming by their professional association. The wrestlers use their immense weight to knock opponents out of the ring, but some had become too fat to compete. The average wrestler in the top division weighed a record 149.5 kilograms, with the heaviest at 273 kilograms.

• **British-born American astronaut Michael Foale** returned to Earth after living through four and a half months of crisis aboard the Russian space station *Mir. See article on pages 40–43.*

• Scientists based in **San Diego, California, United States,** reported that they had developed a technique to grow human organs in the laboratory. The team had already produced human skin, and was now growing ligaments, cartilage, and bone. The method promises to make skin-grafting and transplant operations quicker, cheaper, and safer.

• **Italian prime minister Romano Prodi** resigned after 17 months in office when the Communist Refoundation Party refused to back his plan to cut pensions in 1998. It seemed an election might have to be called, but the communists relented after Prodi promised that, by the year 2001, the working week would be cut to 35 hours.

• **Che Guevara,** one of the leaders of the Cuban revolution of 1959, was given a state funeral in Santa Clara, Cuba, 30 years after his death. Guevara's bones had been found earlier in the year in Bolivia, where he was shot in 1967 while trying to organize a guerrilla war against the government.

• *Thrust SSC*, a British jet-powered car driven by RAF Squadron Leader Andy Green, broke all previous land speed records, including passing the sound barrier. *See article on pages 90–91.*

• Astronomers at the **University of California at Los**

▶ **October:** Hawaiian-born Konishiki was the heaviest sumo wrestler in the sport. He retired a few weeks after sumo wrestlers were told by their professional association to slim down.

Angeles, United States, announced the discovery of the brightest star in the Milky Way, and possibly in the Universe. Named the Pistol Star because of the shape of the gas cloud surrounding it, it is 10 million times brighter than our Sun, but is hidden from our view by a dense cloud of interstellar dust. It was detected by the infra-red camera on board the *Hubble Space Telescope*. The star is 25,000 light years from Earth at the heart of the Milky Way. *See article on pages 40–43.*

• King Juan Carlos of Spain opened the **Guggenheim Museum of Art in Bilbao**. The museum itself, whose exterior features extraordinary curves and flowing lines covered in burnished titanium, was hailed as one of the great buildings of the 20th century. The works on display – all from the 20th century – include a sculpture of a Yorkshire terrier puppy, 12 metres high, entirely covered by 70,000 pansies.

• Four months of civil war in the **Congo** ended in victory for the forces of General Denis Sassou-Nguesso, the country's former dictator, who returned to be sworn in as the new president. Sassou-Nguesso had led a rebellion against the government of the elected president, Pascal Lissouba.

• **Papua New Guinea** suffered its worst drought in 50 years as the El Niño weather pattern in the Pacific delayed the seasonal monsoon rains. Crops failed, and more than 400 people were reported to have died of malnutrition. Australia increased its aid to the stricken country in response.

• After talks with representatives of West African governments, **Sierra Leone's military leaders** agreed to a cease-fire in the country's civil war, and to restore Ahmed Tejan Kabbah as president by April 1998. Those who ousted the president in May would not be tried for their part in the coup.

▼ **October:** people from Lake Murray Station Province, in the west of Papua New Guinea, carry sacks of emergency food supplies back to their village. A severe drought caused a disastrous food harvest, and hundreds of people died of malnutrition.

NOVEMBER

• **The United States and the United Kingdom** sent extra warships and aircraft to the Persian Gulf when Iraq refused to allow three US members of a United Nations (UN) team to enter the country. The UN group was searching the country for nuclear, biological, and chemical weapons. After some weeks on the brink of war, Iraq backed down and agreed to allow the UN inspectors, including those from the United States, to continue with their work. There were fears that by then Iraq had taken the opportunity to hide any weapons it possessed.

• **Louise Woodward,** an 18-year-old British nanny working in the United States, was found guilty by a Massachusetts jury of murdering eight-month-old Matthew Eappen in February. The judge overturned the jury's verdict, but declared Louise guilty of manslaughter and sentenced her to 279 days in jail –

▼ **November:** a US S-3 Viking lands alongside F-14 fighter planes aboard the huge aircraft carrier USS *Nimitz* in the Persian Gulf. The United States and the United Kingdom sent extra warships and aircraft to the area as relations with Iraq became very strained.

the amount of time she had already spent in custody awaiting trial. She would also have to remain in Massachusetts while prosecution lawyers prepared an appeal against the sentence, which was due to be heard early in 1998.

• **French lorry drivers** went on strike over pay, and blockaded 200 ports and border crossings around the country. Road transport of goods across Europe ground to a halt during the week-long action, and governments demanded compensation from France for the loss of trade.

• In the **United Kingdom,** the Labour government proposed a ban on all tobacco advertising, except for that in Formula 1 motor racing. It was then revealed that Bernie Ecclestone, the promoter of Formula 1 racing, had given £1 million to the Labour Party election fund. After taking expert advice, Prime Minister Tony Blair announced that the money would be returned. The government later agreed a compromise in which tobacco advertising would be phased out of Formula 1 over a period of eight years.

• Jenny Shipley became **New Zealand's** first-ever

woman prime minister after challenging the leadership of premier Jim Bolger while he was away at the Commonwealth conference in Scotland. Bolger resigned rather than contest the issue.

• Torrential rains in **Somalia, Ethiopia, and Kenya** brought massive floods and killed more than 1,400 people in Somalia alone. Crops, livestock, and bridges in the region were destroyed, and in Kenya three refugee camps were washed out when the River Tana burst its banks.

• The first oil was pumped from offshore oilfields under the **Caspian Sea.** Controlled by Azerbaijan, the oilfields are believed to be the largest outside the Middle East.

• The German luxury car manufacturer **Mercedes** recalled all 2,600 A Class cars it had sold after it was found that the newly launched model tipped over when drivers tried to dodge obstacles, even at low speeds.

• **Queen Elizabeth II and Prince Philip** of the United Kingdom celebrated their 50th wedding anniversary. A walkabout in London and "people's lunch" with Prime Minister Tony Blair and other distinguished citizens was followed by an evening ball at Windsor Castle, attended by seven kings, ten queens, 26 princes, and 27 princesses.

• More than 500 people died, 3,600 were counted missing, and thousands more were made homeless when Typhoon Linda struck **Vietnam.** With winds reaching 100 kilometres per hour, the storm was the worst to hit Vietnam since 1904.

• In **Egypt,** 68 people died when members of the anti-government Islamic Group opened fire on visitors to Queen Hatshepsut's Temple near Luxor. Of those who died, 58 were foreign tourists, 25 of them from

▲ **November:** a Vietnamese man and his daughter sit in despair after Typhoon Linda swept through their village destroying their home in the southern province of Ca Mau.

Switzerland. The terrorists were later killed in a two-hour gun battle with police.

• **Chinese engineers** diverted the course of the world's third longest river, the Yangtse. This was the first stage in constructing the Three Gorges dam, the world's largest, which will be 2 kilometres long and 185 metres high. It will create a reservoir containing 22.5 million cubic metres of water covering nearly 650 square kilometres. More than a million people now living there will have to leave their homes.

• The governments of **Russia and Japan** agreed to end the state of war that has officially existed between the two countries since 1945, in the final days of World War II. A peace treaty will be signed by 2000.

▶ **November:** Louise Woodward, a British nanny working in the United States, cries as she recounts the events surrounding the death of baby Matthew Eappen. A Massachusetts jury found her guilty of his murder, but the verdict was reduced by the judge to one of manslaughter.

DECEMBER

• In **Hong Kong** more than one million chickens were slaughtered in an attempt to stop the spread of the so-called "bird flu" virus. The highly dangerous disease previously affected only birds, but in the past eight months four people had died after catching the virus, and there were fears that it could quickly spread.

• British prime minister Tony Blair held **historic talks** at 10 Downing Street with Gerry Adams, president of Sinn Fein, the political wing of the IRA. This was the first time an Irish republican leader had been to Downing Street since the partition of Ireland in 1921, when the south became an independent

▼ **December:** workers clean up Hong Kong's biggest chicken market, Cheung Sha Wan, on 30 December 1997 after all its chickens were slaughtered in an attempt to stop the spread of the killer "bird flu" virus to human beings.

republic and the north voted to stay part of the United Kingdom.

• In **South Africa,** President Nelson Mandela stepped down as leader of the ruling African National Congress, handing over power to his deputy, Thabo Mbeki. Mbeki is expected to become the country's president when Mr Mandela retires from politics in 1999.

• Hutu rebels murdered more than 300 Tutsi refugees in a camp near Gisenyi, **northern Rwanda,** confirming fears that violence was once again rising in the country. As many as half a million Tutsis were killed by Hutus in massacres in 1994.

• More than 700 children in **Japan** suffered convulsions and seizures after watching a cartoon on television. Doctors reported that the rapidly flashing red eyes of one of the cartoon characters had triggered the fits in children who suffered from light-sensitive epilepsy.

• The people of **South Korea** chose Kim Dae-jung, a former political prisoner, as their new president. This was the first time since South Korea was founded in 1948 that voters had elected a candidate who was not from the military-backed governing party.

• Representatives from 160 countries met in Kyoto, Japan, to discuss ways of halting the process of **global warming**. Ten days of difficult negotiations produced an agreement to cut world-wide emissions of damaging "greenhouse gases" by 5 per cent within 15 years. Environmental campaigners condemned the deal because it allowed countries to trade emission targets and so avoid cutting their own pollution levels.

• **Bush fires** swept across the state of New South Wales, Australia, destroying homes, burning farmland, and blanketing Sydney, the country's largest city, in smog. Six thousand firefighters tackled more than 200 blazes, and two firefighters lost their lives after being engulfed by flames.

• A court in Paris, France, convicted **Carlos the Jackal,** described as the world's most wanted terrorist, of the murder of two French secret service agents in 1975 and sentenced him to life imprisonment for the crime. Carlos is believed to have been responsible for the deaths of at least 15 people in France alone between 1975 and 1983.

• Roman Catholics in **Cuba** were allowed to

▲ **December:** firefighters deliberately light and control small blazes to create fire breaks to help prevent forest fires from reaching homes in Menai, a suburb of Sydney, Australia, on 3 December 1997.

celebrate Christmas for the first time in nearly 30 years. Officially an atheist nation (where the people don't believe in God), Cuba abandoned Christmas in 1969. President Fidel Castro restored the traditional holiday for one year only in honour of the Pope's historic visit to the island in 1998.
- Police in **Harare, Zimbabwe,** used tear gas to disperse angry crowds demonstrating against threatened tax increases, in one of the worst riots in the country's history. People were becoming increasingly unhappy with President Mugabe's government, because of rising food costs and widespread unemployment, as well as corruption. There was also strong opposition from the country's white farmers to Mugabe's plans to seize their land and give it to the black population.
- Eight hundred people – men, women, and children – were rescued at sea after their ship ran aground off the southern coast of **Italy.** Most were Kurds from Turkey and Iraq, attempting to enter Italy illegally.

◄ **December:** Thabo Mbeki (left), the new leader of the African National Congress (ANC), embraces the outgoing ANC president Nelson Mandela on 20 December 1997.

The Presidents' Summit

Oprah Winfrey was there, and so were John Travolta and Tony Bennett. Colin Powell, Nancy Reagan, President Clinton, and many ex-US presidents were there. In April 1997, Philadelphia, Pennsylvania, was filled to bursting with thousands of the most powerful and famous people in the United States. What do they all have in common? Concern about the future of America. They were in Philadelphia for the Presidents' Summit for America's Future – to try to ensure that the America of tomorrow is a better place. The Britannica Children's Yearbook asked a team of young reporters from Children's Express to go to the summit and report what happened there. In the following article words in italics are quotes from young people who attended the summit.

Philadelphia is known as the birthplace of America. It was there, in 1776, that the Declaration of Independence was signed, which marked the end of the United States as a British colony and its beginning as a free and self-governing country. Some 221 years later, it was chosen to host a summit that launched an ambitious plan to help the young of America. Groups of people representing each of the 50 North American states attended, each one including at least one person under 25. Altogether, there were 1,700 people there.

The need

The summit was chaired by retired General Colin Powell, who was the first African-American to lead the US military as Chairman of the Joint Chiefs of Staff. He believes that the greatest threat to America today comes not from foreign attack, but from young Americans who do not believe in the "American dream". The

◀ Ex-US presidents George Bush (left), and Jimmy Carter (right) were among the influential people who went to Philadelphia to support President Clinton's Summit for America's future.

▲ General Colin Powell chaired the Presidents' Summit. As the first African-American to head the US military, he is a positive role model for at-risk children, many of whom are black.

purpose of the summit was to bring America's youth together, and to put them into the spotlight. It was also geared towards community service, and giving back to those less fortunate.

"I think the purpose was definitely a noble one, but I thought it was very interesting that at a summit where children were supposed to be put first, none of the honorary chairs such as Colin Powell, or George Bush, or Bill Clinton, met with the youth delegates, and that kind of bothered me. I think it should have been more focused on children."

Many of America's young are in need. The education they receive is often lacking, and many live in poverty. There is an alarmingly high number of teenage pregnancies, and more and more young people are being arrested for violent crimes. Some are even being convicted of murder. Why? Many believe that the young people, and especially the poor, have lost their sense of purpose. They have no hopes of a better future, and care little for themselves or others. Yet other young people from similarly poor neighbourhoods do succeed. Why is it that they can make a go of it? Part of the answer is that these people do not have to go it alone. While they are growing and developing they receive help and advice, often from their families, but also from others in the community.

"We, kids, are in dire need of some help, and recognition for what we are doing. On one hand, there are some of us who are really struggling but on the other hand, there are some of us who are really making it on our own merit, and I think we really need to be acknowledged for that."

The summit's goals

So what did the summit plan to do? The summit set out five goals for the future. It wants to see every child have the following:

• An adult mentor. (The mentor may be a parent, teacher, or just a volunteer who lives near-by.)

• Safe places to go and things to do out of school hours.

▼ Teenage pregnancies are one of the growing problems among young people in the United States. Only a few have the backing of a school-age parent centre like this one in El Paso, Texas.

▲ Millions of at-risk children in the United States live in cramped and insanitary conditions. Nine children share two small rooms in this high-rise apartment block.

• Good medical care to ensure a healthy start in life.
• The chance to learn skills, both inside school and out, that will help to find a job in the future.
• The chance to do something in the community to help others.

"Supposedly, if you grow up with the on-going relationship, the safe place, healthy start, then when you get older, you will have learned that you should give back to the community. And community service teaches you something that the classroom won't, it teaches you how to treat other people, so it is almost like a course in human rights."

▼ General Colin Powell joined the clean-up crew on Germantown Avenue, a run-down area of Philadelphia that was given a face-lift as part of the summit's initiative.

Many big businesses have promised to help make the plan happen. The Timberland boot company has pledged to give each of its employees 40 paid hours each year to work in the community. Coca-Cola has promised £80 million towards improving education in poor areas, and Ronald McDonald House Charities will give £159 million towards preventing child abuse and teenage suicide. An organization called Brothers and Sisters, that provides mentors to young people, has pledged to double the number of volunteers to 100,000 by the year 2000. There are many, many more promises of help, and the summit hopes that eventually every company and individual in America will offer assistance of some kind.

Getting the work done

The weekend's activities kicked off with "A Day of Service" when everyone at the summit, including the celebrities, set to work on Germantown Avenue, a poor and neglected area of Philadelphia. They built a children's playground and cleaned and smartened the area up. The first evening included the "Taste of Philadelphia" event when more than 100 restaurants treated everyone at the summit to dinner before they watched a gala performance put on by the celebrities.

▼ The three-day summit focused on community service and the need for both young and old people to get together to improve their environment.

▶ Daniel Ornstein, a reporter from Children's Express, interviewing a Presidents' Summit delegate outside Philadelphia's Independence Hall.

"On the first day, when everyone cleared up Germantown Avenue, they were trying to make a point. Look at the poor state of the city. By clearing it up, symbolically we are going forth into a new era."

"The 'Taste of Philadelphia' was incredible, you could really see why it is called 'the city of brotherly love'. They really gave us the best of what they had. They had 100 of the nicest restaurants in Philadelphia giving out free food. It was ironic, though, with so many homeless people around the convention centre. There were so many more useful ways to use their resources."

The main event of the summit took place on the second day, on the lawn of the historic Independence Hall, the spot where the Declaration of Independence was signed over 200 years earlier. It poured with rain, but amid a sea of umbrellas, the "President's Call to Action" went ahead. One after another, celebrities and dignitaries called on Americans to sit up, take notice, and lend their support. Last to speak was President Clinton. He finished by saying "… a lot of the problems facing our children are problems of the human heart, problems that can only be solved when there is a one-to-one connection, community by community, neighbourhood by neighbourhood, street by street, home by home. The most important people are those who teach the student to read, who save the health of the infant, who give help to families when all help seems gone. The most important title today is not Senator, Vice President, General, Governor, or President. As Harry Truman reminded us so long ago, the most important title any of us will ever hold in this country is the title of citizen."

"The speeches were inspiring in the cheesy way that all speeches are inspiring. The first couple of days of the summit, and even the day afterwards, I felt like I was going to go and give food to the homeless people. But then, I forgot all about it."

While television stations and newspapers were busy getting the message out to everyone not at the summit, the state delegations were hard at work. Their task was to work together to turn the message of the summit into concrete plans of action. They met to discuss all sorts of ways to reach the summit's goals once they returned to their home states. They took part in discussions on many different subjects, from the role of youth to the role that technology has to play in America's future. Above all they looked for ways to get ordinary people, especially the young, interested and excited enough to take part. Teenagers talked of their own experiences, of how mentoring and community work had helped them.

What's next?

There was certainly abundant enthusiasm and energy at the summit, but will it really change anything?

The summit started something that will take a long time to finish. But it was a powerful start, and the people there plan to spread the summit's message in their own communities by organizing local mini-summits. But it is going to take a great deal of hard work to keep the ball rolling, to get people doing something to help the community now, before they lose interest. It's like a house. If you let it sit too long unattended, the basement leaks, the roof needs repair, and the pipes get clogged. America's youth are much the same; we have neglected our house, our young people. The summit represented an investment in our house, insurance for the future. We must do the necessary repairs.

"Ordinary folk are role models"

The most interesting and moving interview given to the Children's Express journalists wasn't with any of the celebrities attending the summit in Philadelphia. It was with two men from a small programme called "The 500 Role Models of Excellence". Created in 1994, the programme is based in the Dade County, Florida, public school system. Its basic aim is to "save at-risk teenagers by giving role models to kids who need them". What is excellent about the organization is that it meets the summit's goals: to mentor, protect, nurture, teach, and serve. While other people told us about what they were going to do, these people told us about what they'd done. The programme operates in almost all of the schools in the district; tutoring kids, taking them on field trips and, sometimes, to jails "so they can see, if you take the other road, how things will turn out".

Paul Wilson, aged 18, was helped by the programme and is now working for it. "I was what you would call a trouble-maker when I was young. My father wasn't around much to

▲ Street gangs are common in Los Angeles and rivalry between groups can lead to violent conflict. Each gang develops its own hand signals to identify its members.

mentor me so I had to depend on other people and negative images," said Paul, a student at Florida A&M University. "College was the furthest thing from my mind." The programme turned his life around. "Because of the role models project, I'm a sophomore in college with a full academic scholarship, so I know the importance of role models and mentors."

Pierre Rutledge, an adult mentor with the group, said that when his father died, his mother was left to raise Pierre on her own. "My role model is my mother. My mentor was a gentleman who's deceased now, named Dewey Knight, Jr. He happened to live directly across the street from me. I think something that is very important – and why you have programmes like this that flourish – is that role models should not be Michael Jordan or Charles Barkley. They should start at home, but if you don't have that, that's why we're here. We're fathers. We're brothers. We're uncles. Ordinary folk are role models, whether we realize it or not." Rutledge went on to say that if you're a kid living in a ghetto with a single mother, America says you're going to be a failure. "It's not true. We are able to survive."

▼ While "short-sharp-shock" tactics persuade some young people to mend their ways, the harsh regime makes others angry or depressed.

Children's Express is an independent, non-profit news service, reported by young people aged eight to eighteen, whose tape-recorded interviews, commentary, and roundtables are edited by teens and adults. For more information, visit the web site at http:// www.ce.org. Read another Children's Express article on pages 92–96.

Tiny technology

by Roland Pease, BBC World Service Science Unit

Scientists believe they may one day be able to construct machines too small to be seen – by building them out of individual atoms and molecules. If they are right, these machines will be faster, more efficient, and more useful than anything we have today. They call this futuristic dream nanotechnology (from the Greek word *nanos*, meaning "dwarf"). At nanoscale, even the full stop at the end of this sentence is enormous.

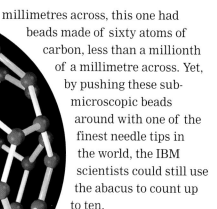

In 1996, researchers at IBM reinvented the abacus – the world's oldest form of computer. But what made this abacus different from the ones used since Babylonian times was its size. It was a million times smaller. While traditional abacuses have beads of wood or metal a few millimetres across, this one had beads made of sixty atoms of carbon, less than a millionth of a millimetre across. Yet, by pushing these sub-microscopic beads around with one of the finest needle tips in the world, the IBM scientists could still use the abacus to count up to ten.

◀ A computer graphic of the buckyball – the 60-atom carbon molecule named after US-architect Buckminster Fuller who designed geodesic domes using the same construction. The carbon atoms, arranged in five- and six-atom rings, are shown in blue, and the chemical bonds that bind them together are represented by coloured rods.

▼ The tiny mechanical devices that measure sudden changes in velocity and trigger the action of air bags in the event of a vehicle collision are just one group of micromachines that are already in everyday use.

▼ IBM nanoscientists Teresa Cuberes, James Gimzewski (project leader), and Reto Schlittler with models of their molecular abacus and the buckyball molecule that is used as the counting bead. At the same scale, the "needle" used to move the beads around would be the size of the Eiffel Tower in Paris, France.

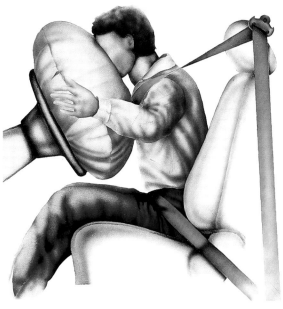

Visualizing the invisible

To give an idea of just how small nanotechnology can be, the 60-carbon-atom bead used in the IBM abacus – a football-shaped molecule called buckminsterfullerene – is just 0.7 billionths of a metre in diameter. That's 0.7 nanometre in the units used by scientists. To make the comparison clearer, think of how much smaller a grapefruit is than the whole Earth. Now shrink the grapefruit by the same amount again and you've got something the size of a buckminsterfullerene molecule (the "buckyball"). And yet scientists believe they can work with such small building materials. US-Nobel Prize winner, Professor Richard Smalley, one of the chemists who discovered buckminsterfullerene, describes nanotechnology as "a branch of architecture where the bricks are atoms, and where every atom is precisely where you want it".

The idea of working at such a small scale may seem crazy – but it should be possible because our own bodies are made up of huge numbers of micromachines. Take a muscle, for example. Every time you tighten a muscle, billions of molecular levers push against each other, each making the tiniest movement but adding up to the kind of strength that enabled Greek weightlifter Pyrros Dimas to lift 180 kilograms above his head in one continuous movement (the "snatch") to set a new world record in the 83-kilogram class. The energy to work these levers comes in the form of little molecular batteries called ATP, which get used up and recharged hundreds of times a second. There are many other miniature molecular machines working away inside our

◀ Andrei Chemerkin of Russia takes Olympic Gold at the Atlanta games in 1996 with a "clean and jerk" (two-stage lift) of 260 kilograms in the 108 kilogram heavyweight division. Such amazing feats are all down to the billions of molecular levers – nature's micromachines – that operate human muscles.

bodies, keeping us healthy and fit. The challenge for scientists is to try to copy nature.

Radical hero

The radical concept of making molecular machines was first proposed by the US-Nobel Prize winner, physicist Richard Feynman, one of the most brilliant scientists of this century. In 1959, Feynman gave a lecture with the title, "There's Plenty of Room at the Bottom". His theme was miniaturization. The entire content of the *Encyclopaedia Britannica* could be written on the head of a pin, he said. More challenging, but still conceivable, was the idea of inscribing all the books in the world in a grain of dust – by using all the atoms inside it as well as those on its surface!

At the time, Feynman's talk must have seemed bizarre. In those days, the transistors used in electronic circuits were quite new and came singly in little cases you could hold in your fingers. Circuits with more than one transistor on a slice of silicon were only just being tried. But in today's world of incredibly powerful computer chips his ideas don't shock us so easily. Why shouldn't they be

◀ Richard Feynman (1918–1988) was one of the most brilliant scientists of his age. He worked on the atomic bomb project between 1942 and 1945, shared the 1965 Nobel Prize for Physics for his work on quantum electrodynamics, and predicted the development of nanotechnology almost 40 years before it arrived.

▲ These miniature micromachine components – photographed next to the leg of a fly – are made out of silicon using similar methods to those used to make integrated circuits (computer chips). At this scale, silicon is as strong as steel, but much easier to work with.

possible? After all, the latest chips contain up to 7.5 million transistors, with connecting wires less than a thousandth of a millimetre across – 100–200 times finer than a human hair.

Micromachines

Miniaturization was created by the £530 billion world-wide electronics industry, but scientists have found that the techniques used for making electronic circuits can also be used to make minute mechanical devices. Complete motors and gear wheels can now be made on the same incredibly small scale. They are called micromachines. One example is a microscopic steam-powered turbine with blades the size of human red blood cells. One day, devices like these could be used to drive tiny electric generators – creating miniaturized power stations that could eventually replace batteries as a means of powering electronic circuits.

Although the cogs and pistons in these miniaturized machines look just like those in the "real" world, many of the engineering problems get turned upside down. The weight and inertia of the moving parts – a major problem in large machines – become insignificant at nanoscale. On the other hand,

any roughness or stickiness on the surfaces of the moving parts immediately becomes a huge problem.

However, even these micromachines are big compared with the things Richard Feynman dreamed of. To go even smaller, scientists needed a new way of making things, and the breakthrough came at IBM's research laboratories in Switzerland where two physicists, Gerd Binnig and Heinrich Rohrer, invented the scanning probe microscope – the most powerful microscope ever devised. Using the probe, scientists could see for the first time ever the individual atoms in molecules and on the surfaces of crystals. Not surprisingly, their invention of the scanning probe microscope gained Binnig and Rohrer a Nobel Prize.

Shoving atoms around

The new microscope did more than just reveal individual atoms: it also enabled the scientists to move them around. That is because it works in a completely different way from any other microscope. It uses a fine needle, moved by sensitive electronic controls, to trace over or "feel" the atoms on a sample. The tip of the

▼ Heinrich Rohrer (left) and Gerd Binnig (right) with the scanning probe microscope. The microscope opened the door to the science of nanotechnology.

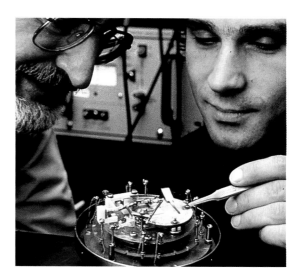

needle is just a single atom wide, and with the best controls, a scanning probe can detect variations in height even smaller than the size of an atom.

By the end of the 1980s, Binnig and Rohrer's colleagues had used the probe to write the IBM logo in atoms. They did it by pushing 35 atoms of the element xenon into place with the probe tip. This was even better than Feynman had predicted. His ideas were based on the notion of moving around little piles of a couple of hundred atoms, and here were scientists handling them one by one!

Not long afterwards, the same scientists found that they could shuttle a xenon atom back and forth between the tip of the probe and the surface beneath it. As it moved, the atom behaved like a little electrical switch that turned an electric current on and off. It was the smallest

▲ The world's smallest company logo – the initials "IBM" picked out in 35 individual atoms of xenon arranged with the tip of the world's sharpest needle.

switch in the world. Since then, scientists have also used a scanning probe tip to cut a single molecule in two. This kind of control would have been unthinkable not long ago. One possible use of such techniques would to be to build electronic circuits ten times smaller than is possible today.

Microscopic microscopes

The most amazing development in the past two years has been to combine the technologies of scanning probes and micromachines. Scientists in the United States have made miniature versions of the scanning probe microscope. They have not shrunk the probe tip itself – that could not be any smaller – but all the machinery that moves and controls the tip has been made so small you would need an ordinary microscope to see it. And that is not all. Using micromachine production methods, they expect to build hundreds or even thousands of these

scanning tips on a single silicon chip. This could open up an entirely new form of computer memory, a kind of silicon Braille in which thousands of tips, working together would build up Morse-code-like piles of atoms to record the data and then switch to microscope mode to read them back. An extension of the idea would be to make tiny chemical factories on such chips, with the probe tips moving molecules around and processing them.

Building up

Chemists are used to working with molecules of a nanometre size or smaller. It is what they do every day. And while physicists and engineers are only just learning how to handle single molecules, chemists are used to handling billions of them at a time. Chemists therefore have all the basic tools needed to build tiny mechanical devices out of molecules. However, there is a big difference between making a large lump of plastic and making a nanodevice. The degree of control involved is very much higher. So what chemists have been concentrating on is making molecules that are not only useful in themselves but that fit together automatically without needing tiny probes or any other outside help. It is called self-assembly, and it is something that all the molecules in our body do.

Josef Michl, a Hungarian working in the United States, has been developing what he calls a molecular construction kit. In the best traditions of science, it started with a mistake: a chemical reaction that produced a different result than he had expected. But when Michl realized the product was a tiny molecular rod, he saw a way to connect the rods, just as children build toys out of wooden sticks and connectors. For the past ten years he has been building up a complete kit of rods and

▶ Professor Richard Smalley now heads the Nanoscale Science and Technology Center at Rice University in Houston, Texas, in the United States. In 1996, Smalley and his colleagues Harold Kroto and Robert Curl received the Nobel Prize for Chemistry for their discovery of a new form of carbon, the buckyball.

connectors with different lengths and shapes, so that he can make molecular frameworks ("scaffolds") of any shape or size. His computer calculations show it may one day be possible to hang little molecular fan blades off such a scaffold, and spin them with a tiny jet of gas.

At Birmingham University in Britain, another team has already made molecules with moving parts. They have found ways of interlocking ring-shaped molecules so that they can slide around one another. Besides making a compound that resembles the five intersecting rings of the Olympic emblem (it is called Olympiadane), they have also made molecular shuttles and molecular train sets, in which the movement of the rings can be controlled by electrical voltages. Each molecule effectively

▼ Professor Fraser Stoddart and his team at Birmingham University, England, created this incredible nanoscale model of the Olympic symbol – "Olympiadane" – in which the five interlocking ring-shaped molecules are free to slide around each other.

behaves like a molecular abacus, with each position of the rings representing a different number.

Where do we go from here?

Some research teams are concentrating on new materials that will be far superior to those we have today because of the way they are designed at the nanometre scale. Richard Smalley, one of the scientists who discovered the buckyball, is now working with tiny hollow tubes of carbon that are a hundred times stronger than steel and can be bent double without breaking. Other chemists are interested in something they call molecular electronics, where they hope to replace silicon microelectronics devices with far smaller chemical components that might do a far better job.

Nanotechnology is developing very fast, and scarcely a week goes by without some new development, but it is still not clear where it will lead. What does seem clear is that it is going to be very important in the future. Some experts are predicting a global market for nanotechnology of £50 billion by the year 2000. With those kinds of rewards waiting, it is not surprising that many engineers and scientists are joining the tiny technology race.

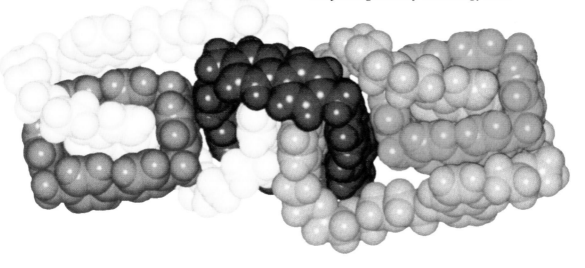

A year in space

In 1997 people watched the Russian space station *Mir* lurch from one near-fatal disaster to another; television screens around the world showed amazing "live" pictures from the planet Mars; new equipment updating the *Hubble Space Telescope* revealed the brightest star; and scientists said farewell to the *Pioneer 10* spaceprobe. Rosy Border reports.

Mir – the on-going story

Throughout 1997 millions of people followed the saga of *Mir*, the Russian space station, as astronauts dealt with crisis after crisis. A ship at sea can be a worrying place to be if something goes wrong; but imagine coping with problems in a metal tube 400 kilometres from Earth, reachable only by space shuttle. Then perhaps you will have some idea how the *Mir* astronauts felt.

NASA, the US space agency, had to think carefully about sending British-born US-

▲ US-astronaut Michael Foale is helped into his space-suit by cosmonaut Vasily Tsibliyev, *Mir*'s commander. After a cargo craft collided with one of *Mir*'s service units, the crew of the damaged Russian space station turned it towards the Sun to help boost power supplies.

▼ The Russian space station *Mir* seen from the space shuttle *Atlantis* in March 1997.

astronaut Dr Michael Foale to the space station after a series of disasters including a fire on 23 February 1997, leaking chemicals from the cooling system, and failures of oxygen generators and other life-support equipment. In May they decided to risk it. Dr Foale, who had already been on four space missions and logged over 600 hours in orbit, was cheerful about the *Mir* mission: "Life on board is cramped with no personal privacy, rotten food, and no women – just like my old boarding school," he told reporters at the time.

Mir, which was originally built to last five years, is 11 years old and showing its age. Dr Foale described his mission as "like a very dirty camping trip in an old car. All the systems are very old, but have been updated over the years, like putting new parts in an old car." That camping trip proved longer and tougher than he could have imagined.

In June 1997, an unmanned cargo module called *Progress*, described by NASA as "the space equivalent of a garbage truck", bumped into *Mir*'s *Spektr* module and damaged the power supply. The accident forced the astronauts to close down the *Spektr* module, where they had their sleeping quarters, and Dr Foale lost many of his personal belongings. The crew found themselves doing a lot of DIY repairs to keep *Mir*'s life-support systems going. Then someone – nobody is saying who – accidentally pulled out a cable which supplied electricity to a computer which controlled *Mir*'s position. At once the spacecraft started drifting and tumbling, so that its solar panels were no longer facing the Sun and the electricity failed. The crew stumbled about with torches, switching off all non-essential electrical systems to conserve precious power. They fixed the fault; but the computer crashed again later after a faulty part failed. There were further computer glitches and power failures. The Russians admitted that *Mir* was showing its age and that vital parts, built to last five years, were still in use after 11 years because of shortage of money. "We used to change *Mir*'s computer parts after five years, but now we have to use them until they die," said Viktor Blagov at mission control in Russia.

While all this was going on, Dr Foale's wife, Rhona, and their children, Ian aged two and five-year-old Jenna, stayed in touch with him by e-mail and video conferences. Dr Foale had also developed a computer program which enabled him to send drawings to his children and for them to send drawings back to him. Meanwhile Ian would often point up at the stars and say "Daddy!"

In September the *Atlantis* space shuttle sent US-astronaut David Wolf to relieve Dr Foale and deliver vital supplies, including a new computer, repair gear, and a big bag of fresh fruit. After 145 days in space, the second-longest stay for any US-astronaut, Dr Foale said that crewing the space station *Mir* had been like plunging into cold water – fine when it is over "but not much fun".

Remote control rover

For hundreds of years Mars has been known as the Red Planet. In 1997 pictures transmitted from the surface of the planet confirmed the findings of the *Viking* landing of 1976. Mars is indeed red – and its sky is red too. NASA sent a

spacecraft called *Pathfinder* almost 500 million kilometres to Mars. Anxious scientists bit their nails as the lander was parachuted to the surface and touch-down was cushioned by giant air-bags. At once it started broadcasting "live" pictures of a rocky, reddish landscape and a dark red sky to television screens around the world. Then a six-wheeled buggy, rather like a remote controlled toy car, called *Sojourner* started to explore. There was more nail-biting when the scientists discovered that *Sojourner* was tangled up in the air-bags. But despite the enormous distance involved they managed to free the buggy. Then the computer on *Sojourner* refused to communicate with the computers at mission control. The controllers tried the oldest trick in the book – switching things off and on again. It worked. "We feel like we've been invited back to the party," said *Sojourner* operator Matt Wallace. Soon *Sojourner*, guided by lasers and feeding pictures to mission control in the United States, was in business.

Sojourner used the energy of the Sun to trundle around by day at a leisurely 0.03 kilometre per hour – about one centimetre per second – taking photographs, "sniffing" rocks

▼ The rover vehicle *Sojourner* examines a large rock on Mars' dusty red surface. The rover weighs 9 kilograms, is 63 centimetres long, and 48 centimetres wide. It is powered by a solar panel, allowing a few hours' movement per day, and is controlled by an operator on Earth.

with its X-ray spectrometer, and examining the soil. The next remote control project may be to send probes to take samples from passing comets, or to dig beneath the ice on one of Jupiter's moons. These projects are much cheaper than sending astronauts to do the same job; and of course nobody's life is in danger.

Sweeping the sky

Stargazers were treated to a spectacular sight in 1997 – a comet as bright as the brightest star that could be seen with the naked eye. Comet Hale–Bopp, a 40-kilometre-wide snowball of dust, ice, and gases travelling at over 160,000 kilometres per hour may well be the brightest comet that we are likely to see in our lifetimes. It had a bullet-shaped head and two tails and was named after US-astronomers Alan Hale and Thomas Bopp, who first spotted it in 1995.

Repairmen in space

In February 1997 the space shuttle *Discovery* blasted off from Cape Canaveral, Florida, on a

▼ The space shuttle *Discovery* lifts off at the Kennedy Space Center, Cape Canaveral, Florida, on 11 February 1997. The shuttle carried a crew of seven on a 10-day mission to service the *Hubble Space Telescope*.

▲ Comet Hale–Bopp over Mount Fuji, Japan's highest mountain, on 31 March 1997. At this time the comet was as luminous as the brightest stars.

10-day mission to fit new components to the £87.5 million *Hubble Space Telescope*. The commander, Kenneth Bowersox, carefully steered the shuttle alongside the 13-metre-long telescope. Then astronaut Steven Hawley reached out with *Discovery*'s 15-metre crane arm and gently grabbed the telescope and manoeuvred it into *Discovery*'s cargo bay. Astronauts Mark Lee and Steven Smith donned space suits and began installing £125 million worth of new components to improve *Hubble*'s already amazing performance.

Almost immediately the new instruments produced spectacular pictures of the birth and death of stars. A special camera called NICMOS (Near Infrared Camera and Multi-Object Spectrometer) photographed an exploding star, and a region in the Orion nebula where new stars are forming. Another instrument, the imaging spectrograph, produced wonderful pictures of events around a black hole in galaxy M84, 50 light years away.

In September 1997 NICMOS discovered a star which may be the brightest in our Galaxy, though it cannot be seen by the human eye because of the interstellar dust that hides it. The star, called the "Pistol Star" because of the shape of the gas cloud that surrounds it, is 10 million times brighter than the Sun. It lies

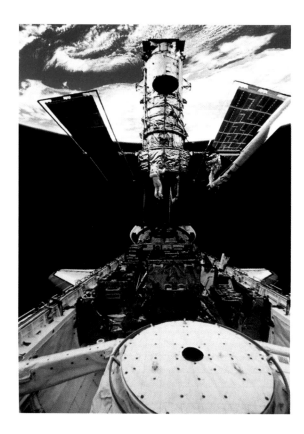

▲ US-astronauts Steven Smith (at centre) and Mark Lee (perched on the Remote Manipulator System robot arm) add new components to the *Hubble Space Telescope*.

with a decorated cake for the craft. *Pioneer 10* was travelling at 45,000 kilometres per hour and its signals took nine hours to reach Earth when scientists watched its signal fade until there was only a blip on the computer screen.

It was an emotional moment for the team, many of whom had been tracking the spacecraft on its mission of exploration for 20 years. *Pioneer 10* carried a message for any intelligent life forms it met – a plaque showing a man, a woman, and a plan indicating where the spacecraft came from. The spacecraft passed close to Jupiter in 1973 and sent back stunning pictures. In 1983 it flew beyond Neptune and Pluto. But it will be 30,000 years before *Pioneer* has its first close encounter with a star – the "red dwarf" star Ross 248 in the constellation Taurus.

Pioneer's plaque has been described by scientists as a "cosmic message in a bottle". Dr Wesley Huntress of NASA said, "Not only has *Pioneer 10* made many major scientific discoveries in the far reaches of space, but we're proud that it has managed to stay alive 10 times longer than the original mission called for, a tribute to the designers, builders, and operators."

25,000 light years from Earth and has a radius of between 149 and 224 million kilometres. In stellar terms the Pistol Star is living fast and will die young. It gives off as much energy in six seconds as the Sun does in a year, and will probably explode in about three million years. Mark Morris of the University of California in Los Angeles said: "Massive stars are so luminous that they consume their fuel at an outrageous rate, burning out quickly and often creating dramatic events, such as exploding supernovas."

Farewell *Pioneer*

The *Pioneer 10* spacecraft, launched in 1972 on a two-year mission, is now 10 billion kilometres from Earth and the scientists who have tracked it all this time have held a retirement party

▼ The Pistol Star, possibly the brightest star in our Galaxy, was the most dramatic find of the Near Infrared Camera and Multi-Object Spectrometer which was added to the *Hubble Space Telescope* in February 1997.

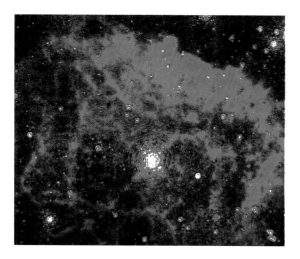

Albania's Home of Hope

In 1997 there were riots on the streets of towns and cities in Albania after so-called "pyramid" investment schemes collapsed and thousands of the Albanian people lost their savings. Many were killed as the country plunged into anarchy and violence. Mike and Judy Smith, who run a children's home in the industrial town of Elbasan, Albania, found themselves at the centre of the storm. Judy Smith tells their story.

It was a beautiful late October day on the Greek island of Corfu in 1989 when my husband Mike and I gazed across the narrow stretch of water towards the little-known land of Albania. I was a primary school headteacher from South Wales and we were taking an autumn holiday during the half-term break. Feeling energetic, we had hired bicycles and were making our way up the hilly east coast road to the resort of Kassiopi. As we rested we wondered about the Albanian people and their way of life. Something stirred within us.

In April 1992, I was given the chance to visit Albania with an aid organization. When we arrived at the airport I was amazed to see sheep and goats wandering over the airport runway. It was like stepping back in time. Everything that we take for granted in our daily lives was in short supply. Hospitals lacked basic equipment and medicines. School children had to work in badly equipped classrooms with no heating or glass in the windows. In the homes cooking and washing facilities were very basic, and many houses had stoves which burned wood cut from roadside trees. I saw Albanian mothers fighting to buy a loaf of bread for their ragged children. My heart was touched by the poverty and when I returned I said to Mike: "I have to go back."

When I returned to my school after the summer holiday in Elbasan I found it hard to adjust to life at home. My pupils had computers, designer trainers, holidays abroad, and plenty of pocket money. The children in Albania had so little in comparison. We had both been looking forward to our retirement and I had recently said to a friend: "If you think that I want to be involved with children after a lifetime as a teacher, you are wrong!" Then, in

▲ A map showing Albania's position in Eastern Europe.

▼ Mike and Judy Smith with some of the children in their care in the early days at the Home of Hope.

Albania – Europe's land of mystery

Albania is a small rugged country, which lies to the east of the Adriatic Sea, bordering Yugoslavia to the north, Macedonia to the east, and Greece to the south.

The country had been a communist republic led by a strict dictator called Enver Hoxha between the years of 1944 and 1985, when Hoxha died. Throughout this period Albania was almost completely cut off from the rest of the world. The people were very poor but they were told by the government that life was better there than it was in the West. Following the collapse of communism in other Eastern European countries, students toppled the giant statue of Hoxha in the central square of Tiranë, Albania's capital city, sparking off an uprising against the government. In 1990, political parties other than the Communist Party were allowed, and in 1992 the Albanian Democratic Party was elected to power and formed a government, under the leadership of Sali Berisha. In 1997, violent protests spread throughout the country following the

▲ Life in Albania is some years behind most of Europe.

collapse of "pyramid" investment schemes. Nearly every Albanian family had invested in the schemes and many had lost their life savings. As the country plunged further into violence and unrest, thousands tried to escape to the safety of the neighbouring lands of Italy and Greece. President Sali Berisha was criticized for allowing the investment schemes and there was an attempt to assassinate him.

In elections held in July 1997, Sali Berisha's government was defeated by the socialists and Rexhep Mejdani became president.

▼ The huge statue of Enver Hoxha in Tiranë's Skanderberg Square, before it was destroyed by student protesters on 20 February 1991.

▲ Children playing in the sandpit at the Home of Hope.

▲ Judy Smith buying fruit and vegetables at a street stall.

February 1993 we were asked to be directors of a new children's home at Elbasan, an industrial town 95 kilometres from Tiranë. Albania was calling us, and we felt that we had to go. We sold our house near the sea in South Wales, arranged to leave our jobs, and on 23 July 1993, set off in a second-hand van on the long journey across Europe to Albania. When we were tired we slept on the twenty-eight banana boxes containing our belongings.

The Home of Hope opens

On 1 August 1993 the Home of Hope opened at Elbasan. I spent these early days making curtains, putting up cots, and learning the language. Mike was busy doing plumbing, electrical, and other practical jobs.

We were asked to take our first child, Erjus, an eight-month-old boy, by the police. He was followed by Anxhela, a little girl whose father had been murdered and whose mother had gone away. These first two children were soon joined by many others from very different backgrounds – some were orphans but others had parents who were unable to look after them. One two-year-old girl weighed only five kilograms and we had the joy of seeing her develop into a strong, happy child who was able to return to her family. We had so many babies and toddlers in the Home of Hope at one time that we were washing over 100 nappies a day. Children that came from the hospital never cried! They had learned that there was no point – no-one ever came. When they realized that, at the Home of Hope, we responded to their tears, they soon learned to cry for attention. I had to teach our young Albanian workers that a baby being bottle fed needs to be cuddled so it knows that it is loved.

The troubles begin

There have been many changes in Albania in the last five years. Food and household goods such as televisions and washing machines can now be bought in the shops, but most people cannot afford to buy them. When the

◀ Moza is an unmarried mother and cannot keep her baby with her at home because illegitimate children are often rejected by the families of the father and the mother in Albania. Her baby has been cared for at the Home of Hope since it was 10 days old.

Albanian people heard of the "pyramid" investment schemes, which promised to double their money in three months, many invested all the money they had. Early investors received the money they were promised but before long so many were due to be paid that the schemes collapsed. Early in 1997 thousands of people found that they had lost all their money.

Everyone became very angry and blamed the government for allowing the schemes in the first place. Some had been unhappy with the way that the government had been elected and attacked the police and the army in violent demonstrations. The trouble started in the south of Albania when weapons and ammunition were seized and criminals were set free from the prisons. Almost everyone was armed.

Noises in the night

On the night of 13 March 1997 we heard firing and explosions all around us. Erjus, now four

▲ At the gates of the Vefa Holding office in Tiranë, Albania, in February 1997, investors in "pyramid" investment schemes show a guard their documents and demand to have their savings returned.

▼ In 1997, thousands of frightened Albanians tried to escape from the violence in Albania aboard any available ship sailing to a safer location.

▲ At the height of the violence, a young Albanian fires a gun looted from the barracks in Elbasan.

▼ Erjus, who came to the Home of Hope when he was only eight months old, sleeping peacefully in his bed.

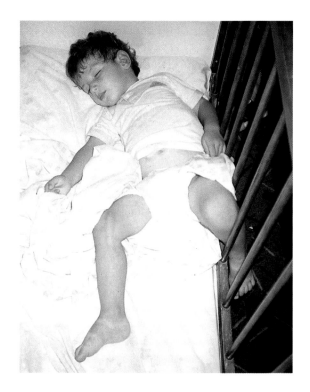

years old asked: "What is that noise?" I told him: "It's the soldiers". "Are they working?" he asked. I said: "Yes". He went back to sleep. The firing continued for many days. Bullets were raining down all over the town; some landed in our garden. It seemed a long way from our house to the gate to answer callers. The guard of the warehouse next to us was shot dead and everything in the warehouse was stolen. We were very frightened when our home was surrounded by masked gunmen but they did not attack us. Gang warfare was taking place around the town and many people were killed.

By 19 March it was too dangerous for our workers to come to work and we were afraid for our safety. We asked the British Embassy to evacuate us. One of the Special Air Service (SAS) officers guarding the embassy said that they would come to collect us early the next morning. We spent the night getting together the clothes, nappies, baby milk, and other

Trefon's story

Trefon and his twin brother were born in Elbasan's maternity hospital. Their parents lived in a shed in a remote village and couldn't care for two tiny babies at home. The twins were transferred to the children's hospital but they were not strong. After seven months Trefon's brother died. By this time the children's mother was seriously ill with gangrene. All her toes were amputated leaving her unable to walk properly or care for her remaining son. Trefon lived in the hospital until he was two years old. We found him in a small unpainted grey room with two other two-year-old boys. In March 1993 they all came to the Home of Hope.

Trefon was unable to sit up, swallow solid food, or recognize his own name. He had been tied to his cot and his body and legs were those of a six-month-old baby while his head, which he rocked constantly from side to side, was a normal size. When he first came to us he gazed around and we realized that it was the first time in his life that he had seen colours. "He thinks that he is in heaven," someone said.

The little boy soon responded to the love and care that he received. We exercised his legs daily and within a year he began walking. Then we noticed that whenever Trefon wanted to look at a book or a small toy he held it very close to his face. He needed quite strong glasses and because he breaks them so often he is well known to the optician as a very regular customer. He now has two pairs of glasses: one pair that he wears and another pair that is constantly being repaired. Because he did not begin to talk until he was three and a half years old and his speech is not clear he will soon travel to a clinic for hearing tests and he may need a hearing aid. Despite all his problems, Trefon, who is now six years old, is a very lively little boy who loves to inspect and take apart anything mechanical. He has a very big appetite but seldom puts on weight. Perhaps he eats for himself and his twin brother who died.

◀ Trefon, who came to the Home of Hope when he was two years old, had many problems when he arrived. He is now a happy and healthy little boy who enjoys playing on his tricycle in the garden.

essential things that the children would need. We had no sleep.

The evacuation

The soldiers arrived at 6.30 a.m., heavily armed and equipped with satellite radio equipment. The children could not understand why they had been dressed in warm outdoor clothes before breakfast. "We're going on holiday," we said, and quickly climbed on board. "Where is the old lady?" cried the officer in charge. I didn't realize at first that he meant me.

Our convoy set off on that dark, misty morning on the winding road which climbs high over the mountains from Elbasan to Tiranë. The driver said: "If we meet any trouble we will drive straight through." The adults were busy with travel-sick children but when they had time to think they wondered: "Where are we going to end up? What will become of the children's home?"

As we started to descend towards Tiranë two Chinook helicopters escorted us at treetop height in case we were attacked. When we reached the safety of the British Embassy, we felt a huge sense of relief. The children celebrated by eating chocolate bars and drinking Coke given to them by the embassy staff.

A place of refuge

We could not after all be taken out of Albania as this would have created diplomatic problems. Our Dutch assistant, Jolanda, telephoned friends in Holland who had been running a guest house in Tiranë. It was only a short distance away and was now empty. They said that we could stay there. It was fully equipped and suited our needs well although we had to sleep the little children on the floor as they might have fallen out of the bunk beds. For the children it was almost like a holiday, but for our five workers it was a busy time. Mike and I had a three-month-old baby in our room and had to practise our feeding and rocking skills twice each night. Each day we took the children to a school playground where they were able to run

▲ Mike and Judy Smith, with some of the staff at the Home of Hope, help the children at breakfast time.

around. At night we listened to the sound of the heavy gunfire but in the daytime it was quiet.

Home again

We kept in touch with friends at Elbasan by telephone and after six days decided to return home. The guest house was fine but the children were missing their toys, their own beds, and space to play. On the return journey we were escorted by military policemen and the British ambassador, as travel was still dangerous. When we arrived back at the Home of Hope we found that the guards had taken food, equipment, and some of our own things. However, the buildings were intact and we were home. The children could play in the garden again but whenever there was gunfire nearby they ran inside. Sometimes even now the children are woken by the noise but there is always someone to comfort them.

The new government was elected in June 1997 and normal life is slowly returning to the people of Elbasan. We have filled in the bullet holes, mended the cracks, and repainted our outside walls a cheerful pink.We thank God that we are all safe. Even on the worst days there has been fun and laughter for the children. The future of Albania is uncertain but the Home of Hope will continue to love and care for its children.

▼ At the Home of Hope in Elbasan, Albania, bullet holes and cracks in the walls have been repaired and the walls have been painted a cheerful pink.

China – a new beginning?

Deng Xiaoping, China's "paramount leader" since 1978, died on 19 February 1997. By the time he died, China was the world's fastest-growing major economy. Even though he had no formal position as China's leader, Deng Xiaoping had governed China since 1978, and was internationally acclaimed as the architect of reforms which transformed an ailing state economy into a thriving market economy. Dr Harriet Evans, Senior Lecturer in Chinese Studies at the University of Westminster in London, describes life in China today and looks back at its recent turbulent history.

The China that Deng Xiaoping started trying to modernize in 1978 had been led by Chairman

◀ Mao Zedong (left) and Deng Xiaoping pictured together in 1959. The two men came from similar revolutionary backgrounds, but they had very different views about the kind of society that China should become.

Mao Zedong for many decades. Mao Zedong was one of the founding members of the Chinese Communist Party in 1921, and was responsible for many of the policies which took the Chinese forces to victory against the Japanese invasion (1937–1945) and against the ruling Nationalists in 1949. Chairman Mao died in 1976. Hailed during his lifetime as the "Great Helmsman", he emphasized the importance of ideology – the way people think – and class struggle, to get rid of the influence of the exploiting classes. He wanted everyone to have

▼ Soldiers of the People's Liberation Army read out loud from the "Little Red Book", the political teachings of Mao Zedong, during the Cultural Revolution.

the same economic, educational, cultural, and social opportunities.

Mao's China

For many years, people thought that Chairman Mao was a great leader who would improve the lives of China's millions of desperately poor peasants. His portrait was displayed everywhere, from the walls of people's houses to the front gate of the old emperors' palace in Beijing. Yet in the years that he ruled China, the standard of living of many ordinary people showed little improvement. Despite claims that Chinese socialism was better than the capitalist systems of the West, average wages did not rise at all between 1957 and 1976. In fact, Mao Zedong implemented many policies which were completely disastrous. In 1958, for example, he masterminded the Great Leap Forward, an experiment to push China's industrial production into the modern age, and in the process created such shortages and chaos that an estimated 40 million people died of starvation and nutrition-related complaints. In 1966, he launched another experiment called the Great Proletarian Cultural Revolution, which sought to change the ways people thought about society, education, and culture. But this also proved to be disastrous. With Mao's encouragement, school and university students were organized into groups of Red Guards. Schools were closed, and universities, offices, and factories became political battlegrounds, controlled by Red Guards claiming to uphold Mao Zedong's revolutionary road. Thousands of young people were sent to the countryside to work in the fields and "learn from the peasants"; teachers, writers, artists, and other professionals were publicly criticized for their wrong "ideology", and were often beaten up, and sent to labour camps in the countryside. As millions of Red Guards travelled

▼ People queuing to visit the mausoleum where Chairman Mao's body was laid to rest. He died in September 1976 after a long illness.

▲ This is a poster publicizing the one child per couple policy introduced in 1979. The words on it translate to "Control population increase, construct a civilized society".

through China, cities became the scene of violent fighting, political chaos, and terror.

Mao Zedong died at the age of 83 in September 1976, and his closest political allies, known as the Gang of Four, were arrested less than a month later. Throughout the country, ordinary people welcomed the end of an era of terrible political pressure. They also welcomed the return to power of Deng Xiaoping who had twice been removed from power by Mao Zedong, first during the Cultural Revolution, and again in 1976.

The Deng era

Deng Xiaoping (1904–1997) came from the same generation of revolutionaries as Mao Zedong, but despite their shared background, he had very different views about the kind of society he wanted China to become. Deng thought that Mao Zedong attached too much importance to

political struggle, and ignored things that really mattered in people's lives, such as education and standards of living. Deng believed that Mao's goal of equality between all people was impossible to achieve while China was still a poor country. He believed the most important thing was to improve the economy and lift China out of poverty and technological backwardness. To this end, he thought that people had to be encouraged to work hard with incentives such as increased wages and bonuses. He also wanted other countries to invest in China and to share their technological expertise with China. In the countryside, he wanted to abolish the collective farms – the rural "people's communes" where large communities worked the land – and give back to peasants their own private plots of land. Deng realized, too, that China's population growth rate had to be drastically reduced if standards of living were to rise. In 1979 he introduced the world's strictest population-control policy, decreeing that Chinese couples

▲ An aerial view of the busy cosmopolitan district of Hong Qiao in Shanghai. With a population of more than seven million, Shanghai is China's biggest city.

were only allowed to have one child. Mao Zedong now became widely talked about as a tyrant, who had prevented China's people from developing. Deng Xiaoping was hailed as China's new "saviour".

China today

China in the late 1990s is a very different place from the country it was two decades ago. As late as the mid-1970s the main shopping street in its capital city, Beijing, had no advertisements, few street lights, and shop fronts that looked like ordinary houses. Central Beijing is now a modern cosmopolitan centre, much like other capitals throughout the world. It displays expensive, glass-fronted shops, ritzy international hotels, loud disco music, high-speed ring roads, and flashing billboards advertising everything from Coca-Cola to Japanese computers. The same kind of changes

are evident in the clothes people wear: twenty years ago, men and women alike wore grey, green, or blue jackets – the so-called Mao jacket – and trousers, short or bobbed hair, flat shoes, and no make-up. Bright colours and patterns were reserved for small children. Now, street fashion is as varied as in any international urban centre, with designer-label T-shirts and jeans, elegant dresses, and beautifully tailored Western-style business suits.

By the early 1990s, Deng's reforms had resulted in the tripling of average yearly incomes. However, China remains a country of extreme contrasts and differences. Deng's reforms have had very uneven results. While luxury high-rise blocks have sprung up in large cities, pollution and other environmental problems have become worse. Privatization of the urban economy has brought enormous profits to a small number of people, but has also led to increased unemployment and social instability. Incomes are still much higher in the towns than in the countryside. The "single child" birth-control policy has been much more successful in the big towns than in rural areas. This is mainly because whereas urban couples have a pension to support them in old age, in the countryside the elderly look to their children to provide money. Seventy per cent of China's vast population – at more than 1.2 billion it counts for more than 20 per cent of the world's total – live in the countryside. Most of China's poor people come from the rural regions. Recent estimates suggest that one in ten of China's population lives below the internationally recognized poverty line. Of China's 182 million illiterate adults, 70 per cent are women, most of whom live in rural areas. Huge numbers of peasants have no access to medical care or pension benefits and many have left the land altogether to join the vast "floating" population who flock to the big cities in search of employment.

The non-Hans

Another big contrast is between the Han majority of the population of the People's

◀ A farmer in arid Inner Mongolia, where only hardy crops such as corn can grow, ploughs his field with a camel. Like many farmers in the poor northwestern region of China, he cannot afford expensive farm machinery.

Republic of China, and the 56 ethnic minorities, or "national minorities" as they are officially called. While they occupy some 60 per cent of China's territory, including the vast western areas, those who are not Han represent only about eight per cent of the total population of China. While economic reform has brought progress to many minority areas, improvements have been uneven. The gap between the Han regions near the coast, towards the south and southeast, and the western regions such as Yunnan and Guangxi, has widened. Many non-Han peoples, such as the Tibetans and the Uighurs in Xinjiang, speak their own language, have their own religion and culture, and eat a very different diet from the Han peoples. Many of these people would like to set up their own country and manage their own affairs without interference from central government in Beijing.

Political stalemate

Accompanying all these changes, the social and cultural mood of China is very different from that of twenty years ago. Travel, the possibilities of studying abroad, being able to see foreign films and buy foreign books, and the introduction of modern telecommunications and the Internet, have hugely changed China's cultural and social life. Political changes, however, have been less apparent. Students, teachers, and the mass of workers asked repeatedly for democratic reform throughout the 1980s. Time and again, Deng himself referred to the need for "reform of the political

▼ A migrant who has come to Beijing to seek work, rests among his belongings in Tian'anmen Square. Huge numbers of peasants have left the land to join the "floating" population who flock to the cities in search of jobs.

▶ A family of the Yao minority eat their lunch in their home in the Longsheng district of Guangxi Province, in southwestern China. Average incomes in this area have risen in recent years, due largely to the increase of tourism in the region.

system" to keep up with the pace of economic change. However, despite Deng's speeches, there was little political reform during his time in power.

Tian'anmen Square

On 4 June 1989, Deng Xiaoping showed the world that he was prepared to use violence to preserve the Communist Party's rule. He ordered the army to suppress a massive pro-democracy movement that had gathered in Beijing's famous Tian'anmen Square. The movement began in April with a students' parade honouring the memory of Hu Yaobang, an open-minded party leader who had recently died. Student leaders called for a democratic government, an end to officials' corruption, and a stop to political censorship of the press. Many students went on hunger strike. The public's support for the students grew, and for a while the hundreds of thousands who filled Tian'anmen Square

seemed on the verge of toppling the Communist Party. Yet Deng Xiaoping and other hardline leaders declared martial law in May, and two weeks later, on the night of 3–4 June, sent in tanks to violently suppress the movement. Several hundred people died, and many more were arrested and imprisoned in the weeks that followed. Despite world-wide condemnation of the massacre in Tian'anmen Square, the Chinese government continues to imprison people who speak out in favour of democracy.

In the year that it became part of the People's Republic of China, Hong Kong symbolizes many of the extraordinary contrasts of contemporary Chinese society. On the one hand Hong Kong represents the prosperity that China's cities aspire to. On the other, its return to Beijing's rule highlights the concerns many people in China share about the political and social pressures they face. And as the new millennium approaches, there is little indication that China's leaders are willing or able to resolve this contradiction. As the state decides to sell off state-owned property, opening the way for full privatization of the economy, its leaders still have little to say about political reform.

Medical matters

The oldest doctor in the United Kingdom

Archaeologists at Colchester in Essex, England's oldest recorded town, have dug up a surgeon's kit dating from about AD 50. The instruments, which were buried with their doctor owner in a burial ground for high-ranking Britons, are not for the squeamish. They include a saw for amputations and tidying up the ends of broken bones, hooks for removing tonsils, tweezers, probes, a spatula, and a set of needles. There is a spud – a sharpened spoon for gouging out tissue – and a mystery object like a big hairpin with turned-out points, which experts think was used to hold the surgeon's incisions open during operations.

In the same grave were some rods, half copper and half iron, which archaeologists think may have been divining rods. "Doctors consulted the gods and used divination techniques," said museum curator Ralph Jackson. "Foretelling the future would have gone hand in hand with medical practice."

HBO helps Ben

Hyperbaric Oxygen (HBO) has helped deep sea divers suffering from "the bends" – a serious and very painful condition that occurs when a diver comes to the surface too quickly – for years. The treatment involves putting the patient in a pressure chamber. Compressed air is pumped into the chamber, giving the sensation of being eight metres under the sea. A hood is placed over the patient's head and pure oxygen is pumped in. This increases the blood supply to the brain.

Doctors believe that children with severe brain damage can show amazing improvement after receiving HBO treatment. Over 200 children with cerebral palsy have already been treated. Benjamin Marks, aged four, who was born paralysed and without muscle control, showed signs of improvement within hours of his first HBO treatment. "Doctors wrote him off," says his mother. Then she and her husband heard about HBO and bought a second-hand chamber which Ben used several times a week. From being small for his age Ben has grown six centimetres and has now started to crawl.

Computers kill pain

The Starbright Foundation in the United States introduces sick children to each other through their computers. They can play, "talk", and take part in school lessons together. The scheme was set up in response to medical research that has shown that children cope much better with pain while they are engrossed in computer games. This helps them to get better, as painkillers often make the children feel tired and weak.

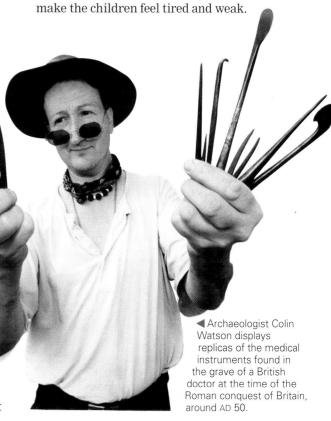

◀ Archaeologist Colin Watson displays replicas of the medical instruments found in the grave of a British doctor at the time of the Roman conquest of Britain, around AD 50.

Miracle at sea

On 9 January 1997 Tony Bullimore, British yachtsman, was rescued from the freezing waters of the Southern Ocean. For five days he had sheltered in a tiny air pocket in the upturned hull of his capsized yacht, battling against hypothermia, frostbite, and dehydration. Common sense, sheer determination, and a lifetime's experience of sailing got him through. This is Tony Bullimore's own account of his adventure – the biggest survival story of the year.

In the early part of 1996 I made up my mind to compete in the Vendée Globe, the non-stop single-handed sailing race around the world. The race started from Les Sables d'Olonne, on the west coast of France, on 3 November 1996. I had eight months to prepare. My shore crew worked long hours to refit and completely overhaul my racing yacht, *Exide Challenger.* I was planning to sail 65,009 kilometres non-stop

▲ The *Exide Challenger* on sea trials in 1994.

▼ On board the *Exide Challenger* in the harbour at Les Sables d'Olonne on the eve of the start of the single-handed round-the-world Vendée Globe Challenge race.

and it was vital I had no problems.

On the morning of the day the race began, I had an early breakfast with my wife Lalel in the little house we had rented in Les Sables d'Olonne, before we set off for the harbour. When we arrived it seemed as though all hell had been let loose there. Whichever direction I looked, there was a sea of faces – thousands of people had turned up to watch the start of the Vendée Globe. At mid-morning an 80-metre fishing boat towed *Exide Challenger* out of the harbour. A few hundred metres from the shore, I released the towline – now I was on my own. I sailed on to the start area. By now, although my mind was relaxed, adrenaline was starting to speed me up. I needed to hear the starter's gun and get on with the race. The atmosphere was electric, with helicopters zooming in with cameramen on board and spectator boats honking their horns in farewell. All of a sudden the starter's gun blasted and I was off. *Exide Challenger* surged towards the starting line and I started to crank on the winches and trim the sails to get more speed.

The North Atlantic Ocean

It was a hard slog out of the Bay of Biscay and into the North Atlantic Ocean. But a couple of weeks later I had reached the equator, the area known as the Doldrums because there is never much wind in the equatorial zone. It was important that I studied the weather patterns carefully to ensure that I chose the right course to steer through the Doldrums. If I got it wrong, I could add days on to my sailing time.

The South Atlantic Ocean

Once I had crossed the equator, I was in the South Atlantic. I sailed the *Exide Challenger* as hard as possible towards the Southern Ocean. On the way, I had a few problems. My water maker (equipment to turn sea water into fresh water) packed up, one of the two fuel tanks leaked, and my Satcom C (satellite communication equipment) stopped working. All these problems would make it more difficult to sail around the world non-stop, but I was determined to keep going. I thought of the great nineteenth-century clipper ships that passed this way on their passage to Australia or New Zealand. They had managed without high-technology equipment and I would just have to do the same.

New Year's Eve

On Tuesday, 31 December, I sailed past Heard Island in near-perfect weather conditions. I had the opportunity to check over the boat, make a few repairs, and prepare myself for what I knew would be difficult days ahead. What I didn't realize was just how hard they would turn out to be. I tried to radio through to Heard Island to report my position and to wish everyone on the island a happy New Year. There was no reply and I found out later that the island was uninhabited at that time of the year.

By Saturday, 4 January, the weather conditions were deteriorating and the wind strength was rapidly building. For the last couple of days the barometer had been steady at around 1010 millibars but now it had dropped to 990 millibars and was still falling. This was a sure sign that heavy weather was on its way. I checked that *Exide Challenger* was on course and then I went below to make sure that all the loose equipment was safely stowed away. I didn't want objects flying around the cabin in a storm – that could be dangerous.

The winds continued to strengthen and the seas were looking uglier by the hour. It was now blowing over 50 knots. I was sure that this was going to be a blockbuster of a Southern Ocean storm that could last for several days. Conditions outside were near freezing but I had to go back on deck to check that everything was

▼ Sailing off into the horizon and towards the Southern Ocean at the start of the Vendée Globe race.

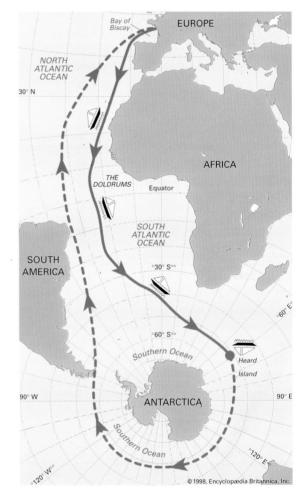

▲ I popped up to the surface of the water on one side of the boat as the Australian Navy rescue team knocked on the hull on the other side. It wasn't long before they spotted me!

▶ This map shows the route of the Vendée Globe challenge race. I was about 1,600 kilometres east of Heard Island when the storm broke and the *Exide Challenger* capsized. The broken line indicates the route I should have followed to complete the race.

in order. This time I put on the safety harness which was attached to a line clipped to a padeye on the deck. Without it I could easily be washed overboard by one of the enormous waves rolling over *Exide Challenger*. One of the halyards (a rope to lower the sails), had come adrift at the bottom of the main mast. It was swashing around on the deck and I had to secure it before it got washed overboard. This was dangerous work and it took me 15 minutes to reach the mast, curl up the rope, and tie it up. I climbed gratefully back into the cockpit, cold and soaked through, but glad that everything was now in order. It was time to have a mug of tea and maybe a doze.

Trapped

All of a sudden, there was a mighty crack and before I could think what had happened, *Exide Challenger* had capsized and I was sitting on the ceiling of the cabin (the coachroof). I waited for

▲ Cold, hungry, and very grateful, I am helped aboard the rescue boat by Chief Petty Officer Peter Wicker and Leading Seaman Clearance Diver Alan Rubb.

the boat to right herself but she couldn't. The crack I heard was the keel breaking off. Without it there was no chance of rolling upright again. As the boat heaved and pitched in all directions, I tried to think how on earth I was going to get out of this mess alive. Here I was, 2,400 kilometres from land, trapped in my capsized racing yacht in the middle of an almighty storm. I had to be calm and work out my best chance of surviving until I was, hopefully, rescued. At least the port holes and hatches were all shut and battened down and there was little water getting in. I started to gather the equipment that had been thrown everywhere. All of a sudden there was a large crash as a coachroof window smashed. Thousands of gallons of water flushed into the cabin with tremendous force and within seconds it was up to my chest. For a few seconds I stared at it blankly, frozen in shock. My body temperature was rapidly dropping and I could feel the freezing cold. I came to my senses. I had to reach my survival suit and get it on as soon as possible. The water had damaged the power supply from the batteries and all the lights had

gone out. I had to wade through the torrents in almost total darkness. I reached the engine room and the cuddy, a small stowage area I used for storing my clothes and some of my food supplies. I found the survival kit and within minutes I had it on. I felt my body temperature stabilizing and this gave me more confidence.

May Day, May Day

My next job was to get one of the distress beacons working and on to the surface of the sea. I grabbed a beacon and flipped the emergency switch. A small red light started to flash steadily on and off, sending out a May Day message. I tied it to a long rope to make sure it stayed alongside *Exide Challenger* and then, clutching it, dived under the freezing water to push it through the broken window. I unwound the rope until I was as certain as possible that the beacon was floating on the surface.

All my hope lay in my distress signal being picked up by the rescue services, but even if it was, I knew it could take five to six days for a ship to reach me. I had to prepare myself to survive the treacherous conditions. I needed food and drinking water, and above all, I had to keep myself as warm as possible. Searching around the small cabin, I managed to find a can

▼ Wrapped in a foil blanket to overcome the mild hypothermia I am suffering, and equipped with an oxygen mask, I lie on the floor of the rescue boat thanking my rescuers.

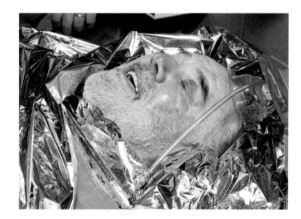

▲ The crew of the Royal Australian frigate HMAS *Adelaide* look on as Peter Wicker, Alan Rubb, and I pull up alongside. I will always be grateful to them for saving my life.

▶ I point to my injured foot (damaged by mild frostbite) as I am helped off HMAS *Adelaide* after we had docked in Fremantle. I was back on dry land at last.

of baked beans, a couple of bars of chocolate, and a few sachets of water – not much but it was better than nothing. Most of the equipment and supplies were rapidly being ruined by the sea water and some were being sucked out through the broken window into the ocean itself.

Numbed pain

I had to get the life-raft to the surface and ready to use, in case the *Exide Challenger* completely filled with water or began to sink. It was firmly lashed to the floor of the upturned cockpit, now several metres under water. Armed with a knife to cut the rope, I dived under and swam towards it. I could only stay under for about 90 seconds before I had to come up for air. My lungs were bursting and I was freezing cold. Again and again I swam down. Once, as I came up for air, I grasped hold of the frame of the entrance hatch and a sudden surge of water forced the hatch shut on my little finger. I felt a second of

blinding pain before I saw my finger float away. All I had left was a stub of jagged bone and blood. For once I was grateful for the cold, it numbed my hand so that I hardly felt any pain. I dived again for the life-raft and finally managed to cut it free, but I couldn't get it to the surface because it was pinned to the upside-down cockpit floor by its built-in buoyancy. I had no choice but to abandon my plan. Weariness overcame me, I could think of nothing but the cold and how much I wanted to sleep. I climbed on to a narrow shelf just out of the water. There was no room to move but I stretched out, with my shoulders jammed against the hull, and slipped into fitful sleep as the sea water continuously rolled over me.

Saved

The days passed, I lost count of how many. With *Exide Challenger* lurching violently in every

▶ My wife Lalel and I are reunited. She went through her own terrible ordeal during the days that I was missing. As soon as she heard I was safe she flew to Australia to be with me.

direction, I felt as though I was inside an ice-cold, out-of-control washing machine. My body temperature had dropped alarmingly and my feet had no feeling left in them. At least a hundred times every couple of hours I would bang them against the side of the boat to keep the blood circulating and frostbite at bay. The boat was sinking lower and lower into the water, I had run out of chocolate, and had to rely on the Survivor watermaker to quench my thirst. At times I truly believed I would die squashed onto the shelf, but I battled hard with such thoughts, forcing myself to be hopeful.

At last it came – a loud banging on the side of the hull. I quickly rolled off the shelf and into the water. I put my ear against the hull and heard a muffled shout. My heart began to thud and I muttered "don't blow it, Tony. This is your big chance." I shouted as loudly as I could, over and over again "I'm in here!" But I didn't know if anyone could hear me and I was terrified that they would go away. I had to get out of the boat. I took a deep gulp of air, and swam out and up to the surface. After days in darkness the brightness outside was blinding. As my eyes focused, the first thing I saw was the warship *Adelaide* of the Royal Australian Navy. It was one of the best moments of my life. A bearded man swam towards me and pulled me through the water to an inflatable dinghy. Arms reached out to drag me aboard; at last I felt truly safe. I looked up at my rescuer. "This is wonderful," I said, "if you didn't have a beard, I'd kiss you."

I will be back

Once on board the *Adelaide* I was quickly given medical treatment and then I had a mug of hot tea and a plateful of crispy toast, dripping with butter. It was heaven. Everyone on board was so kind and helpful and gave me a true feeling of well-being. There is no doubt in my mind, if it had not been for the combined efforts and skills of the Australian Defence Forces and the Maritime Rescue Co-ordination Centre of Australia, I would not be alive today.

After a few days recuperating on board the *Adelaide* I sat on deck and looked out across the Southern Ocean. We were roaring through the sea, making for Fremantle. My mind wandered back to *Exide Challenger* and all that I had been through. Would I sail these seas again? A broad smile spread across my face and I mumbled, "I will be back – I have some unfinished business."

▼ Within two weeks of my rescue I was back on the water again and in June 1997 I took part in my first race since *Exide Challenger* capsized – the "Race Around Europe".

64

Dolly the duplicate

In March 1997, genetic scientists in Edinburgh, Scotland, announced that one of their lambs, Dolly, was a clone of an adult animal. The news echoed around the world. But what is a clone, and why was Dolly so important? Could – and should – we ever clone humans? Steve Parker explains.

◄ Dolly, the world's first clone, or exact copy, of an adult mammal. Dolly has exactly the same genes as a six-year-old ewe. Despite the difference between their ages, the two sheep are identical twin sisters.

Dolly, a lamb of the breed called Finn Dorset, was born in July 1996. She looked like any other lamb. Indeed, many people cannot tell the difference between one sheep and the next. But in Dolly's case, this similarity did not stop at her general sheep-like appearance. She was a clone – an exact genetic copy of another sheep. This other sheep was not the one who gave birth to Dolly. That was a substitute, or surrogate, mother, who had received Dolly as a tiny embryo during an implant procedure. Dolly then grew in her womb.

Mother and sister
Dolly had the same genes as a different sheep, a six-year-old ewe. This ewe was Dolly's true genetic double. Or, more accurately, and perhaps more strangely, she was Dolly's identical twin sister. She and Dolly were clones.

Confusing? In the world of genetic research, ordinary terms like "parent" and "twin" take on new significance, and the word "clone" crops up repeatedly. It helps to understand what cloning means, in order to appreciate why Dolly became so famous and what she could mean for the copying of other animals.

What is cloning?
Genes are instructions for growing, making, and maintaining a living thing. They are found inside each microscopic unit, or cell, which makes up every plant or animal. Genes exist in the form of chemical codes of the substance DNA (de-oxyribonucleic acid).

Clones are living things that have exactly the same genes as each other. So they are as identical to each other, in their shape, size, appearance, inner structure, and body chemistry, as it's possible to be.

Different genes
In the normal method of breeding, called sexual reproduction, the genes of the two parents come together and combine in various ways in each offspring. The genes may also change slightly, or mutate. This means each offspring has its own unique selection or set of genes. It is genetically

▼ A few months after Dolly hit the headlines, the Roslin Institute, in Edinburgh, Scotland, introduced Polly to the world. She was cloned from the cells of an embryo which had been genetically engineered to carry a human gene. Polly is pictured here with her surrogate mother, a Scottish Blackface sheep.

▶ These monkeys were cloned in the United States at the Oregon Regional Primate Research Center in Beaverton. Despite looking very similar, they are not clones of each other. Each came from a different embryo.

different from its parents and from its brothers and sisters.

This happens across most of the living world, from daisies to oak trees, from houseflies to blue whales, and includes ourselves. It's why we have a family likeness, but we are all slightly different and unique individuals.

The same genes

Clones have the same genes. There are various reasons for this. Some occur in nature, and have done so for millions of years. For example, a strawberry plant grows and sends out long stem-like runners. Where these touch the soil, they may

sprout roots, and a new strawberry plant gradually develops. This new plant grew directly from its "single parent" strawberry, with no mixing or changing of genes. It is a clone of the parent.

This type of process happens in many plants, and is called vegetative or asexual reproduction. Gardeners make great use of it when they split and divide plants, or take cuttings, and encourage them to grow into new, whole plants. This is, in effect, cloning.

Preserving the same genes

Why do it? The gardener usually wants the offspring plants to have exactly the same features as the original parent plant. These features might include a new and special flower colour, or a new leaf shape, or bigger-than-normal fruit.

Left on their own, the plants would breed in the natural way, by sexual reproduction involving pollen and seeds. This would mix and recombine the genes, producing genetically different offspring, and the special features could be changed or lost.

Twins as clones

Another example of natural cloning is identical twins. These occur in many kinds of animals, and of course in people. They happen during sexual reproduction after the microscopic sex cells, the sperm and egg, come together and join, which is called fertilization. The fertilized egg begins to split or divide, first into two cells, then four, and so on, to form a tiny ball of cells. This gradually develops into a very young baby, or embryo, inside the mother.

Sometimes by chance the tiny ball of cells

▼ These girls are identical twins. They grew from the same fertilized egg which split into two cells. Although one twin is often bigger than the other at birth, they are always of the same sex and look remarkably alike.

divides into two separate, smaller balls which continue to grow. Both develop separately into offspring. Since they came from the same fertilized egg, they both have exactly the same genes. So they are clones of each other. This is why identical twins look so similar to each other, especially in the early stages of their lives. But unlike the strawberry plant, although they are clones of each other, they are not clones of their parents.

Cloning animals

Dolly the sheep was not the first cloned animal. Cloning has been carried out in frogs since the 1950s, and in mammals such as sheep and cows, which have more complicated genes and cells, since the mid-1980s. It is done by taking a tiny developing embryo, or ball of cells, and splitting it into several separate cells. This is like making lots of identical twins. It is done in a laboratory glass dish under the microscope, using incredibly fine probes and similar tools.

Each cell is cultured – kept in ideal conditions with warmth and plenty of nutrients, in a culture dish. The cells continue to divide, and each one develops into a new embryo which has exactly the same genes as the original embryo.

At a suitable stage of development, the embryos can be inserted or implanted into surrogate mothers. They continue their growth into babies until they are ready to be born.

More and more clones

Rather than implant this first batch of embryos into mothers, it is possible to repeat the cloning procedure on them. This produces yet more batches of genetically identical embryos, numbering hundreds, even thousands.

This is sometimes necessary because cloning is a procedure fraught with chance and failure. Not all the divided-up balls of cells may continue to develop into embryos. Of those that do, not all will continue their growth when implanted into surrogate mothers. From

▲ Bill Ritchie is the senior technician at the Roslin Institute. Using highly sophisticated equipment, he extracted the minuscule cell and injected it into the egg, resulting in the development of Dolly.

hundreds of cloned balls of cells, only two or three offspring may finally be born.

The importance of Dolly

Cloning could have benefits in several areas, particularly in medicine and farming. For example, a farmer could choose the cow which produced the most milk and clone her to make a whole herd of champion milk-producers. But in the type of cloning described above, the original embryo had two parents. It was produced in the normal way of sexual reproduction, by a sperm from the father bull joining the egg from the mother cow. Their genes got mixed, shuffled, and changed. So the mother may be a good milk-producer, but her cloned offspring may not. They are genetically identical to each other but not to her. One idea behind Dolly was to clone, not a developing early embryo, but a fully grown adult who had shown that it had desirable features and proved its worth.

Cells that can do anything

This next step, cloning a fully grown adult rather than an early embryo, may sound simple. But there's a problem – at the level of the microscopic cells which make up every living thing.

All of the cells in a living thing, such as a sheep, contain the same full set of genes. But in the egg cell and early embryo stages, these cells are unspecialized or "undifferentiated". All of their genes can be active and working. Each cell has the potential to differentiate, or divide and develop. It can become any one of the many kinds of highly specialized cells found in the adult body, such as nerve cells, muscle cells, blood cells, and so on.

Specialized cells

As the embryo continues to develop, its cells go through the process of differentiation. They become different from each other in shape, structure, and function, specialized to do various tasks. The only active genes are those for the cell's specific role, as a bone cell, liver cell, or other specialized cell.

So in the adult body, cells are fully differentiated and specialized. Each type has much of its genetic code switched off. However, to clone embryos which will then grow and develop into whole new individuals, the full gene

▲ Seoul, March 1997. South Korean environmentalists stage a protest against the cloning of living things. The protesters wore sheep costumes and carried signs reading "Stop the copying of animals".

set needs to be able to be switched on and working.

Switching on genes

It was thought that the switched-off genes of differentiated cells, in an adult, could not be switched on again. So cloning from the cells of an adult could not be done. That is, until Dolly was born.

Dolly was the result of research led by Ian Wilmut and Keith Campbell into the genetics and reproduction of farm animals. This was carried out at the Roslin Institute in Edinburgh, Scotland. The announcement of Dolly's birth rocked the realm of science, and also the wider world. It meant the problem of switching on all of the genes, in a specialized or differentiated cell, had been solved. It also meant that the farm animals, crops, and genetically engineered living things could be cloned after they had reached adulthood and shown that they had desirable features. This would be a vast improvement on the far more hit-and-miss method of cloning them as embryos. It could have the potential of huge benefits for humankind.

▼ Dr Ian Wilmut with Dolly. Dr Wilmut is the head of mammal cloning work at the Roslin Institute. Even before human cloning was ruled illegal in Europe, the Institute said it would never attempt to do it.

But it also raised the sinister possibility that one day, human beings could be copied or cloned from other adult human beings.

Controversial cloning

Most scientists agree that if cloning can be carried out on an adult sheep, then it could be done on an adult human. Sheep and humans are both mammals. In biological terms, their cells are extremely similar. Tests to clone a human from another adult human might only take two or three years.

It could be done – but *should* it? Cloning is wasteful. Dolly was the result of 277 tests. To work on humans would mean the loss of many human eggs and embryos, which pro-life groups say is nothing short of murder. And this is only one of the arguments against research into cloning humans. Combined with genetic engineering, the subject raises all kinds of possibilities that many people find horrific.

The best soldiers could be cloned to make an invincible army. Cloned teams of champion athletes and sports players would be unbeatable. Various races of slave beings, sub-humans, and hybrid combinations of humans and animals, could be cloned for all kinds of tasks.

▼ Identical twin sheep, Morag and Megan, were born at the Roslin Institute in 1995. They were cloned from a cell taken from an embryo where the cells had already started to become specialized.

▲ Anti-cloning politicians from the environmentalist Green Party make their feelings clear at the European Parliament. They wore white masks giving them a similar "cloned" appearance.

Raised from the dead?

There is another, perhaps even stranger, possibility. Genetic material in cells can be preserved by freezing. In theory, still-intact genes from the cells of a dead animal or human could be put back into living cells and then cloned. Experiments on cloning cows in Denmark have used cells from adult cows that had been dead for about half an hour. But with specially prepared and then preserved cells, this time interval could be extended to weeks, even years.

Misunderstandings

Rather than discuss the benefits and drawbacks of cloning sheep and other farm animals, many people leapt ahead to thinking about the possibilities of altering and cloning humans and bringing them back from the dead.

Would cloned humans be exactly the same as each other? Identical twins, who are natural clones, give clues. They look very similar. But they cannot be in exactly the same place at the same time and always have the same experiences, even when they are in the womb. As they grow, they learn different things,

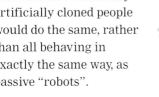

▶ President Clinton warned against "trying to play God" when he imposed a ban on US federal funds being used to finance human cloning experiments.

develop their own personalities, likes and dislikes, and become individuals. Presumably artificially cloned people would do the same, rather than all behaving in exactly the same way, as passive "robots".

Problems

Towards the end of 1997, leaders of the European Union decided to suspend all research into cloning adult humans. But in many parts of the world this step has not yet been taken. In the United States, President Clinton imposed a ban on using federal funds to finance human cloning experiments. However, a religious group that believes that the Earth was created by aliens, has set up a company called Clonaid which may fund research into cloning humans.

Another step along the road?

The fuss arising from Dolly the cloned sheep can be seen as another stage in the development of artificial reproduction and cloning techniques. This happened with the first freezing of sperm cells in the early 1950s, which caused an outcry then. In 1995 identical twin sheep, Morag and Megan, were born at the Roslin Institute. They had been cloned from a cell taken from an embryo, but a late embryo where the cells had already started to differentiate or become specialized. Like Dolly, they appeared in newspapers and on television programmes around the world.

From time-honoured selective breeding of farm animals and crops, to artificial insemination of animals, and humans, and then test-tube babies, surrogate mothers, gene therapy for inherited diseases ... science and its possibilities tend to stay ahead of public thought and opinion. Only when the issues are fully understood and debated, including the science, and the morals and ethical rights and wrongs, can society make its decision. Some stages become accepted, while others are banned.

Before long, there is another "advance". In a few years, we'll be debating the next stage. Which will be ...?

Why clone?

In farming and livestock

● One prize animal could be cloned to produce thousands of identical offspring in one season. The cow in the herd which produces the most milk would be cloned into a whole herd of champion milk-producers.
● Cloning rather than breeding would not interrupt the competition schedules of very valuable animals like racehorses.

In conservation

● Cloning might be used to produce extra numbers of endangered animals or plants. If some died, they could more easily be replaced.
● Combined with genetic engineering, cloning could be used to make endangered species more resistant to disease or bad conditions.

In medicine

● Cloning might produce cells that could be put into the body to heal parts that do not normally mend, such as severed nerves or damaged heart muscle.
● It could help scientists to understand why some cells multiply out of control, as in cancers.
● Transgenic animals, which have been genetically altered to make useful medical

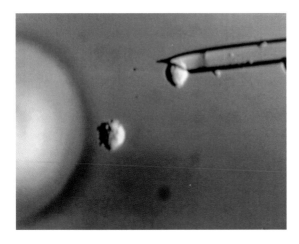

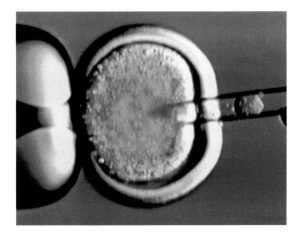

▲▼ These greatly magnified photographs, taken through a microscope, show a microneedle sucking up an embryonic sheep cell (top), a sheep egg being injected with the embryonic cell (centre), and the sheep egg once it has fused with the cell (bottom).

substances and drugs, could be cloned in large numbers. This would cut chance and wastage.

• Cloning could copy genetically engineered animals with organs that are suitable for transplanting into humans.

• Large numbers of genetically identical laboratory animals could be produced for testing new drugs or the ways that genetic diseases are passed from parents to offspring.

How Dolly was made

Dolly was cloned from the cells of her "double" ewe which were in this ewe's milk-producing or mammary tissues, commonly called the udder. The cloning was the result of a series of stages involving microscopes, chemicals, and other laboratory equipment.

1 The specialized mammary cells were made inactive, or quiescent. This was done by putting them in a laboratory culture dish and starving them – depriving them – of nutrients. Apparently, this simple trick unblocks all the genes and makes them active again.

2 The genetic material was removed from another cell. This was an egg cell from another sheep. The genetic material was sucked out with a fine tube or pipette, seen through a powerful microscope. This is called enucleation.

3 The quiescent mammary cell and the enucleated egg cell were squashed together and given a tiny electric shock. This stimulated the cells to merge into one, and then split or divide – the same effect as when a sperm fertilizes an egg. But no sperm or other genes were involved.

4 An egg cell was used because it contains all the substances and chemicals for growth of a new individual, from the very beginning. But the enucleated egg cell had no genes – these came from the quiescent mammary cell. The newly combined egg-mammary cell began to divide as normal and make a ball of cells, then an early embryo.

5 The embryos which continued to develop were put into surrogate mothers and one grew to full term and was born – Dolly.

Sea world

The fastest whale in the world?

A humpback whale has amazed scientists by swimming the 4,466 kilometres from Alaska to Hawaii in just 39 days. Humpback whales rarely exceed eight kilometres per hour, but they are famous long-distance swimmers, migrating from Alaska to Hawaii to breed. Normally they do the trip in about 102 days; but this whale – known only as 339 – sliced 63 days off the average.

Scientists can identify individual whales by unique black and white patterns on their tail flukes. One of the scientists photographed whale number 339 off the coast of Alaska and sent the pictures to Hawaii. Then 339 was spotted in Hawaiian waters only 39 days afterwards.

Where is 339 now? Nobody knows. The scientist who took the photo commented, "That whale has also been seen in Mexico. He – or she – certainly gets around."

Hunting the giant squid

There are many seamen's stories and legends about the monstrous giant squid. But the giant squid is no traveller's tale – scientists are sure it is alive and well and living in the deep waters off New Zealand. Apparently, it is 20 metres long, with eyes the size of dinner plates, and a long, bird-like beak. Its tentacles resemble tree trunks fitted with suction cups.

Scientists are using specially equipped ships, underwater cameras, and a computer-aided mini submarine to track the monster; but their chief helpers are sperm whales fitted with special cameras called Crittercams. "Sperm whales eat squid," said a scientist, "so we let the whales be our hound dogs and lead us to them. ... It is amazing that this big animal exists and we know so little about it. We know more about dinosaurs than we do about giant squid."

Keiko prepares for freedom

The killer whale who leapt to fame in the film *Free Willy*, is himself preparing for freedom after nearly 20 years of captivity. Keiko the whale was just two when he was captured in 1978 and starred in the film that was a world-wide hit. But there was no freedom for Keiko, who remained in a Mexican zoo. His teeth were worn from chewing the pool sides and he had breathing and skin problems. In 1996 he was rescued and preparations began to equip him for life in the ocean. Four full-time trainers are working to build up his flabby muscles and wake up his sluggish brain ready for release. "Seeing him use his brain is like watching someone wake up from a deep sleep," said a trainer. Not everyone is sure Keiko will survive in the wild; but a special transmitter will be attached to his dorsal fin to enable scientists to check up on him.

▼ Steve O'Shea, a curator at the Ministry of Agriculture and Fisheries in Wellington, New Zealand, examines an 8-metre giant squid, caught about 500 kilometres off New Zealand's South Island in early January 1997.

Banks for the poor

More than one out of five people in the world – 1.3 billion people – struggle to live on less than 70 pence day. Most have no regular jobs. Some earn a pittance by running their own tiny businesses. They might shine shoes, weave mats, or bake bread. But even to set up such modest businesses they need to have a small amount of money to start with – to buy polish, weaving material, or flour. The banks won't risk lending to the very poor because they don't trust them to repay the money, so the poor turn to money lenders who take almost all their profits. One Bangledeshi man, Muhammed Yunus, saw how many people could easily be freed from this trap, if only someone would give them a chance. Sheila Davie of the organization RESULTS reports on how his idea is changing so many lives.

▲ In goes the card and PIN and out comes the money – banking has never been easier for those with money. But despite giving the impression that they are eager to lend money, traditional banks rarely take the risk of lending to the poor.

▼ A poor woman sorts through stinking rubbish at a dump in Guatemala City, Guatemala. Many people believe that microcredit schemes, which help people to help themselves, are the best long-term solution to poverty.

▲ This Bangladeshi family used their loan from the Grameen Bank to buy a bicycle rickshaw to carry paying passengers. The small investment provides them with both an income and dignity.

Sophia lives in a small village near Chittagong in Bangladesh. She used to be extremely poor, making bamboo stools for a living but barely earning enough to buy food and clothes. To buy the bamboo Sophia borrowed money from a trader. One day a man stopped beside her and asked why, when she worked so hard and made such beautiful stools, did she have so little money to show for her effort. Sophia explained that the trader would only lend her money if she would sell the completed stools back to him cheaply. He made sure that he never paid her enough to allow her to buy the bamboo from anyone else. She earned just one penny for each stool she made.

The man was shocked at this terrible situation. He could see that Sophia had the skill and energy to produce beautiful goods and knew that she should make more money from them. All she needed was enough money to buy the first lot of bamboo. Then she could sell her stools to whoever she wanted and charge a fair price for them.

An experiment in trust

The man who spoke to Sophia was Professor Muhammed Yunus, a

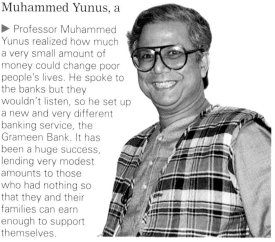

▶ Professor Muhammed Yunus realized how much a very small amount of money could change poor people's lives. He spoke to the banks but they wouldn't listen, so he set up a new and very different banking service, the Grameen Bank. It has been a huge success, lending very modest amounts to those who had nothing so that they and their families can earn enough to support themselves.

◄ Two borrowers from the Grameen Bank working on the loom they have bought with a loan. Once they have made the loan repayments, they still have enough money to live on.

▼ FINCA (the Foundation for International Community Assistance), believed that village banking could work as well in the United States as it does in developing countries. They were right; already the small loans it provides have helped many people, particularly in poor rural areas. These women, in rural Minnesota, used the money to set up a small business producing and selling dried flower arrangements.

young economics teacher at the University of Dhaka in Bangladesh. He listened to her story and asked why she didn't borrow money from a bank. Sophia told him that the banks would not lend to people like her who had nothing to use as collateral (money or possessions that the bank can take if the borrower fails to pay back the loan).

Professor Yunus decided to help and lent Sophia some money of his own. She bought bamboo from the market and sold the stools she made from it to her own customers. Before long she had repaid Professor Yunus and was making enough profit to buy her own materials, feed herself, and even to save a little.

The professor told his students at the university about Sophia. He described how there were thousands of Bangladeshi people, mainly women, in a similar situation and suggested they set up a small money-lending service. If the loans were repaid they could prove to the banks that it was safe to lend to the poor.

Over a number of years Yunus and his students made many very small loans. Every single one of them was paid back. The experiment was a huge success.

Grameen – the biggest from the smallest

Professor Yunus took his message to the local Bangladeshi banks. He said "the poor have proved they can borrow and repay money; now will you give them loans?" But the banks still thought it was too risky. So Professor Yunus decided to set up a bank that would only lend to poor people. Back in 1975, when the Grameen Bank (meaning "Rural Bank" in Bengali) first opened, almost everyone thought it would fail. They could not believe that the poor would repay their loans and thought that women especially did not know how to handle money.

How wrong they were. Twenty-two years on, the Grameen Bank is hugely successful. Every month it makes loans to over two million poor people (most of these are women, who have proved to be more reliable than men). The word spread and now there are similar banks in many countries.

Village banks

Lending small amounts of money is called microcredit or "microlending" ("micro" meaning extremely small). It is one of the most effective ways we have to fight poverty and is beginning to have a big impact in the developing world. And it isn't just in countries such as Bangladesh that the microcredit idea is successful. The idea has been imported to the Western world and now there are banks for the poor in the United States, Canada, and western Europe.

FINCA stands for the Foundation for International Community Assistance. Launched in Central America in 1985, it took Professor Yunus's idea another step forward with the system of village banking.

A village bank is a group of 20–35 members, mostly mothers, who meet once a week or so.

▲ Guatemalan women gather to pay in money to a savings club and microcredit project in Totonicapan in the west of the country. FINCA, a group that has set up 2,700 village banks worldwide, was launched in Central America in 1985.

FINCA sets them up with a small amount of money that they can borrow. They must invest the money carefully in businesses and then the bank provides a safe place for them to store any savings they earn. The village banks are run entirely by the members who elect their own leaders, make their own rules, make the loans, and collect repayments. Most importantly, the members guarantee each other's loans (which means that if one member should fail to keep up repayments, the others have to pay it back). So as well as giving direct financial help, the village banking scheme teaches borrowers a great deal about the responsibilities of business.

Seeing how well village banking worked in Central America, FINCA decided to introduce it to the United States.

▼ The first lady of the United States, Hillary Clinton, and her daughter, Chelsea, visited Bangladesh in 1995. They travelled to the village of Rishpara in the western district of Jhenidah where Professor Muhammed Yunus introduced them to a group of women who are members of the Grameen Bank.

La Capilla village bank

Before she joined the village bank in Quito, Ecuador, Mercedes earned only a very small income from gardening. She and her two daughters lived on corn, potatoes, and bananas. Mercedes received a £60 loan from La Capilla ("The Chapel") village banking group after she had spent four weeks training. She used the loan to buy a few chickens to raise a flock. Soon she began to earn money selling the chickens she raised, and their manure as fertilizer. Before long her daughters and niece were helping in the business, and the family put the savings back into the bank. They saved £100, far more than they needed to get a second loan. With that Mercedes bought plants for her gardening business. She found many new clients and soon that too became a flourishing business.

Now Mercedes' family has £200 saved with the village bank. They have a much higher standard of living, and know the true value of investment.

FINCA in the United States

Could village banking work in the United States? It was certainly risky to launch an idea that relies so much on people's trust in a society where people move around a lot, and often hardly know their neighbours. How could they be expected to work closely together and guarantee each other's loans? But FINCA took the risk and it has paid off. It seems that people in the United States welcome the sense of community that village banking brings.

The most striking difference between microcredit in the United States and elsewhere is the size of the loans members can borrow, between £295 and £3,500, around 20 times larger than those offered in developing countries. But these amounts are small in a country where the

▲ Hillary Clinton co-chaired the first-ever microcredit summit in February 1997. The Clintons are very enthusiastic about microcredit, the system of lending small amounts of money to people so that they can set up in business.

big banks rarely consider business loans of less than £18,000. In the United States, borrowers have to complete a loan application, detailing exactly how they plan to spend the money. It is demanding, but good practice. If they really make a go of it, they may find themselves successful enough to be applying for far bigger loans from commercial banks one day.

Whether the borrower is from Bangladesh or the United States and whether the loan is for £30 or £3,000, it is a start that poor people cannot get any other way. It can make the difference

▶ Judy Proudfoot, from Alexandria, Minnesota, was able to set up her own business "Proudfoot Wearable Art", thanks to help and advice from a FINCA organization.

between wretched poverty and running a thriving little business that brings in enough money to feed and clothe a family and build a decent house.

The goal

So far 13 million people have benefited from microcredit. It is a revolutionary way to tackle the massive problem of world poverty – to help people to help themselves.

So great is the enthusiasm behind it that in February 1997, a Microcredit Summit took place in Washington DC. It brought together nearly 3,000 people – heads of state, bankers, politicians, and microcredit workers and borrowers. Its aim was to find a way to reach a

▼ A young mother signing an agreement for a small loan at a village bank. The bank is run by a group of 20 or so members who are lent money by FINCA to invest in their own small businesses.

Judy's story

Judy struggled for years to raise her children while living on public assistance in Chicago, Illinois. She is a woman of quiet dignity who has known great sorrow, including the death of a child. She was anxious to build a better life for herself and her children.

To supplement her meagre welfare money, she began to sell shoes door-to-door. But Judy did not have the capital to invest in enough shoes to make the business work. Despite her ambition and natural ability to sell, she could not earn enough to support her family. Judy was referred by her caseworker (social worker) to the Women and Self-employment Project (WSEP). WSEP is one of many microcredit organizations helping women to create their own jobs in some of the poorest communities in the United States. Judy's first loan was for £380. She spent two and a half years finding plenty of reliable customers and gradually building up her shoe-selling business with larger and larger loans until recently she was able to open a store. Today she operates her own retail business. Her youngest son, who often goes with his mother to the WSEP borrowers' meetings, has plans to go into business too.

further 100 million of the world's poorest families to offer them the essential start that a tiny loan can provide. If that target is reached then we will have taken a hugely important step towards tackling world poverty.

RESULTS is an international grassroots lobbying organization and charity that played an important role at the Microcredit Summit. RESULTS campaigns on many issues to do with poverty and the developing world and has supported microcredit for many years.

Hong Kong – the handback of power

by Robin Lustig, BBC broadcaster

On 30 June 1997, the Crown colony of Hong Kong returned to Chinese rule after 156 years as a British possession. Prince Charles, the Prince of Wales, the British prime minister, Tony Blair, and the last governor of Hong Kong, Chris Patten, joined the president of China, Jiang Zemin, and the Chinese prime minister, Li Peng, in solemn ceremonies to see the British Union Jack lowered for the last time and the red flag of China raised in its place. It was a unique event in recent history – a territory and all the people living in it were transferred from one country to another, because of a treaty signed 99 years ago.

Hong Kong is made up of a main island, several smaller islands, and 850 square kilometres of the Chinese mainland. The name comes from the Chinese words *xiang gang*, which mean "fragrant harbour". More than six million people live in Hong Kong, and it's one of the most crowded places anywhere on Earth. Over 95 per cent of

▲ A map of China, Hong Kong Island and the New Territories.

▶ The last British governor, Chris Patten, holding a folded British flag as he receives a salute during a ceremony marking his departure from Government House in Hong Kong on 30 June 1997.

the population are of Chinese origin.

The story of how Britain came to be linked with Hong Kong goes back to the 1830s, when British trading ships sailed up and down the coast of China buying silks and tea for sale in Britain. In return, they sold the addictive drug called opium from India to the Chinese. Many Chinese became addicted and then the merchants supplied even more. In 1839, the Chinese government tried to stop the opium trade, confiscating 20,000 chests of British opium and burning them at Canton. The British government then went to war to protect its trading interests. The Chinese forces were much weaker than the British, and in 1842 the Treaty of Nanking was signed, giving Hong Kong Island to Britain. It wasn't very important at that time – the British foreign secretary, Lord Palmerston, called it "a barren rock with hardly a house upon it" – but it did have a useful deepwater harbour which was valuable to the trading ships. This harbour later became even more important as Hong

▶ This wax seal accompanied the Treaty of Nanking, which was signed in 1842 when Britain won the first Opium War between Britain and China. As part of the settlement, Britain was given control of Hong Kong Island.

▼ This painting shows the British warship, *Nemesis*, destroying Chinese war junks at some time during the Opium Wars of 1839–42 and 1856–60.

Kong developed into a thriving trading centre.

Once Britain had been given Hong Kong, the opium trade flourished again. But the Chinese didn't want China to be opened up to foreigners – they referred to them as "barbarians" – and in 1856 another war started. A second treaty called the Convention of Beijing was signed in 1860 which gave Britain Kowloon, the tip of the Chinese mainland opposite Hong Kong Island, to be held forever. By this time other countries, such as Germany, Russia, and Japan, all wanted to start trading with China as well, and the British felt threatened. For China, this was a time of humiliation and repeated invasions. In 1898, Britain signed a third treaty which gave it control of a much larger area of China. This land was called the New Territories, but it was given to Britain for only 99 years. That time was up at midnight on 30 June 1997. In theory, Britain could have given back only the New Territories, but because nearly half the population of Hong Kong live there, and because it was the largest part of the colony, there wouldn't have been much left. That is why all of Hong Kong has now been handed back to China.

Colonial rule

In its early years as a British colony, Hong Kong was not regarded as very important, although it did have a good natural harbour and could be used as a trading base free from Chinese

control. In the 1920s and 1930s, it became known as the "Paris of the East", and a popular place for adventurers who wanted to make a lot of money. Some people, both British and Chinese, became very rich, because the British government was so far away that no one paid much attention to what they were doing. Although the Chinese emperors did

◀ British merchants made huge profits in silver by illegally smuggling opium into China in the 1830s and 1840s. Many Chinese people became addicted to smoking the drug.

▼ Hong Kong Island at night resembles the centre of New York, in the United States. Huge shiny skyscrapers crammed together along the waterfront, look across to the Chinese mainland.

▲ Hong Kong's thriving stock exchange attracts investment from all over the world.

not want to have anything to do with foreigners, some other Chinese people did – and they went to Hong Kong where they could learn more about the outside world. Sun Yat-sen, a revolutionary who wanted an end to the rule of the emperors of the Manchu dynasty, said in 1923 that what he saw there convinced him that change was needed in China: "I began to wonder why it was that foreigners have done such marvellous things with this barren rock in only 70 or 80 years, whilst China with several thousand years of civilization has not even one place like Hong Kong."

During World War II (1939–45), Hong Kong was occupied by Japan, but after the war ended, Britain regained control of its colony. In 1949, the Communist Party came to power in China and 750,000 Chinese fled to Hong Kong. It was their presence and hard work which enabled the territory to flourish and develop into one of the fastest-growing economies in the world. Many of the newcomers came from the Chinese city of Shanghai, which was the most important business centre in China. They transferred their businesses and money to Hong Kong, because they feared that the communists would take everything away from them. Among the people

who arrived in Hong Kong at this time was Tung Chee-hwa, whose father owned a big shipping business. Tung is now the chief executive in Hong Kong, a position rather like prime minister in Britain.

Modern Hong Kong

During the 1950s, China was once again isolated from the rest of the world, and Hong Kong was the only place where trade could take place between China and other countries. Many small factories were built, with workers working very long hours for low pay. The goods that they produced were very cheap. At first the quality of the goods was often poor, but in recent years Hong Kong products have enjoyed a better reputation. The territory became one of the most important banking and financial centres of the Asia-Pacific area with a stock market attracting investment from all over the world. At the same time high technology industries such as electronics were developed and trading links were opened up with many other countries, including Japan, Singapore, and the United States. Today, Hong Kong Island resembles the centre of New York, with huge shiny skyscrapers, all crammed together along

▼ On 30 June 1997, a firework display lit up the Hong Kong skyline as part of the celebrations marking the handback of power from Britain to the Chinese.

the waterfront, looking across to the Chinese mainland. The harbour is one of the busiest stretches of water anywhere in the world. Ferries bustle to and fro, and huge container ships carry goods to and from every corner of the globe.

The main exports from Hong Kong are clothes, toys, games, computers, radios, watches, and sports shoes. More than one-third of all Hong Kong's trade is with China, and more than half of the money from overseas

▲ Lorryloads of Chinese soldiers arrive in Hong Kong before the handback of power from Britain to China at midnight on 30 June 1997.

which is invested in China comes through Hong Kong. Some of the richest people in the world live in Hong Kong, and the people there generally enjoy one of the highest standards of living in Asia. But there are still many people who are very poor and live in tiny apartments where a whole family has to eat, sleep, and wash in a single room.

The future

Many people were worried before Hong Kong was returned to China that the way of life there would change after the British left. But the Chinese government promised that it would respect Hong Kong's special characteristics for at least 50 years. It developed an idea called "One Country, Two Systems" to explain that although Hong Kong is now a part of China, its people will not be expected to live in the same way as the rest of the country. Hong Kong keeps its own currency and taxes, and many of its own laws, upheld by a separate police force. Many people feel that very little has changed so far.

The biggest changes are in the political life of Hong Kong. In the last few years before the handback the colonial government began to

▼ Hong Kong's Chief Executive Tung Chee-hwa (centre) displays a calligraphy work during a celebration of the first day of Chinese rule on 1 July 1997. Chinese President Jiang Zemin is on the left.

introduce reforms which allowed the people of Hong Kong a greater say in how they were ruled. China thought that the changes were being rushed through at the last minute, and the Legislative Council, or parliament, was abolished when the Chinese took over. Now there is a provisional council in its place, until new elections are held in 1998. Although China approved the Basic Law drawn up with the United Kingdom in 1990, which guaranteed certain freedoms to the citizens of Hong Kong, including the right to have an independent legal system, a free press, and the right to peaceful protest, some people doubt that China will let Hong Kong keep these rights. They cannot forget that in 1989, when Chinese students were demonstrating against the government in Tian'anmen Square, Beijing, the army moved in to stop them and many were killed.

▼ In June 1997, thousands of people gather in Hong Kong's Victoria Park to attend a candle-lit vigil in memory of the student protesters killed by Chinese troops at Tian'anmen Square, Beijing, in 1989.

For China, the return of Hong Kong marked the end of more than 150 years of national shame. The Chinese people believe that Hong Kong has always been a part of China and that now it is coming home to the mother country. For Britain, the handback of power was something that had to happen because of the treaty signed 99 years ago. For the people of Hong Kong, it marked the beginning of a period of uncertainty. No one knows for sure what China will do; some are optimistic because they believe that Hong Kong's continued prosperity and stability are as vital to China as they are to the people of Hong Kong. They also believe that China can use Hong Kong's economic success to help its own growth. Others are fearful because, after Tian'anmen Square, they do not believe that China will respect the personal and political rights that they have at the moment. But most people seem fairly confident that China's leaders mean what they say when they promise that Hong Kong will be able to continue with its own special way of life.

AIDS – new hope for a cure?

by Neil McKenna

Doctors and scientists racing to find a cure for the deadly disease AIDS, have discovered that they can stop HIV – the virus that causes AIDS – in its tracks by using a powerful cocktail of three different drugs. As yet this is not a cure, but the therapy seems to be an effective treatment. Scientists are hopeful that these drugs may eventually eliminate HIV from the body.

Every day, around 8,000 men, women, and children are infected with the human immunodeficiency virus – or HIV for short. HIV is the virus that causes AIDS. By the year 2000, there are going to be at least 40 million people in the world infected with HIV. The vast majority of cases of HIV are found in the

▲ Around the world at least 1.5 million children have been infected with HIV (human immunodeficiency virus) – the virus that causes AIDS.

▼ The HIV virus (coloured yellow) attacks the T-lymphocytes (coloured blue) in the white blood cells that form part of the body's natural defence against disease.

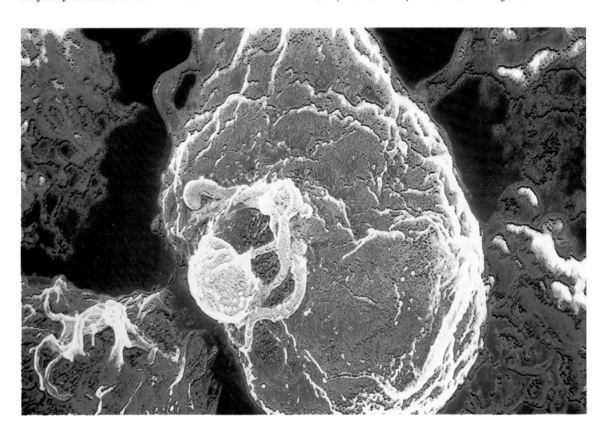

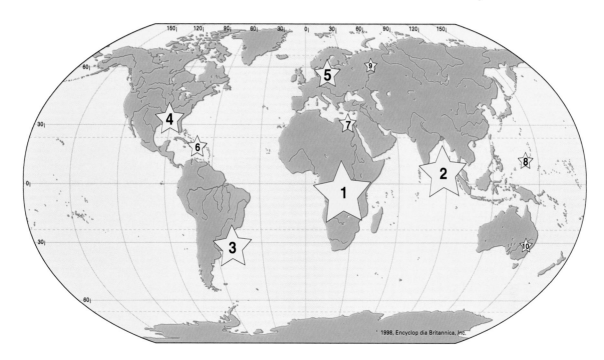

▲ Map showing the AIDS "hot-spots" around the globe. The figures below show the number of people suffering from the AIDS/HIV virus in each area.

❶ Sub-Saharan Africa – 14 million cases
❷ South and Southeast Asia – 5,200,000 cases
❸ Latin America – 1,300,000 cases
❹ North America – 750,000 cases
❺ Western Europe – 510,000 cases
❻ Caribbean – 270,000 cases
❼ North Africa and Middle East – 200,000 cases
❽ East Asia and Pacific – 100,000 cases
❾ Central and Eastern Europe and Central Asia – 50,000 cases
❿ Australia and New Zealand – 13,000 cases

poorer countries of the developing world – in Africa and Asia.

Globally, at least 1.5 million children have been infected with HIV, and around 500,000 have gone on to develop AIDS. Many of these children have already died. Many hundreds of thousands more children in the developing world have lost both their parents to AIDS.

All efforts to halt the spread of AIDS have, up to now, proved unsuccessful. Only a handful of countries – mostly the industrialized countries of the West – have been able to slow down the frightening speed with which the disease spreads through the population.

A scientific detective story

The story of the AIDS epidemic began in June 1981 in the United States when scientists at the Centers for Disease Control, in Atlanta, Georgia, became alarmed by a big increase in cases of a rare form of pneumonia among homosexual men in Los Angeles, California.

A year later, growing numbers of people within certain groups – homosexual men, haemophiliacs (people whose blood doesn't clot properly so that they bleed heavily when they cut themselves even slightly), and injecting drug users – were experiencing a sudden collapse of their body's immune system – the

◀ In April 1984 Dr Robert Gallo, of the National Cancer Institute in Maryland, USA, announced that his laboratory had isolated the HIV virus.

body's natural defence against disease. Doctors called this condition Acquired Immune Deficiency Syndrome – or AIDS for short.

Scientists were confused. What was the link between these cases? What caused the immune system to collapse and why did it seem only to affect these particular groups of people? The first real clue came in December 1982 when it was proved beyond doubt that a person had contracted AIDS as a result of a blood transfusion. So, whatever triggered AIDS, the scientists thought, was passed on through the blood.

Two teams of scientists led by Dr Luc Montagnier working in France, and Dr Robert Gallo in the United States, struggled to find the answer. Both teams of scientists –

◀ Five years ago US-assistant professor Dr Mahlon Johnson was infected with the HIV virus when he cut himself while performing an autopsy on an AIDS-infected patient. Massive doses of virus-beating drugs have reduced the HIV in his blood to a level so low that it cannot be measured.

Dr Montagnier in 1983 and Dr Gallo in 1984 – found that in all cases of AIDS a virus was present. HIV had been discovered.

By 1987, it was clear that AIDS was a major problem in Africa, in Latin America, and in parts of Asia, especially Thailand. And unlike the Western countries where AIDS had at first only been found amongst homosexual men, haemophiliacs, and injecting drug users, the vast majority of people infected with HIV in the developing world were heterosexual.

AIDS has now reached every country in the world and threatens the health of millions – especially those in Asia's crowded cities where HIV is spreading fastest.

The deadly virus

The HIV virus is clever and deadly. When HIV enters the bloodstream it attacks the white blood cells of the immune system which are the body's defence against disease. HIV inserts its own genetic coding into the immune cells with devastating results. Every time an HIV-infected immune cell is activated to fight disease, it produces new particles of HIV, which in turn infect other immune cells. Scientists believe that each HIV-infected cell can produce as many as 10,000 particles of HIV before it dies.

It's a continuous and lengthy process. People with HIV can look and feel perfectly well for several years after their first exposure to HIV. But all the time the body is fighting a losing battle against a rising tide of HIV-infected cells.

When the immune system has too few uninfected cells to defend itself from all the

▼ In December 1982 the first proven case of AIDS resulting from a blood transfusion, led to the routine testing of blood for the HIV virus in many countries.

▶ At the Aaron Diamond AIDS Research Center in New York City, USA, Dr Nathan Landau has discovered that some people will never contract AIDS because they are born with a gene called CKR-5 that protects them from infection.

bacteria, viruses, and parasites around us, the immune system collapses, and the patient is said to be suffering from AIDS. With no natural defence against a wide range of infections, he or she becomes ill and finally dies.

How HIV is passed on

HIV is quite hard to transmit. Unlike viruses such as the common cold or influenza, HIV cannot be passed on by coughing, sneezing, or kissing. Most cases of HIV infection world-wide are passed on through sexual intercourse.

HIV can also be transmitted through infected blood and blood products. In countries where the medical blood supply is not thoroughly tested for HIV, people have contracted HIV from blood transfusions. In the early 1980s many haemophiliacs in the United States and Europe were infected with HIV after using a blood-clotting agent made from HIV-infected blood.

Medical equipment which has not been properly sterilized after exposure to HIV-infected blood can also cause infection. HIV can be transmitted between injecting drug users because of their habit of sharing syringes to inject drugs which can transfer small amounts of HIV-infected blood directly into the bloodstream.

HIV can also be transmitted

▶ Dr David Ho of the Aaron Diamond AIDS Research Center, New York, believes that attacking the HIV virus with "combination therapy" in the first weeks of infection, may eliminate the virus completely within two or three years.

from mother to baby in three ways: while the baby is still in the womb; during the birth of the baby; and while the mother is breast-feeding the baby.

Treatments

In the early days doctors concentrated on trying to prevent and treat the infections that resulted from AIDS. But their real aim was to develop an anti-viral drug which can stop HIV's relentless spread through the body.

In 1987 a drug called AZT, which belongs to a group of drugs called nucleoside analogues, was found to slow down the reproduction of HIV cells. But AZT alone was not enough to stop HIV.

In the past two years a new generation of anti-viral drugs called protease inhibitors has been used to treat HIV. Protease inhibitors work by attacking an enzyme (the protein found in living cells) in HIV called protease, which is essential to the spread of the virus.

Both types of anti-viral drugs were found to slow down, but not stop, the reproduction of HIV. Why? The problem is that HIV can very quickly change itself, or mutate, in the body – in a matter of days or even hours – which means that the anti-viral drug is powerless against its new form.

Combination therapy

Taking their cue from the treatment of cancer, where doctors use several different drugs at the same time, AIDS scientists discovered as early as 1992 that two anti-viral drugs taken together were more effective than just one. And if two were more effective than one, what about three anti-viral drugs? And how about combining different types of anti-viral drugs – nucleoside analogues (such as AZT) and protease inhibitors – in this triple cocktail? Scientists gambled that the HIV virus would not be able to change itself fast enough to withstand the combined firepower of three anti-viral drugs.

The gamble paid off. The news of the benefits of triple combination therapy was unveiled in Canada at the Vancouver International AIDS Conference in 1996 and has since become almost standard treatment for people with HIV in Western countries. The effects of triple combination therapy have been remarkable. Some people who have been infected with HIV for many years, have found that levels of HIV in their bodies have been reduced so much that they cannot be detected.

Combination therapy is not without its drawbacks. Side effects of the drugs are common and often extremely unpleasant – a person undergoing combination therapy may feel sick and dizzy almost all the time. They may have to take up to 24 tablets a day at precise intervals, sometimes on a full stomach, sometimes on an empty stomach. If doses are delayed or missed, even for a day, this can have devastating effects, giving HIV an opportunity to develop resistance to one or more of the drugs in the combination.

Children with HIV face a special set of problems when it comes to combination therapy. Although children with HIV tend to fall ill with AIDS sooner than adults because their immune systems are not fully developed, very little research on combination therapy for children has been done. Doctors do not know what the correct doses for children are. Many of the anti-viral drugs licensed to treat adults are not yet licensed for use with children.

Combination therapy is also very expensive, costing many thousands of pounds a year to treat each person. This means that for the vast majority of men, women, and children with HIV who live in the poorer developing world, combination therapy is too expensive to be an option.

Some leading AIDS researchers, like Dr David Ho of the Aaron Diamond AIDS Research Center in New York City, believe that combination therapy is the key to a cure for AIDS. His hope is that if combination therapy stops HIV from reproducing itself for long enough, the virus will eventually die in the body. Up to now this has not happened – it seems that in every case of people coming off combination therapy, HIV has reappeared.

◀ US-actor Paul Michael Glaser, whose wife and two children developed AIDS as a result of an HIV-infected blood transfusion, has insisted that his one remaining son, Jake, be given combination therapy, even though the treatment is not yet approved for children.

It is still early days. No one is sure what will happen after a person has been on combination therapy for many years. Will the treatment eventually kill the last remains of HIV in the body, or will there always be a tiny amount of the virus left, ready to flare up when the powerful effects of combination therapy are withdrawn?

Prevention rather than cure

For most of the world's population, HIV still spells a death sentence. Even though treatments are now available in the world's wealthy countries, only the very rich in the poorer developing world will be able to take advantage

▼ Campaigners for a cure for AIDS march in Vancouver, Canada, before the opening of the 11th International Conference on AIDS.

There have been many theories to explain the origins of HIV. These range from the idea that HIV was developed by military scientists for the purposes of biological warfare, to the belief that it is a virus from outer space.

There are two less sensational but more likely theories. The first argues that HIV was contained in an isolated population, probably in Africa, until the huge social and medical changes of the 20th century allowed the virus to escape and thrive in the wider world. The other theory is that HIV is a virus that has jumped the species barrier. Viruses closely resembling HIV are known to infect cats, cattle, and monkeys. It's not unusual for viruses to jump the species barrier. Influenza viruses are thought to begin in domestic fowl and spread to pigs before they are transmitted to human beings.

of combination therapy.

Prevention is better than cure in the developing world, and most international aid agencies are spending money informing people how to protect themselves from HIV. Scientists are also searching for a vaccine that will protect people from HIV and a number of such vaccines are undergoing clinical trials. The problem with a vaccine for HIV is the virus's ability to change itself. There are two major strains of HIV in the world, and dozens of minor types. Finding a single vaccine that would protect against all the different types of HIV is a difficult task.

It's taken scientists just 15 years from the first, baffling appearance of AIDS to arrive at an understanding of what HIV is, how it works, and how to control its reproduction. Such progress is miraculous in the history of medicine. Given such progress, perhaps a cheap and effective vaccine, and a complete cure for AIDS, may not be too far away.

Thrust through the sound barrier

On 15 October 1997 in Nevada's Black Rock Desert, United States, *Thrust SuperSonic Car (SSC),* a black, ten-ton, jet-propelled car surged through the sound barrier and into the record books for the second time in a few weeks. British RAF fighter pilot Andy Green had become the first man to set a supersonic land speed record, almost 50 years to the day after United States Air Force pilot Chuck Yeager first flew through the sound barrier in a Bell X-1 research plane.

On 25 September 1997, *Thrust SSC,* with Andy Green at the controls, smashed the world land speed record with a 1,149.2 kilometre per hour (kph) run. Then on 13 October *Thrust* broke through the sound barrier with a storming 1,229.79 kph over a measured mile (1.6 kilometres). US-challenger Craig Breedlove, whose record bid had been dogged by technical and financial problems, had planned to run his *Spirit of America* car next; but he gallantly stepped aside to give the British team a chance to make its repeat run at once. The rules, set down by the Fédération Internationale Automobiliste, required a second record-breaking attempt to be made within an hour to make the record official. *Thrust* made the return run and broke the barrier again – then the team found that the run had been made just 1 hour 50 seconds after the first run. It was a devastating blow – *Thrust* had broken the sound barrier twice, but it didn't count.

It's official

In the cool Nevada dawn of 15 October 1997, one day after the 50th anniversary of Chuck Yeager's record-breaking achievement, *Thrust* tried to go supersonic again. "Mach 1", or the speed of sound, varies according to the surrounding temperature. So, to make the task a little easier, the team decided to make their bid early in the day, when the speed of sound was a little lower. That morning it was 1,203.93 kph.

Two sonic booms were heard in some parts of the desert, but near the measured mile where the record-breaking time was logged, there was only a faint pop. Bill Sherlock, a pilot who was flying above *Thrust* at the time, said that shock waves were clearly visible from the air and "totally shook the aircraft". This time the team managed the first supersonic run at 1,221.99 kph. Then team leader Richard Noble said, "You've just seen a supersonic run but we've got to be back within the hour. This is where the tension starts." The minutes ticked away as the team members and technicians raced to re-fuel the car, turn it around, and re-attach the parachute it needs to slow it down – all within the allotted hour. Then, with five minutes to spare, *Thrust* started the return run. This time it was official. *Thrust* had clocked an average speed of 1,227.98 kph over two runs. While an aircraft trailed a huge "Mach One" flag overhead, Andy Green with Richard Noble, who had devoted six years to the project, were carried shoulder high by their team mates.

▼ On 15 October 1997, on the Black Rock Desert, *Thrust SSC* team leader Richard Noble (right) cheers the new supersonic land speed record holder Andy Green, who is carried on the shoulders of his crew.

Thrust SSC proves itself

It had been a tense time for everyone. The team had spent five weeks out in the desert, battling with computer and technical problems, as well as unusually bad weather. Ron Ayers, the team's aerodynamics expert, had admitted that he had been unsure how well *Thrust* would behave at Mach 1. Would the car be tossed around like a leaf in the wind, or would its special suspension system, designed to raise the tail-plane and hold down the nose as *Thrust* exceeded the speed of sound do its job?

They call it a car, but *Thrust* is unlike any car that you have ever seen. Picture instead a black space rocket or guided missile on aluminium wheels, with two mighty Rolls Royce Spey Phantom engines capable of a theoretical top speed of 1,367.9 kph.

Ron Ayers, known for his design of the *Bloodhound* anti-aircraft missile, had taken on the challenge of designing a safe supersonic car as a retirement hobby. That hobby had involved fiendishly complex calculations on a computer, and sonic tests with a scale model bolted to a rocket trolley to convince him that, despite what everyone else said, it was possible to break the sound barrier on land as well as in the air. Watching *Thrust* prove him right was, he said, "more fun than mowing the lawn".

▲ On 15 October 1997, the British *Thrust SuperSonic Car*, driven by Andy Green, broke through the sound barrier on land. US-pilot Chuck Yeager was the first man to fly through the sound barrier 50 years before on 14 October 1947.

▶ Craig Breedlove, the US-challenger for the land speed record, stands next to his car, *Spirit of America*.

Model talk

Many teenagers dream of becoming a model. They imagine being spotted in a crowd and whisked away to a life of fame, fortune, glamour, and travel. For a few it really happens. How do they cope with the transformation from school student to supermodel? Janet Kelly and reporters from Children's Express investigate.

The 1990s has been the decade of the supermodel. Beautiful models are now just as famous and adored as the movie stars of previous eras. And in recent years, Western cultures have become more and more obsessed with very youthful images of beauty. The adolescent mixture of adult and childlike looks is in demand and people as young as 12 are being sought by the modelling agencies. British supermodel Kate Moss was "discovered" at JFK Airport in New York City when she was just 14, although her agency didn't allow her to model full-time until she was 16.

A British schoolgirl, Rachel Kirby, recently started modelling on the international fashion scene when she was 12. A newspaper covered the story, and there

British model Twiggy, whose real name is Lesley Hornby, led the fashion world in the late 1960s. Her wide-eyed looks and exaggeratedly slim figure had a huge impact on the modelling world.

▲ Kate Moss is among the leading models in the world. Talent-spotted at the age of 14, she modelled only part-time for two years. Now she is so famous that photographers and reporters follow her both on and off the catwalk.

was a great deal of debate as to whether she was too young to be modelling with adults.

Too young to cope?

What are the dangers for young models? Youngsters often grow up fast once they start modelling. Suddenly they are earning their own money and mixing with older, more worldly and glamorous people who may drink, smoke, or take drugs. Newcomers soon learn to look and act a lot older than they are. The pressure on them is intense. The work itself is hard, plus there are the added worries of putting on weight or breaking out in pimples. Some girls leave school to become full-time models. A few years later they may no longer be in demand. Perhaps their particular "look" has gone out of fashion or they are simply considered to be too old. They have missed out on their education, their modelling career has abruptly ended, and without qualifications they have little chance of finding another job.

It is often said that sex sells, and photographic shots may call for models to look sexy, alluring, and older than their years. On the catwalk, the fashions of many designers are very daring – and, many people believe, too suggestive to be modelled by young teenagers.

In Paris, France, girls must be at least 16 to model. Elsewhere, most large, reputable agencies are reluctant to take girls or boys on to model adult clothes until they are 14. Most agencies keep a careful eye on their young protégées and try to protect them from the dangers.

Children's Express chatted to models who see the temptations but, so far at least, have managed to survive, and even enjoy, the crazy world of fashion.

Hannah Ware

Hannah Ware was signed by a leading model agency when she was 12. She is one of the youngest models in the business, and has appeared in most teenage magazines, and taken assign-ments in France, Germany, and the United States. Although she is often described as a younger version of supermodel Helena Christensen, Hannah insists that modelling will only be a small part of her life. Here she talks about the pressures of working in a ruthless industry.

"I never take time out of school to do modelling because study is my first priority. I don't take a modelling job if it clashes," says Hannah, "unless it's loads of money!"

Hannah's career began when her mother took her along to the Storm model agency off London's trendy King's Road. The agency was worried about launching her when she was so young, but they took the plunge, and since then Hannah hasn't looked back.

"I was really flattered that they took me on at such a young age. I don't think it's spoiled me in any way," she insists. Hannah is confident the fashion industry won't change her because she doesn't take it too seriously. "It's just a hobby, I haven't been taking loads of bookings."

Despite the pressure of being part of an industry where image is everything, she claims her attitude towards her appearance hasn't changed. "There is a lot of pressure on girls to be thin. I haven't changed my diet though. I eat just as much as I used to." Hannah dismisses any suggestion that she might buy more expensive products because of the pressure to look good – with her earnings at £36 per hour already, she could well afford to. "I still wear the same cheap brand of mascara. I don't wear much make-up anyway – just mascara and lipstick, nothing too heavy," she explains.

Her minimal approach to make-up explains her dislike of most of the photographs of herself that make it into print. "They just don't look like me. Make-up can change the way you look so much; I look 21 in some of my photos."

▼ Schoolgirl models, some as young as 13 years of age, wear designer Vivienne Westwood's "Red Collection".

◄ "I really am aware that people might think that I am big-headed and all I have to think about is modelling." Hannah Ware pictured (centre), on holiday with her sister and brother, and (right) at a photo-shoot. ▶

Although Hannah's fame seems to have barely changed her, others find her success harder to deal with. "Girls who don't know me are often very nasty. They assume I'm really boring and obsessed by my looks. I've heard a lot of rumours about me which are really stupid," she admits. But real friends are a source of support and are enthusiastic about her work. "They're excited when they see me in a magazine but I tend not to talk about it with them, unless they ask me a question. I don't bring it up in conversation because I really am aware that people might think that I am big-headed and all I have to talk about is modelling."

Hannah's parents are happy with her new-found success as long as her school work doesn't suffer. Her younger brother is so proud of her that he shows her pictures to all his friends at school. But Hannah is keen to protect her sister from insensitive remarks. "It annoys me that people have to compare us because we are completely different. She doesn't want to be a model but she feels bad sometimes because people say, 'your sister's a model; how come you're not like her?'"

The money and the glamour of the fashion industry have failed so far to tempt Hannah into making modelling her full-time career. "It's not something which satisfies me that much, it's quite

▶ Charley Speed: "I am so happy that modelling came along. I feel secure, I love the money, I like being able to travel, and I like meeting so many people."

shallow." But she hopes her experiences in front of the camera will help her in the future. "I'd like to get into the business as a photographer. I've had a good start, seeing how they work."

Charley Speed

Charley Speed is 18. He has starred with Kate Moss in a huge advertising campaign for the designer Calvin Klein, and is hot property in the fashion industry. Yet he claims his feet remain planted firmly on the ground.

"I hated having my photograph taken as a child. Hated it. I didn't know what to do," says Charley Speed. "I still don't", he laughs, although events over the past 12 months tell a different story.

Since he won an important modelling competition when he was only 16, Charley's urchin-like looks have been blazoned across the pages of several teen magazines. They have taken him down the catwalks of New York, Paris, and Milan and earn him thousands of pounds a day. No wonder he is pleased with his life right now.

"I am so happy that modelling came along," he says. "I feel secure, I love the money, I like being able to travel, and I like meeting so many people," he enthuses. Having dropped out of college shortly before he was offered his first big contract, Charley jumped at the opportunity. He soon proved himself a natural model.

"I never feel any pressure to look good," he says, seemingly relaxed in an industry well-known for snapping up youngsters and swallowing them whole. "The clients are either going to like you or they are not," he states simply, adding that he is too lazy to go to the gym as his agent would like. He admits that his relaxed approach could have much to do with the fact that he is male. "There is more pressure on the girls in the business," he says, although he is quick to point out that girls on the whole can also earn a great deal more money. Charley doesn't feel

▲ Sophie Dahl, the grand-daughter of the author Roald Dahl, brought a different image to magazine fashion pages. She began modelling when she was 19, and her rounded, wholesome look contrasts with the ultra-slim figures that have dominated the fashion world for so long.

▶ Critics claim that ultra-thin models such as Jodie Kidd (right) become unhealthy role models for teenage girls. In their desperation to achieve a similar look, some develop eating disorders such as anorexia nervosa.

that he is being exploited. "If they are making you stand naked in the middle of a river and not paying you, you're being exploited. But that has never happened to me."

Charley has carved out a truly global career for himself; agencies all over the world book jobs for him. He believes "meeting all sorts" has truly broadened his mind. Spending a lot of time in New York has toughened him up. "American male models can be loud and strong. You've got to gain respect from them. You can't be nice.

You shouldn't be rude or stupid. Just keep quiet – until you have been doing it long enough to start being loud yourself."

Despite his glamorous life, Charley insists "I haven't changed since I started out, not at all. I don't want to. I'm not interested in being famous or meeting amazing women (who are a nightmare because they are all so worried about how they look). I can't be bothered to go to big parties, I still do the same things with my friends that I have always done. If it all ended tomorrow, the only thing I'd miss is knowing what my future held."

Juliet Fowler

Juliet Fowler is new to the modelling business. A year ago, when Juliet was 15, she visited the Clothes Show in Birmingham, England, when she was approached by representatives of a major modelling agency. "They arranged test shots and then said they would like to take me on," Juliet explains. "I had thought about modelling but because of school I didn't think very seriously about it." Juliet found out that she could work at modelling just at weekends and during the holidays. This persuaded her to go ahead, but to treat it only as a very casual part-time hobby. For something she is not taking seriously, Juliet's modelling has really taken off. She has done a great deal of photographic work, mainly for magazines, and has been selected for a model of the year competition. When we spoke to Juliet she was off to Nice, France, to take part in the international finals. Does Juliet want to make modelling her career? "It's possible but I'm not sure," she says. "After 18 months at college I may take a year out to model and see how it goes." How have her friends taken to her success? "I haven't told any of them actually. I don't want anyone to know. I didn't take it too seriously at first, I was quite shocked. It is hard work, particularly at the casting stage, showing people your portfolio to see if you're right for the job. There are loads of other models and it is very busy. When you get a job, though, it's brilliant. You turn up between nine and ten in the

▲ Juliet Fowler aged 16: "It is hard work, particularly at the casting stage… When you get a job, though, it's brilliant. Exhausting but fun."

morning to be introduced to everyone. It takes an hour or two to have your hair and make-up done and if it's a fashion shoot you are constantly changing clothes. It's exhausting, but fun."

In the business, Juliet does see other young girls whose only desire is to be successful models. "I would say it's about half and half. For some of them the dream does come true."

Children's Express is an independent, non-profit news service, reported by young people aged eight to eighteen, whose tape-recorded interviews, commentary, and roundtables are edited by teens and adults. For more information, visit the web site at http://ww.ce.org. Read another Children's Express article on pages 30–34.

Amazing rescues

Danger! Toothless crocodile

Even though Solomon, a 5-metre crocodile in an Australian wildlife park, has lost most of his teeth, he almost killed his keeper, Karla Bredl. Karla was making jokes to watching tourists about Solomon's lack of teeth when the crocodile grabbed her by the leg, then by the waist, and pulled her into the water. Her father, Joe Bredl, jumped on its back and gouged at its eyes. He then grabbed a rake and beat the crocodile about the head until it let go. Karla suffered a broken leg, broken pelvis, and internal injuries, but has no plans to give up her work. Meanwhile Solomon will not be destroyed. "He is usually fairly placid, and won't eat anything with bones in," said Joe.

▲ John Elliott, from Didcot, in England, who has cerebral palsy, is lucky to be alive. After collapsing while playing Scrabble on the Internet, he managed to summon help by leaving a message on the Internet which was read by Dee Dobyne of Chicago in the United States.

Seven days on a mountain

A lost tourist survived for seven days on Mount Kenya, thanks to a packed lunch, rain water – and her furry elephant. Helicopters airlifted 22-year-old Jessica Lundquist of Wisconsin, United States, from Mount Kenya National Park, where she had been wandering after becoming separated from colleagues during a climb. Her packed lunch lasted her three days. For the final four days she had nothing to eat or drink except rain water; yet doctors found her in good shape apart from exhaustion and blistered feet. She said later, "I clutched my furry elephant for comfort. It was freezing cold, and I was soaked. I am lucky to be alive."

Web of friendship saves John

The Internet became a lifeline for a disabled man when he lost consciousness during a Scrabble game. It was 2 a.m. in Didcot, Oxfordshire, in England, and John Elliott, who has

cerebral palsy, was playing Scrabble on the Internet. Dee Dobyne in Chicago, in the United States, who read John's message, "I've fallen out of my chair I'm dizzy and my head hurts mgbfgbmmmcghi....////", had no idea where John lived and no way of contacting him except by computer. It took eight hours of anxious enquiries on the Internet and on the telephone, as emergency services and other Internet users tried to trace John. The fact that Elliott is a common name did not help. At last, after checking registers of disabled people, the police traced John. He was conscious although he was still lying on the floor. John, who lives alone, said, "The Internet is my only contact with the outside world. In this case it was literally my lifeline."

◀ Jessica Lundquist (left) hugs a friend at a welcome home celebration at Mellen, Wisconsin, in the United States. Jessica was missing for nearly a week in Mount Kenya National Park.

The digital revolution

We'll soon have television screens with clearer pictures, hi-fi sound, and hundreds of channels to choose from. We'll have home shopping on screen so that we do not need to leave our homes. We'll be able to select camera viewpoints, and instant replays at the touch of a button. Or will we? The digital revolution seems to be just around the corner. But what is it and how will it affect our daily lives? Steve Parker looks at the possibilities of digital technology.

◀ Today's digital cameras need no film or processing. Instead they store images on a disc that can be fed into a computer and then printed out.

Digital technology lies behind today's computers and CD players. It is based on digits, which are whole numbers. It is different to analogue technology, which is based on quantities that can vary in a continuous way, like a wave shape that constantly goes up and down. If you imagine that you are going upwards, digital is like a number of steps or stairs, while analogue is like a continually sloping ramp. A lot of our everyday appliances – our televisions and telephones in particular – are still based on analogue technology.

Differences between digital and analogue can be shown by taking a look at the different types of wristwatches. An analogue watch has the traditional hour and minute hands on a circular face. A digital watch has a digital code – a display of numbers. Digital wins over analogue in two ways.

Digital precision

The first is that it is more precise. What's the time? On an analogue watch, it's just after half past the hour – well, nearly. On a digital watch, it's exactly 31 minutes and two seconds past the hour. Digital's precision is extremely important when dealing with many millions of radio signals or electronic pulses every second. It permits far fewer errors to creep in.

Digital reproduction

The second advantage of digital over analogue technology can be shown by this imaginary experiment. Ask someone to draw the time, by sketching the positions of the hands on an analogue watch or clock. Then pass this sketch to another person, who copies it. Pass it on again, and so on. Like a game of Chinese

▼ Fibre optic cables seem set to become the most efficient method of carrying digital signals around the world. Each strand is capable of carrying complex signals in the form of light pulses.

whispers, the information will probably change. With each redrawing or reproduction, the watch hands "wander" slightly from their original positions, and these wanderings add up. In analogue form, the copy of the copy gradually gets less clear and less accurate. People who try to make too many copies of copies of a video or audio tape know this. It happens with any form of information in analogue form.

Now imagine the same experiment with a digital watch. The time is in numbers, so even if it is copied many times, its accuracy should not change. This is very important when copying or converting information many times – from the sound waves of a voice, to electronic signals in a studio, to radio waves for broadcast, to electronic signals again in a television receiver, and finally into sound waves for the listener.

Indeed, many television and movie studios may convert their scenes from analogue form into digital code, for handling by a computer. Then they can add in special effects, edit out unwanted parts, and copy the pictures each time, without loss of quality.

Going digital

At present most televisions, radios, telephones, video and audio tapes still use analogue systems. Computers and CDs, plus Nicam sound for television, are digital. But the use of digital information will spread. It gives greater precision, reliability, and quality. Modern electronics can digitize pictures, sounds, words, and other information, and compress or squeeze them into smaller and faster batches of coded signals. This allows hugely greater amounts of information to be broadcast as radio or television programmes.

More and more of more and more

Around the world, huge broadcasting conglomerates and electronics companies are preparing for the biggest revolution since television began to invade our homes in the 1950s. They are launching yet more satellites

▲ Digital technology's capacity to carry a greater number of signals has enabled scientists to develop GPS (Global Positioning System) satellites. Here a walker checks his location with a hand-held satellite navigation receiver. Each satellite sends out a signal with its identity, position, and the exact time from an atomic clock. The receiver reads the data and can instantly calculate his or her position anywhere in the world to within 100 metres.

into space, erecting more terrestrial transmitter towers, and digging more cables underground, to bring us hundreds of channels with thousands of programmes daily.

The broadcasts will be digital rather than analogue, allowing more channels to be squeezed into the already crowded airwaves, with better picture and sound quality, less prone to interference and bad reception. Telephone networks, including mobile telephones, are undergoing a similar change. It's called the "digital revolution".

Choice or quality?

For example, the group or band of wave-like analogue radio signals which now carries one typical television channel, could be used for up to ten digital channels of the same picture quality. This would increase our choice of viewing enormously.

Alternatively, the same batch of analogue signals could be used for two or three digital channels with much higher quality, clearer, more detailed pictures and sound. This is known as HDTV, high-definition television.

A third possibility is a mixture of some extra digital channels, perhaps 50 or 100, plus some digital HDTV channels, all broadcast alongside each other in the "bit stream" – the high-speed

▼ ASTRA is a European satellite system transmitting around 70 television channels, and 40 digital radio channels.

▲ Around the world, thousands of kilometres of fibre optic cables are being laid, not only in towns and cities, but also across oceans to link continents.

transmissions of digital code in the form of radio signals.

The price of going digital

The digital revolution seems to be just around the corner. But it's been a long time coming, and even now, it's still in something of a world-wide mess. Different governments, electronics manufacturers, satellite operators, and broadcasters argue about many aspects. What should happen, and when? Which technologies, microchips, and circuits should be used as standard? Should there even be a standard, or should each group go its own way and leave the result to competition and market forces? Will our existing satellite dishes, terrestrial aerials, set-top decoding boxes, and television sets be useful in the future or thrown on the scrap-heap? How much might the new equipment cost? How many people could afford to buy it?

Choose your seat

What will these hundreds of television channels

▶ Many people who have invested in satellite dishes for a greater variety of television coverage may have to buy new equipment in order to be able to send as well as receive signals.

show? Of course, there will be many new programmes. Some of the channels may also carry the same programme at the same time, but in different forms. The viewer can switch between them to choose the combination of features he or she likes best – camera angles, split screens, insets, action replays, subtitles, national language, and even the commentator's voice. Another possibility is to select different options for a mystery movie or detective story, so that each time you watch it, there's a different middle or ending, and it keeps you guessing.

Two-way television

Yet another tele-revolution will be interactive TV. Instead

▼ In 1996, Time Warner's Full Service Network (FSN), the first interactive cable television channel in the United States, flopped after a two-year trial. Although this experiment was an expensive failure, interactive television seems set to become part of our lives in the future.

of the television set being one-way, simply receiving programmes and information, it will be two-way. You will be able to send information as well, probably by choosing items and menus on screen using a remote-control device with many buttons. Several groups of big companies are developing this technology, especially in the United States, Europe, Japan, and Australia.

◀ President Clinton speaks of the future of cable technology while addressing the crowds at the National Digital Television Center in Denver, Colorado, on 19 June 1997.

digital cameras mounted near the television set, select from the current music charts, order tickets for sports events or the cinema, enquire about the latest news from any corner of the globe, take part in educational programmes, book your next holiday – the possibilities are endless.

For interactive television, each viewer must be able to send signals out via the television set. Beaming signals from individual users up to satellites may be possible within a year or two. But each viewer needs suitable transmitting equipment, which will not be cheap. This will also turn each home into a mini ground-station capable of satellite communication, and it's not clear if special licences and precautions will be needed.

A more down-to-earth route is from the set, along the telephone line or cable, out into the world-wide telecommunications network. So cable television operators say their system already has a built-in advantage. It can easily carry information two ways along its fibre optics. The only extra piece of equipment required may be a new phone line. Then interaction, Video On Demand (VOD) and even, for computer users, Software On Demand (SOD), is just a short step away.

Window on the world

What could you do with interactive television? Vast amounts, say its supporters. You could go virtual shopping and order the goods, check your money in the bank and move it from one account to another. You could even hold a video meeting with friends in other houses using

The world through a screen

It will be very different from today's text-based services, where you can choose pages to read, but not send out messages or order goods. You will be able to chat, learn, shop, and interact through the screen. With home delivery, food and goods can be brought around to your house. You pay using electronic cash or "smart" bankcards from the decoder or box in your room. Need you ever go out at all? The television screen could become your window onto the outside world.

TVs, computers, and the Net

Interactive television is not the same as having a computer and being on e-mail or the Internet. Computers and televisions both have screens. But the computer has computing power, processing circuits, memory discs, and other equipment. So it is more expensive. In the near future a typical computer may cost two to three times more than an interactive television set with a similar-looking screen. Making either the television or computer screen high-definition quality increases the price again. But you couldn't play a full-scale, fast-animation, all-action computer game on an interactive TV, or

MON AUG 11 9:38 PM

webtv

TV Listings

Settings

Web Home

34
DSC

Swift, Smart and Deadly
9:00 PM – 10:00 PM

DEVILLE

2 FOX   5 CBS   11 ABC   54 PBS

▲ WebTV, the US-company backed by Microsoft's billionaire founder, Bill Gates, enables the consumer to watch television in one window, while "surfing the Web" on the rest of the screen.

download large amounts of information or games from e-mail or the Net. At least, not yet.

Coming together

Already you can buy a computer which also works as a television. In a few more years, computers and televisions may merge even further. You could use the same screen, keyboard, mouse, and remote-control – or perhaps by then, voice commands – to do almost countless tasks. All of those activities mentioned above for interactive television, plus computer-based activities such as word-processing, drawing and graphics, downloading information such as encyclopædias, sending and receiving e-mail, accessing and spreading information through

the Net, making animations, and chatting or playing games on disc will be possible with anyone, anywhere in the world, via ordinary phone lines and the expanding telecommunications network of the "information superhighways".

A global business

Groups of companies are developing and promoting digital technology in anticipation of this explosion in television services. Publishing giants and manufacturers are developing new products and new ways of packaging existing ones. Governments and lawyers are grappling with the legal implications of this expansion in communications.

It's a global fight for business, and the winners will wield enormous influence and power. They will control our access to the outside world from the television and computer screens in our homes.

Awards

A selection of top awards presented in 1997 for outstanding work

Nobel Prizes

Chemistry: John E. Walker, Paul D. Boyer, and Jens C. Skou for their research into how living cells store and release energy.

Economics: Robert C. Merton and Myron S. Scholes for creating, in the early 1970s, a formula for measuring how much stock options are worth.

Literature: Dario Fo, the Italian playwright who satirizes the Italian state, politicians, and the Roman Catholic Church.

Medicine: Dr. Stanley B. Prusiner for research into how proteins called prions cause disease.

Peace: Jody Williams and the International Campaign to Ban Landmines for their efforts to stop the use of land mines throughout the world.

Physics: Steven Chu, William D. Phillips, and Claude Cohen-Tannoudji for developing a method to slow down the movement of atoms so that they can be observed more easily.

Pulitzer Prizes

Journalism (Public Service Award): *Times-Picayune* of New Orleans, Louisiana, USA, for its series on why the world's stocks of fish are threatened.

Drama: No award.

Fiction: Steven Millhauser for his novel *Martin Dressler: The Tale of an American Dreamer,* the story of a 19th-century man's rise from shop boy to wealthy hotel owner.

General Non-Fiction: Richard Kluger for *Ashes to Ashes: America's Hundred-Year Cigarette War, the Public Health, and the Unabashed Triumph of Philip Morris,* about the tobacco industry's denials over the last 100 years of the harm caused by smoking cigarettes.

History: Jack N. Rakove for *Original*

▲ Arundhati Roy was awarded the Booker Prize for *The God of Small Things,* a novel set in modern Kerala, southern India.

Meanings: Politics and Ideas in the Making of the Constitution.

Biography: Frank McCourt for *Angela's Ashes,* his account of growing up in Limerick, Ireland.

Poetry: Lisel Mueller for *Alive Together: New and Selected Poems.*

Music: Wynton Marsalis for *Blood on the Fields.*

Booker Prize

Arundhati Roy for *The God of Small Things,* a novel about a family tragedy set in modern Kerala, southern India.

Academy Awards (Oscars)

Best Actress: Frances McDormand in *Fargo.*

Best Actor: Geoffrey Rush in *Shine.*

Best Picture: *The English Patient.*

Best Director: Anthony Minghella for *The English Patient.*

◄ Geoffrey Rush was named Best Actor for his portrayal of the classical pianist David Helfgott in the film *Shine.*

Terror in Peru

A party for more than 500 rich and powerful people held at the Japanese ambassador's home in Lima, Peru, ended in disaster when 14 armed terrorists burst in and took the guests hostage. The siege lasted for 126 days until the terrorists were killed by Peruvian commandos who stormed the ambassador's house in a dramatic rescue. Two soldiers and one of the hostages – a Peruvian judge – were also killed, and five others were injured. David Sapsted reports.

On 17 December 1996, the Japanese ambassador, Morihisa Aoki, held a party to celebrate the birthday of Japan's emperor, at his residence in the smart Lima suburb of San Isidro. His guests included politicians and other important people from Peru, diplomats from many countries, and Japanese business people. Most were chatting, eating, and drinking in a large marquee set up in the garden at the back of the house.

The partygoers thought that they were reasonably safe – there were armed guards on the gates to the ambassador's house, which was itself surrounded by a high wall. Although there had been many terrorist attacks in the past, they felt secure because the government of President Alberto Fujimori of Peru had cracked down hard on armed groups over the previous few years. Peruvian troops had arrested many in attacks on their jungle bases.

The siege begins

But the guerrillas did not come in through the gates. At eight o'clock in the evening there was a huge bang as they blasted a hole in one of the walls with explosives and rushed into the grounds of the house. Some of them went to the marquee where they fired shots into the air and made the men and women at the party lie on the ground. Others went round to the front of the house where they exchanged gunfire with the guards. One of the rebels was injured in the shooting.

It was all over in a few minutes and the victorious terrorists herded the hundreds of terrified hostages inside the house at gunpoint. Most of the terrorists were young – two were teenage girls and the others were in their twenties and thirties. But the leader, Néstor Cerpa Cartolini, was a rather chubby, 43-year-old man who immediately told the government by telephone his main demand in return for the safe release of the hostages – he wanted more than 400 members of his group, including his wife, released from the Peruvian jails where they were being held.

Cartolini and his followers came from the Tupac Amaru Revolutionary Movement, the

▼ Cerpa Cartolini, the rebel leader, freed hundreds of the original hostages. He refused to release 72 of the most influential hostages including President Fujimori's brother Pedro, Peruvian officials, foreign diplomats, and the Japanese ambassador.

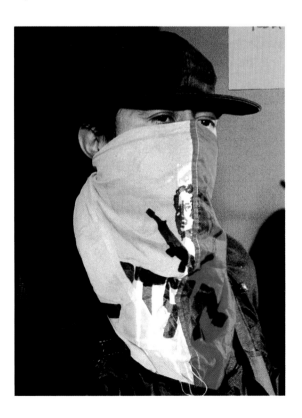

smaller of two guerrilla groups in Peru which have been trying to overthrow the government for 20 years. Both groups have been involved in many terrorist bombings and killings. Tupac Amaru, named after the last Inca ruler of Peru, and the

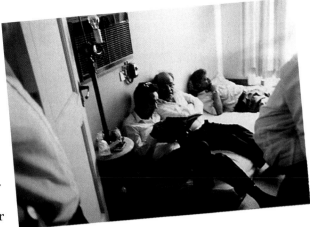

◀ One of the worst problems the hostages faced was boredom. They managed to fill the long hours of the 126-day siege by reading, writing letters, and listening to the radio.

Shining Path guerrillas want to install communist rulers because they believe that this is the only way to help the peasant farmers and many poor people living in the country.

Within hours of the attack on the ambassador's home, Cartolini began releasing the hostages. First, all the women were allowed out. Then, in the days that followed, many of the men, including the diplomats from Europe, North America, and many other countries, were freed. The house was simply not big enough for all the people being held there.

In the end, the rebels kept 72 people captive, including the most important Peruvians, such as Pedro Fujimori, the president's brother, and Foreign Minister Francisco Tudela, as well as Ambassador Aoki, 23 Japanese businessmen, and the Bolivian ambassador.

Peruvian troops and police had taken up positions around the ambassador's home soon after the rebels had stormed in, but they did not attack. The Japanese government insisted that the siege should be ended without bloodshed and so the business of trying to negotiate a deal began. A group, led by Juan Luis Cipriani, the Archbishop of Lima, was set up to talk to the rebels and the government.

Captivity

Life in the ambassador's home was grim. The government had cut off the electricity early in the siege and there was no air-conditioning at

the height of the sweltering Peruvian summer. There was no lighting apart from candles, and the rebels kept the curtains drawn to stop the soldiers outside from seeing what was going on, so the hostages lived in semi-darkness. A very limited water supply for the showers and lavatories was provided by tanks set up in the gardens by the Red Cross. Most of the captives slept on the floor on foam mattresses. They were not allowed to go outside. In any case, the gardens had been booby-trapped – a land mine killed the ambassador's dog early in the siege.

The Red Cross delivered food twice a day for the rebels and the hostages – raw fish for the Japanese and local food for the Peruvians. Bread, cheese, and flasks of coffee were dropped off during the evening for the next morning's breakfast. They also delivered letters from the hostages' families.

Boredom was the worst problem for the hostages and rebels alike. Without electricity they could not watch television, although each "team" of captives held in different areas of the house for easier control was allowed a transistor radio. For 24 hours a day for more than four months, they tried to find ways to pass the time. They read a lot – the ambassador had a large library and other books were delivered by the Red Cross. They were allowed to write single-sheet letters to their families; they played cards and other games, and they did jigsaw puzzles. The Japanese prisoners started to teach the Peruvians their language and the Peruvians taught the Japanese Spanish. The hostages even started a guitar class which one of the rebels joined. For exercise, some of the younger men organized runs along the ground floor of the house and then up the stairs to the second floor, where most of the hostages slept. Even so, the hours passed very slowly for everyone inside.

Most of the hostages were treated well, although some of the Peruvians were singled out for threats and rough treatment by the rebels. Despite the crowded, cramped, and unsanitary conditions, the health of the men remained good. As the siege dragged on, they were allowed visits by government doctors, who brought medicines. Towards the end of the siege, intelligence agents posing as doctors managed to smuggle in the radios and listening devices that were to prove crucial to ending the siege. Tiny, two-way microphones were hidden inside the books, guitars, and other personal items that were apparently sent in by the hostages' families.

The endless talks

At first, the group of mediators shuttled messages between the rebels and the government. Then direct negotiations began. Cartolini met the president's advisers at a house just opposite the ambassador's home. In early March 1997, almost three months after the siege began, the Tupac Amaru leader abruptly broke off talks because he said that he and his group could hear the sounds of men tunnelling under the house in preparation for a surprise attack.

The government denied that they were digging tunnels but this was a lie. Cartolini eventually resumed indirect talks with the group led by the archbishop and, as the weeks dragged on, it seemed an agreement might be possible. Although the Peruvian government refused to release all of the 400 rebels in jail, there was a chance that some might be freed and that others might have their sentences reduced. Cuba offered the rebels a safe haven and it was rumoured that Japanese businesses, anxious to see the hostages released, had

secretly offered millions of dollars as a ransom.

But, on 19 April, Cartolini suddenly went back to his original demand and announced he would accept nothing less than the release of all his imprisoned comrades. President Fujimori, whose military leaders had wanted to attack from the start, consulted with his advisers who told him that the preparations for a rescue were complete. The stage was set for the dramatic finale.

The rescue

The 140 Peruvian commandos were well prepared to end the siege – they had been practising on a full-size plywood model of the ambassador's house, built on an island just off the coast. In the meantime, more than 20 miners had been digging a network of tunnels under the grounds of the residence from the garden of

▼ Police snipers keeping watch on the Japanese ambassador's residence from the roof of a nearby building early in the siege.

▲ Smoke billows from the roof of the Japanese ambassador's residence on 22 April 1997, as Peruvian troops stormed the compound.

▶ Foreign Minister Francisco Tudela is led to safety by Peruvian troops in the dramatic finale of the siege.

▼ A Peruvian soldier peers out of one of the many tunnels dug beneath the grounds of the residence. The troops were armed with automatic weapons, explosives, and grenades.

one of the villas more than 200 metres away. Cartolini had been right about the tunnels, but he had failed to take measures to protect his group from a surprise attack in daylight. He assumed that any attack would take place at night, or very early in the morning.

On the afternoon of 22 April 1997, President Fujimori gave the order to attack. Many of the hostages, who were being held in the upstairs rooms, had 10 minutes' warning of the rescue thanks to the radios the "doctors" had smuggled in. They were told to get down on the ground and take cover, and to try to open a heavy metal door leading to the balcony outside the master bedroom. The soldiers knew that the time was right because they could hear on the secret microphones hidden in the house that most of the rebels were playing a game of indoor soccer in the large, downstairs living room.

The first explosions came from the tunnel directly below the living room. Before the sound of the blast had died away, there

were more explosions as bombs blew open the entrances from the tunnels into the grounds and the house. Other explosions blasted open the front door of the house, and troops rushed in. Another group of soldiers armed with automatic weapons, explosives, and grenades, raced up the outside stairs to the top floor where the hostages cowered on the floor as smoke and gunfire filled the house. "The whole house shook like cardboard," said an army lieutenant.

The rebels were in disarray, completely unprepared for the attack. Five were killed by the explosion under the living room and others, including Cartolini, were shot dead as they raced upstairs, presumably to carry out their threat to throw grenades into the upstairs rooms and kill the hostages if they were attacked.

On the balcony outside the upstairs bedroom where the hostages were being held, the commandos found the wooden outer door still locked, although the hostages had managed to open the inner metal one. The soldiers blew

▶ Peruvian President Alberto Fujimori talks on a radio on the driveway of the residence after soldiers successfully stormed the residence.

▼ The rescue operation

At 3.23 p.m. local time on 22 April 1997, President Alberto Fujimori gave the order for the rescue operation to begin. The 126-day ordeal was over in 36 minutes.

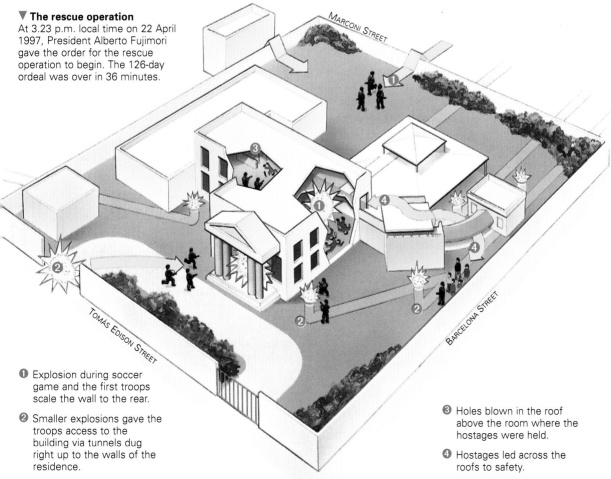

❶ Explosion during soccer game and the first troops scale the wall to the rear.

❷ Smaller explosions gave the troops access to the building via tunnels dug right up to the walls of the residence.

❸ Holes blown in the roof above the room where the hostages were held.

❹ Hostages led across the roofs to safety.

◀ Large quantities of primed plastic explosives were packed into tunnels directly beneath the downstairs living room where most of the rebels were playing soccer. The explosion killed five of the rebels instantly and ripped the room apart.

▼ The body of one of the rebels lies on the roof of the Japanese ambassador's residence near a tree still covered with Christmas decorations.

open the door with a grenade and stormed in. They gradually led the hostages, some crawling on their hands and knees, others carried on stretchers, across the roofs and down an outside staircase to freedom.

Although there were reports that four of the rebels, including the two teenage girls, were shot in cold blood as they tried to surrender, there was little criticism of the operation by world leaders. It was regarded as a remarkable military success, particularly as there had been so little loss of life among the hostages and soldiers. The Peruvian foreign minister was shot in the ankle by one of the terrorists, two soldiers were killed, and the Peruvian judge, who was hit in the leg, suffered a heart attack and died on his way to hospital.

The operation was also seen as a victory for the policy, which all governments say they support, of never giving in to terrorists. President Fujimori argued that he had to take the decision and responsibility for the daring military operation alone, without warning the Japanese government of his intentions, even

though this meant breaking a promise he had previously made to them not to attack unless one of the hostages was harmed in any way. It was an enormous gamble that could have gone terribly wrong, but in the end it was a gamble that paid off. Alberto Fujimori said: "I had to take such a difficult decision ... alone, but conscious that in Peru there could not be a place for terrorism."

Taking drugs – the facts

Illegal drugs were in the news in 1997. In May, US President Bill Clinton attacked certain photographers in the fashion industry for taking pictures of very thin, hollow-eyed models who looked as though they were heroin users. He said that the industry should not make taking drugs seem glamorous in order to sell clothes. In the United Kingdom, Noel Gallagher of the pop group Oasis created an uproar when he said that taking ecstasy was the same as drinking a cup of tea. Yet over 70 young people have died in the United Kingdom from taking ecstasy. It's all very confusing. What is the truth about drugs? Harry Shapiro of the Institute for the Study of Drug Dependence, London, England, tries to answer some of the questions.

What are drugs?

Drugs. When you hear that word – what comes into your head? Heroin? Ecstasy? LSD? Some people might think of medicines that you get from the doctor. But what about alcohol and cigarettes? Or coffee, tea, and cola? Surely they can't be seen as drugs as well? In

▲ A tribal woman harvests the opium poppy in Laos, Southeast Asia.

fact all of these contain substances that can alter the way we feel.

Does this mean that some drugs are legal while others are banned by law?
That's right. In fact the most popular legal drugs such as alcohol and tobacco can be very dangerous. In the United States and the United Kingdom, over half a million people die every year from diseases caused by long-term smoking and drinking. Coffee and tea contain the drug caffeine which is a stimulant and can be addictive. Caffeine is the most popular legal drug used by young people in the United

▶ Opium, grown in the Bekaa Valley, Lebanon is produced and exported illegally. The illegal trade in drugs is very lucrative and is protected by the power of the gun.

◀ This fashion photograph of model Jodie Kidd, wearing pale make-up with dark shadows around the eyes, is an example of the "look" that has been dubbed "heroin chic".

Kingdom, followed by alcohol, and then by tobacco. After these come cannabis and the other illegal drugs.

A young boy inhales glue on the streets of Bangkok, Thailand. The experience of solvent inhalation is similar to being very drunk on alcohol.

How many people use illegal drugs?

It is difficult to be certain about this, but we know that many millions of young people in the United States and the United Kingdom have tried illegal drugs at least once. Cannabis is by far the most commonly used illegal drug, while use of heroin and cocaine is much rarer. Heroin and cocaine are expensive and most young people can't afford them. The peak years for drug use are between the ages of 16 and 30. Before the age of 16 most young people don't have enough money for drugs and don't go out to clubs, concerts, and other places where drugs may be found. After 30, many people have steady jobs, houses to pay for, and families to look after. Their priorities change.

Why do they do it?

There can be many reasons. Here are a few:
• They enjoy it.
• It's fun to experiment and take risks.
• As a protest – their parents and teachers don't like it.
• Because their friends do it.
• Because it's fashionable.
• Because they want to escape from problems.

Can anybody be a drug user?

Yes, they can. The people with the very worst drug problems – those who inject heroin or smoke crack cocaine – often come from the poorest families and neighbourhoods. But lots of people from all kinds of backgrounds try drugs. Most will come to no harm. Certain people may become addicted to drugs because of some kind of unhappiness in their lives.

What drugs do people use?

Drugs can be divided into four groups according to the effects they have:

Painkillers These are the drugs that do exactly as the word suggests – they stop pain. We all know the legal ones we can buy from the chemist or pharmacist such as paracetamol and aspirin. But some very powerful painkillers are controlled under the drug laws (possession, supply, cultivation, and manufacture of these drugs is illegal). These strong painkillers are derived from the opium poppy and include heroin and morphine. They are very addictive.

Depressants These are drugs that slow the body down and make people feel relaxed and sleepy. Alcohol is a depressant. If somebody drinks too much he or she may eventually fall asleep. Sleeping pills and tranquillizers (such as Valium) are also depressants. Powerful painkillers, heroin for example, also slow the body down, which means that they can also be seen as a depressant.

Stimulants These are drugs that speed the body up and make people feel alert and energetic. Caffeine (found in tea, coffee, and some soft drinks and medicines) is a mild stimulant – so is tobacco. The strongest stimulants are controlled under the drug laws. They include ecstasy, amphetamine, methylamphetamine (ice), cocaine, and crack cocaine (smokable cocaine).

Hallucinogenics These are drugs that change the way people view the world. People may "see" unusual images, intensified colours, and hear strange sounds. Time can seem to stretch out so that a minute seems like an hour. Some of

Why have people died after taking ecstasy?

More than 70 young people have died in the United Kingdom as a result of taking ecstasy. Although this figure is very disturbing, most people who use the drug come to no harm at all. Those that have died have done so for these reasons:

• One of the effects of ecstasy is to raise body temperature. When people dance for hours in crowded clubs, dancehalls, or "raves", body temperature rises even more dramatically. A great deal of moisture is lost through sweating (causing dehydration), and in extreme cases the user may suffer from heat-stroke, collapse of the respiratory system (lungs), and death.

• Because of the heat problem, some people think that if they drink a great deal of water

▶ Paul and Janet Betts, the parents of Leah Betts, a teenage girl who died after taking ecstasy, have campaigned to publicize the dangers of taking the drug.

before they take ecstasy, they will be safe. Unfortunately, when people take ecstasy they urinate (pass water) less. When a large quantity of water has been drunk, it is soaked up by the body tissue like a sponge. If this happens in the brain, pressure may build up and cause collapse. In the worst cases a user may go into a coma and die. This is what happened in 1996 to a young English girl called Leah Betts who died on her 18th birthday after taking an ecstasy tablet at a party.

• Because ecstasy is a stimulant and speeds up the body, it is dangerous for people with heart or blood pressure problems to take the drug. They might have a heart attack or a stroke.

Dying as a result of taking ecstasy is very rare. Scientists are more concerned about the possible long-term damage, such as people becoming very depressed years after they have stopped taking the drug.

▼ The drug ecstasy has become closely identified with the "rave" scene – where people dance for many hours to electronic music with a fast repetitive beat.

these experiences can be pleasant, others can be very frightening. Most of the drugs in this group are controlled under the drug laws. They include LSD (lysergic acid diethylamide), certain types of mushrooms and cacti, and PCP (phencyclidine). Cannabis (marijuana) is also included in this group – the very strong varieties can have hallucinogenic effects – but the drug usually acts more like a depressant.

What are the dangers of using drugs?

First you have to think about the drug itself, then who is using it, how it is being used, and finally where it is being used.

• Different drugs carry different risks. A depressant drug such as heroin or alcohol can cause death if too much is taken (this is known as an overdose). A hallucinogenic drug such as LSD, on the other hand, might give users disturbing experiences, which might lead them to behave in a dangerous way. Taking too much of a stimulant such as amphetamine can cause anxiety, panic attacks, and mental disorder. Mixing drugs can also cause an overdose, especially if one of them is alcohol.

• Many of the illegal drugs are not pure. They are mixed with other substances that can sometimes be more harmful than the drug itself. A person using a drug such as ecstasy, for example, has no means of knowing whether the drug is pure.

• Drug use is more dangerous for people with health problems such as heart disease, epilepsy, diabetes, asthma, or liver problems. The state of mind of the person using the drug is also important. If people are worried or depressed before taking drugs, they are more likely to have disturbing experiences. They may take too much of the drug, or put themselves into dangerous situations. If they are depressed all the time they may come to rely on drugs to make them feel "normal".

• Some drug users inject themselves with drugs. This is probably the most dangerous way of using

▼ Melvin Burgess, who won the UK Library Association's Carnegie Medal in 1997 for his novel *Junk* which deals with heroin addiction, believes that authors writing for young people should not be afraid to cover difficult subjects such as drug taking.

▲ Noel Gallagher of the pop group Oasis was criticized for saying that taking ecstasy was the same as drinking a cup of tea.

drugs. Why? Well, the drug is going straight into the bloodstream, so it is very easy to overdose. People who inject drugs often share their needles and equipment with other drug users and this can spread some very dangerous diseases such as AIDS (*see article on pages 84–89*) and hepatitis B. Inhaling solvents (lighter fuels, glues, sprays etc.) can cause sudden death through suffocation (when a plastic bag containing the solvent is placed over the user's head), or from freezing of the airways when an aerosol is sprayed directly down the throat.

• We also have to think about where somebody is when taking drugs. People often hide themselves away because they are afraid that somebody might see them. They might go down by a river bank, or to a derelict building. Accidents can easily happen in such places. And if anything does go wrong help may not be nearby. If people drink or take drugs and then drive a car or ride a bike, they may injure themselves or others.

What does all this mean?
It means that it is not really possible to say "if you take drug X, this will happen to you". We are all individuals. What might be safe for one person could be dangerous for someone else. The safest option is not to use any drugs at all.

Not so dumb animals

Clever pigs

Let's face it, some video games are pretty mindless. And, as if to prove it, a scientist in the United States has taught pigs to play with them. Professor Stanley Curtis of the Pennsylvania State University started by teaching pigs to control the temperature in their sties, and found out that they preferred cooler temperatures than had previously been thought. Then he taught two young pigs, Hamlet and Omelette, to play video games on a special pig-friendly PC, gripping the joystick between their teeth. A hit brought a sweet and a "dwoop" sound; a miss only produced a "nrrr" sound. "Ham" and "Om", as the pigs are nicknamed, took only a few minutes to learn which movements resulted in the reward. After they discovered the key to winning, they rarely "missed".

One of Professor Curtis's colleagues, Dr Sarah Boysen, who has done many similar studies with chimpanzees, is impressed with the pigs. She says that they are equal to the brightest chimpanzees in many respects. "They are able to focus with an intensity I have never seen in a chimp," she said. Meanwhile, Professor Curtis, who grew up on a farm, says he will continue to eat pork; but many people who were involved in the project will never be able to look at a bacon sandwich again.

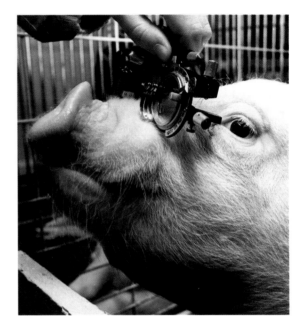

▲ Omelette, a large white pig (the same breed as the pig in the film *Babe*), has his eyes tested. Omelette and his half-brother Hamlet have impressed researchers with their ability to perform relatively complex tasks.

Sheepish

For many years farmers have used grids to keep sheep and cattle from straying. Any animal trying to cross the grid would get its feet caught between the bars – until a flock of sheep in Bramshaw, Hampshire, in England, figured out a cunning way around

the problem. Apparently, when a flock of sheep wants to go across the grid to the lusher grass on the other side of the fence, one of them lies down and the others use it as a bridge, negotiating their way across its woolly back to the other side. Sarah Wyatt told other villagers about the bridge method: "Once the sheep saw grass on the other side of my cattle grid, they obviously decided that nothing was going to stop them getting in."

◄ Hungry sheep in the New Forest village of Bramshaw, about to use their "commando style" tactics (described in the article above) to cross a cattle grid to reach grass on the other side.

Diana, Princess of Wales

The death of Diana, Princess of Wales, in a car crash in Paris on 31 August 1997 shocked the world, but the outpouring of grief and affection that followed was totally unexpected. Here, Lesley Riley looks at why the Princess of Wales captured the hearts of so many – not just in Britain but around the world.

◀ Lady Diana Spencer smiles shyly for the press on a visit to Balmoral castle with Prince Charles before their wedding in 1981.

Much has been written about the princess, especially since her death. The picture painted by many at that time was one of a saint. But this hides one of the secrets of Diana's appeal. She was able to combine a dazzling royal presence with the down-to-earth qualities of a "real" – and by no means perfect – person.

The fairy-tale princess

When the world first became aware of Diana, it saw a shy, pretty, 19-year-old girl, who was

▼ The "fairy-tale" wedding of the Prince and Princess of Wales on 29 July 1981 at St Paul's Cathedral in London, and their kiss on the balcony of Buckingham Palace, were watched by an estimated 1,000 million people on televisions around the world.

working as a nursery teacher in London. In reality, she was no ordinary commoner. Lady Diana Spencer came from one of the wealthiest and most aristocratic families in the United Kingdom. She had known Prince Charles, the Prince of Wales, since she was a young girl, and their romance captured many people's imagination.

Diana's vitality and youthful charm turned the solemn pomp and ceremony of their wedding at St Paul's Cathedral in 1981 into a huge popular celebration of romance, seen on television screens around the world. As she took up her duties as the Princess of Wales, Diana gradually shed her shyness. In public she became more confident, developing her own sense of style and fashion. She was the centre of attention wherever she went, whether working for one of the many charities she supported, or dancing with US-actor John Travolta at the White House in Washington, DC. During one "walkabout" Prince Charles remarked that he was only there to collect the flowers; another time he said he wished there were two Dianas, so that when meeting the public she could be on both sides of the street at once.

Princess Diana may have been born into one of the most aristocratic families in Britain, but nothing could have prepared her for life with the British royal family. Her outgoing temperament, sense of fun, and readiness to express her feelings were always at odds with the House of Windsor's famous formality and stiffness. Beside her, they often seemed stuffy and dull. This may have been the royal family's way of dealing with the strain of being constantly in the public eye. Diana seems to have felt that they gave her little support when she was struggling to cope with the loss of her privacy.

After the birth of Prince William in 1982, Diana became depressed. Secretly, she was suffering from bulimia, an eating disorder that often affects people (usually women) who feel unloved, and who have a low opinion of their own worth. Prince Charles apparently failed to recognize that she was crying out for help. Diana had a second child, Harry, in 1984, but she was still deeply unhappy. The couple put on a show of affection for the cameras, but by the late 1980s it was clear to everyone that there was a rift between them. They agreed to separate in December 1992, and were divorced in 1996.

Despite the sometimes embarrassing

◀ The strain on the marriage between the Prince and Princess of Wales becomes obvious as they look in opposite directions during a visit to Seoul, South Korea.

revelations about the royal couple's private lives, Diana's magic aura survived. Once she had come to terms with her illness and sought help, she found that she had the strength to overcome it. She became fit and healthy again, glowing with energy and confidence.

In the months before her death it appeared that she had achieved some degree of inner peace. She was once more on friendly terms with Prince Charles, and had found purpose in her life through her support of causes and issues such as the campaign to ban land mines. She even seemed to have found a new happiness with Dodi Fayed, a wealthy Egyptian businessman, who also died in the car crash in Paris. The grief that greeted Diana's death was in part, perhaps, sparked by a sense that she had been cheated of the new life that was opening up for her.

▼ Diana, Princess of Wales, enjoys the log ride with William and Harry at a theme park in England in 1994. Her warm, informal approach to motherhood was a complete break with royal tradition.

The natural mother

If Princess Diana brought new zest and glamour to the British royal family, where her children were concerned she broke entirely with its previous customs. For generations, British royal children had been brought up by nannies, governesses, and private tutors. They grew up having little contact with their parents, meeting few children outside the small circle of their own relatives and the families of courtiers. Neither Prince Charles nor Princess Diana had any wish for their children

◄ Running in bare feet, Princess Diana dashes over the finishing line to win the mother's race on sports day at Prince Harry's school in 1989.

to grow up as distant from their parents as Charles had been.

At the same time Diana fully respected the traditions of the royal family, and wanted to be sure that the princes – particularly William, who would one day be king – understood and could deal with all that would be expected of them in the years to come. She believed that the monarchy would be stronger if William and his brother understood what real life was like for many people, especially the less fortunate ones. Her approach was not meant as a break with tradition, but as a way to renew and refresh it.

One of the first signs of the new royal style came in 1983. It was unheard of for a royal couple to take a baby on an official tour, but that year Charles and Diana took William with them to Australia. As they grew up, Diana gave her sons lots of hugs and kisses, took them to theme parks and to Disneyland, on skiing holidays, white-water rafting, and on spontaneous trips to the cinema. She also took them to visit Centrepoint, a hostel in London for young people living on the streets, and to meet AIDS patients in hospitals and hospices.

The princes' education too was different. Diana made sure they did not start their schooling in isolation. Both went to nursery and prep schools and William then went on to Eton, a top British public school. Even though these are exclusive, fee-paying schools for the children of the wealthiest people in British society, William and Harry's education was less isolating than previous generations of royal children. When Diana and Charles separated, they shared custody of the young princes. Diana had been hurt by her parents' divorce when she

▼ Diana's visits to Angola (below) and Bosnia in 1997 gave a terrific boost to the Red Cross's campaign for a worldwide ban on the use of land mines.

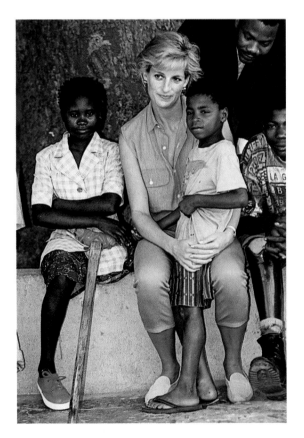

◀ Although Diana, Princess of Wales, sometimes used the press to convey her own messages to the public, the invasion of her privacy by press photographers who followed her everywhere she went was often unbearable.

was six years old, and was determined that her sons would not suffer in the same way. The princess may not have changed the royal family in her lifetime, but her influence on the British monarchy will surely be seen in future generations.

Diana the campaigner

Princess Diana had been a patron of many charities since her marriage, giving time and support to more than 100 organizations. At first, she was seen mainly as a fund-raiser, attracting attention and donations simply through her charm and popularity. Beneath that, however, lay a genuine interest and concern for the suffering and the disadvantaged. From the beginning she worked hard for the many charities to which she lent her name.

Over the years she became more personally involved in certain issues, recognizing that her name and fame could make a big difference to important but unpopular causes. After her divorce from Prince Charles, Diana announced she was cutting down her commitments and would concentrate her energies on just six charities. She had become especially interested in those caring for sick children and homeless youngsters, cancer patients, and people with leprosy and AIDS. Later on she became a roving ambassador for the international campaign to ban land mines, run by the Red Cross.

Diana's charitable work went much further than her public efforts. The media image of a glitzy modern girl who would rather be dancing than discussing world affairs entirely missed the Diana who spent her weekends visiting the

dying in hospices and the homeless in temporary shelters. She seemed able to reach across the enormous divide between herself and those in poverty, sickness, or despair because her sympathy sprang directly from her own experience of unhappiness – and people understood that.

Diana's support for a cause could have an electrifying effect on public attitudes. In 1987 she was photographed shaking hands with AIDS patients at the Middlesex Hospital in London. In 1989 she visited children in the AIDS unit at the Harlem Hospital in New York and held and hugged the young patients. At the time it was commonly believed that the HIV virus that leads to AIDS could be passed on just by touching someone infected with it. Diana's simple actions not only changed the way people thought of AIDS, they gave a great boost to people suffering from the disease. Almost single-handedly, she took away the stigma from AIDS.

Perhaps most effective of all was her work for the Red Cross's crusade for a world-wide ban on land mines. Although the campaign had been running for two years or so before Diana became involved, comparatively few people were aware of the issue until she took it up. In 1997 she visited first Angola and then Bosnia, two of the countries most plagued by land mines. The usual horde of press photographers followed, and the issue of land mines became headline news.

A natural communicator

Since 1980 when press photographers and reporters first learned of Prince Charles's interest in Lady Diana Spencer and besieged her London flat, Diana hated the intrusiveness of the media. The ever-present cameras made her the most photographed person in the world. But Diana also recognized that those images had a power of their own, and soon grasped how to use the relentless attention of the press for her own purposes. One result was the boost she gave to AIDS victims and to the land mines campaign.

With rather less success, she tried to

▲ Many thousands of mourners laid flowers outside Kensington Palace, the London home of Diana, Princess of Wales, as a tribute to her memory.

▶ Diana, Princess of Wales, seen here on her 36th birthday, became the most photographed woman in the world, who often used her glamour and style to promote her chosen charities and campaigns.

she did, but her doing so hardly justified the media's pitiless pursuit of her every move.

But – in the end – it is not Diana's use or abuse of the media that will be remembered. Even those who never met her recognized her winning manner and her gift for putting people at ease. She had a rare instinct for knowing what to say to the people she met, and how to say it. Diana also listened; she reached out to people, even touched them, where previously members of the royal family had kept both a physical and emotional distance. She became the "human face of royalty".

Diana's success in speaking to – and often for – so many different people on so many different levels was reflected in the mountains of flowers and messages left at the royal palaces after her death. The vast majority of these tributes came from people who had never met Diana or even seen her in the flesh. But they felt that they knew her, and that their lives had been touched by her.

In a controversial interview filmed for BBC television in 1995, Diana said she wanted to be "queen of people's hearts". In death, if not in life, she became that. But she would never have been given that place in people's hearts had she not shown that she shared with ordinary people a toughness, a will to survive, and the knowledge that, whether rich or poor, we all sometimes feel the need of a comforting hand.

persuade the British royal family to learn from her experience and use media interest to change its stuffy image. On a personal level, Diana was not above sending thinly-coded messages to the public about her private life. At the height of her marital difficulties, for example, she allowed herself to be photographed sitting alone and forlorn in front of the Taj Mahal, built by one of India's great emperors as a symbol of love for his wife.

Because of episodes like this some commentators have said that Princess Diana was contradictory or confused in her relations with the press. She may indeed have been unwise to make her personal troubles public in the ways that

Animal tales

A seal called Nuisance

A seal was chasing a shoal of fish when she got into a reservoir at Dungeness power station, England. In theory this shouldn't be possible, but a ship had damaged the filter designed to keep her out, and she was sucked 200 metres down a pipe into a big tank. There she stayed. Filters stopped her getting any further and the current was too strong for her to swim back.

Seals can swim for a long time without taking a rest, but sooner or later they need a break and the tank had vertical sides. Would the power station have to shut down to get the seal they had nicknamed "Nuisance" out? The answer, spokesman Bob Fenton said, was to give her an artificial beach.

"We lowered a raft attached to a crane and left it until Nuisance slithered on for a nap. Then we hoisted her out. She was then taken to a rescue centre for seals in Norfolk to check her over before returning her to the sea. They commented on how well-fed she was because the tank was full of fish. Nuisance had been to seal heaven."

Wildlife at risk

Headlines like the one in red above usually go on to blame human beings, but this time the threat comes from a 3-metre tree snake. The snake's bite is not fatal to people, but already it has wiped out 9 of the 11 native species of birds on the United States island of Guam in the Pacific Ocean. The snake originally came from Australia, where it had natural enemies to keep it in check. Unfortunately, it has a habit of hiding on ships and aircraft. Stowaway snakes have reached many Pacific islands and there are fears that it may reach the mainland of the

◄ "Nuisance" the seal seems to be winking as she swims in the reservoir at Dungeness power station in England. Perhaps this is because the tank was so full of fish that she put on weight while she was trapped there.

United States soon. President Clinton has set aside almost £1 million to deal with the problem.

Star tern

A tern recently set a world record for the longest flight by a bird – 25,750 kilometres in 18 weeks. The 115-gramme common tern averaged 200 kilometres a day on its flight from Finland, where it was ringed as a chick in June 1996, to Australia, where it was caught by bird ringers. They checked its ring and realized that the tern had broken the previous record of 22,530 kilometres set by an Arctic tern in 1956. Experts think the tern will stay in Australia until summer 1998, then fly home to Finland.

▼ President Clinton has set aside almost £1 million to deal with the problem of the brown tree snake – the "stowaway" snake that has already wiped out 9 of the 11 species of birds on the Pacific island of Guam.

Science '97

In the world of science and technology in 1997 there were new developments in most major areas. Steve Parker reports on the main stories – and some that didn't quite make the headlines.

Where would you like to meet today?

The Internet, the world-wide network of computers linked by the cables and satellites of the telephone system, continues to grow at enormous speed. From about 2.2 million host computers in December 1993, numbers had rocketed to an estimated 20 million by December 1997. With so many users, the places and ways that people meet on the "web" have become more varied.

How about a chat room? Users communicate by words, typed in via a keyboard. Each chat room has a main topic, such as sports, music, or historical events. Users choose the room which interests them most. In more advanced systems, voices are picked up and changed by a voice-recognition program into text.

Those with a taste for fantasy and games can meet in a MUD. This is a "multi-user dungeon" where each user can become a character, real or imaginary, with a certain "avatar". This Hindu-based word has been adapted to mean a personality that exists only inside the computer world.

MUDs have been mainly word-based. But a new program known as VRML, "virtual reality modelling language", now means that users can communicate and interact with images. You can design your visual avatar, of any human, animal, or alien shape, and of any size or colour – just the ticket for exciting online adventures in the virtual world of cyberspace.

Running out of water?

In the past 20 years, world demand for water has

▼ Waitress Jin Yuhua stands outside the Internet Café in Tianjin, China. Students at the nearby university use the café's computers to communicate via the Internet.

▶ An iceberg floats in Le Conte Bay, Alaska. Some scientists fear that global warming will cause the vast ice sheet floating on the middle of the Arctic Ocean to start to melt within 20 to 30 years.

risen three-fold. Finding the water in the first place, and the business of piping, pumping, cleaning, and disposing of it are multi-billion-dollar industries. But if we ate more chicken and potatoes, and less beef and rice, we could save vast amounts.

Scientists at Cornell University in Ithaca, New York, estimated the litres of water needed to grow or produce one kilogram of various foods. Rice was the "thirstiest" crop, requiring 1,910 litres per kilogram. Potatoes needed only one-quarter as much. Beef needed a massive 100,000 litres per kilogram. Only a tiny proportion was drunk by the cow – most went to grow grassy food. In contrast, one kilogram of chicken meat used only 3,500 litres of water.

Will the North Pole melt?

Surveys show that the Arctic Ocean, the world's coldest and shallowest ocean, is warming. Vast areas of it have risen in temperature by 1° C in just ten years. This could possibly be an early sign of global warming. Or it could be only a sudden but natural variation in temperature. Unless the trend slows down considerably, the vast ice sheet that floats on the middle of the ocean might start to melt within 20 to 30 years. This would raise sea levels around the world and flood low-lying areas, including many coastal regions, seaports, and small islands.

In October 1997, the specially adapted ship *Des Groseilliers* was anchored near the ice sheet off Prudhoe Bay, Alaska. The ship is part of a project called SHEBA, "surface heat budget of the Arctic Ocean". It will be frozen into the spreading winter ice with about 50 scientists and their equipment on board. They will live and work there for 13 months, taking measurements and readings of ice, water, sun, and weather.

Old eggs don't smell

In 1997 officials announced an amazing find of dinosaur remains near Mèze, in southern France. Found by amateur fossil-hunter Alain Cabot, the site consists of hundreds of preserved dinosaur nests, containing thousands of fossilized dinosaur eggs, 65–70 million years old.

There are at least six different kinds of eggs, some bigger than soccer balls (shown on the following page). This suggests various types of dinosaurs bred at the site, which long ago was lush and river-crossed tropical lowlands. The eggs do not stink, of course, because they are fossils and made of solid rock. In 1998 the site will become an open-air museum.

T is no longer rex

Meanwhile the fossil skull of the biggest meat-eating dinosaur ever to walk the Earth was

▼ Scientists have calculated that beef cattle need 100,000 litres of water to produce one kilogram of meat. The production of one kilogram of chicken meat requires only 3,500 litres of water.

displayed at the Academy of Natural Sciences in Philadelphia, in the United States. This honour was long held by famous *Tyrannosaurus rex*, "king of the tyrant reptiles".

But new fossils from Argentina show an even bigger predator, similar to T rex, but with a skull 50 centimetres longer, and a larger body. The new record-holder, *Giganotosaurus carolinii*, lived about 100 million years ago.

Floating frogs

One of science's odder reports in 1997 was the story of the frog that floats in mid-air. Scientists

◀ Scientists in The Netherlands use a powerful magnet to "levitate" a frog.

at the University of Nijmegen, in The Netherlands work with extremely powerful magnets. These very slightly change the atomic structure of nearby objects, turning them into temporary magnets with opposing magnetic fields. Amazingly, scientists were able to create a force strong enough to levitate a frog so it floated in mid-air for a short time, before it made its escape. Grasshoppers, fish, and plants were also lifted by magnets. "If you have a magnet that is big enough, you could levitate a human," said one of the researchers. He added that the frog did not seem to suffer any ill effects from the strange experience of levitation: "It went back to its fellow frogs looking perfectly happy."

Ol' Farmer Robot

Robot and computer experts are working on ideas which may reach the farm – one day. Robo-sheepdog will react to its flock, round them up, and herd them into a pen. But sheep move too fast, over ground that's too rough, for the robots they have developed so far. So designers are making a start with a robot that herds a flock of slow-waddling ducks around a smooth indoor arena.

Robo-pest-destructor will identify and kill animal pests on crops. It crawls around a field, detecting the pests and grabbing them. Then it takes their bodies back to its home base and dumps them into a fermenting chamber. The

◀ Alain Cabot with the dinosaur eggs he discovered at Mèze, in southern France. Thousands of fossilized eggs have been found on the Mèze plain and an open-air museum is now planned for the site.

bodies rot, produce bio-gas, and the robot uses this as environmentally friendly fuel. But again, today's robots are very slow. So they are being tried out on one of our slowest animal pests – slugs.

Caught in the NET?...

New York police have tested a new device to catch and incapacitate suspects without harm. Called non-lethal entanglement technology, it is – well, a NET. Just like the one Peter Parker, alias Spiderman, throws over his victims.

The NET device is like a hand-held launcher that fires the net itself, to spread and drop over the victim. There's an ordinary net about 5 metres across, a stun-net linked to a battery which gives electric shocks via a remote controller, and a sticky net with glue-coated fibres. Watch out, Spidey!

Or phased by reality?

The lightgun "phaser", set to stun or worse in *Star Trek,* may become a real possibility if Hans Eric Herr from San Diego, California, has his way. The gun would use a concentrated energy beam from the type of laser known as an argon-fluoride d-p excimer. The ray would be invisible, because it is ultra-violet, and so slightly out of the range of rays detected by our eyes. But he

▼ New York police have developed a net that can be fired at suspects in order to capture them without harm.

▲ Chess grandmaster Garry Kasparov considers his next move against IBM's Deep Blue chess computer while Chung-Jen Tan, manager of the Deep Blue project, looks on.

suggests it would be powerful enough to change the nature of the air it passes through, and carry an electric current which could stun, burn through clothing, paralyse, or kill.

In theory, that is. At present, this type of laser is bigger than a big refrigerator. But in years to come …

Oldest bits of Earth

The old-age record for Earth rocks was broken in 1997. They came from the Great Slave and Great Bear Lake regions of Canada. They are just over 4,000 million years old, creeping closer to the time when Earth formed from a whirling ball of dust, gas, and debris in space, about 4,600 million years ago. Massachusetts Institute of Technology scientist Sam Bowring said that they were "just like rocks being formed today – there's nothing unusual about them".

Computer beats chess champion

In May 1997, the IBM research super-computer "Deep Blue 2" became the first machine to beat a world chess champion – Garry Kasparov. Fifteen months previously, Kasparov had won the first match. But Deep Blue's "minders" had upgraded its programing and strategy to check out the consequences of 200 million moves every second.

With scores level after five of six games, Kasparov resigned in the last, after less than an hour. He went into the match "blind", unable to find out about Deep Blue's tactics, as he would do for a human opponent. He also said that if he improved his attitude and techniques for playing machines, he would "tear Deep Blue to pieces".

Sadly there will be no best-of-three deciding match. Deep Blue is being reprogramed back to proper scientific studies.

◀ The new Bell-Boeing 609, a cross between a plane and a helicopter, does not need a long runway on which to land.

More muscle makes mice mightier

Genetic engineers continued to produce weird and possibly wonderful creatures during 1997. At Johns Hopkins University in Baltimore, in the United States, mice were altered to remove the gene for the body chemical GDF8. This chemical normally controls and limits muscle growth. So each mouse's muscles grew to almost twice the normal size.

Extra-strong mice may not be especially useful. But the research could lead to better treatments for muscle diseases in humans and animals. It may also lead to farm animals such as chickens, pigs, sheep, and cows with extra muscle giving larger amounts of lean meat.

Tilt-rotor comes of age

After 20 years of problems with technology and finance, the Bell-Boeing 609 finally went into commercial production. It's a tilt-rotor aircraft – a combination of plane and helicopter. Most of it looks like a smallish plane. But at each wing tip is a large engine that can tilt or swivel. Its large propeller-rotors face upwards for vertical take-offs and landings, like a helicopter, then tilt to face forwards for normal flight, like a plane.

Also known as the V-22 Osprey, the craft has been tested by the US Navy and Marines. Its enormous advantage is that it needs no long runway – just a patch of flat ground, like a car

park. It could become common as a short-haul commuter craft, flying passengers between smaller airport-less cities. Or to and from larger airports, where it would not interfere with long-haul planes using the busy runways. It could even land in a school playground. Could school buses become school air-buses?

▼ Rocks found in the Great Slave and Great Bear Lake regions of Canada's Northwest Territories are believed to be over 4,000 million years old (story on previous page).

Inventions '97

Adaptable spectacles, a remedy for colour blindness, and a wind-up radio were among the bright ideas that went into production during the year. William Gould reports.

Superspecs

In the developing world, it can be extremely difficult and expensive to buy spectacles. For people living in a poor and isolated African village, for example, spectacles are a luxury that can cost a year's salary.

Enter Superspecs, or Adaptive Spectacles (Adspecs) to give them their proper name. They are the brainchild of British inventor Josh

▼ Dr Josh Silver tests his Superspecs on a villager in Ghana. Constructed from two pieces of plastic membrane, liquid, and a pair of syringes, they may look a little odd but they do work.

Silver, an Oxford University research physicist. Dr Silver's fluid-filled Adaptive Lenses, the outcome of 12 years' research, are at the heart of the new Adspecs. They have no costly glass or plastic lenses and can hardly boast what one would call "designer" frames, but they do work. Each lens consists of two pieces of plastic membrane sealed into the frames, and the Adspecs come with a couple of syringes full of liquid attached to each lens via short tubes. The liquid from the syringes is pumped into each lens so as to fill the space between the two layers of membrane. This alters the curvature or bulge of the lens and thus varies its magnifying power.

Wearers can use the syringes to alter the power of each lens themselves until their vision is corrected. Dr Silver claims that about 90 per cent of all sight problems can be corrected in this way, eliminating the need for eye tests and costly and complicated lens-grinding procedures. When Dr Silver visited remote

▲ This young girl is taking a colour-blindness test. The dots on the paper, to those with normal vision, form the numbers two and six. People who are colour blind see only a random pattern of dots. The colour lenses, invented in Hungary, have helped many people to see colours correctly for the first time.

villages in Ghana to test the Adspecs on the people there, the results were remarkable. Several villagers he met had lost their livelihoods as tailors, fishermen, traders, and professional people after they had become unable to do their jobs properly because of failing eyesight. Suddenly they found they could see properly again as soon as the lenses were adjusted to suit their eye problems. Their lives were transformed as they realized that they could once more earn their livings.

There is a huge market for Adspecs. The World Health Organization (WHO) estimates that there are about one billion people with sight problems in the developing countries of Africa, Asia, and the Middle East. Josh Silver's Adspecs can be made for less than a pound a pair, making improved eyesight affordable for poor people at last.

Seeing red

Colour blindness, more correctly called colour-deficient vision, is a condition that is passed down the generations and affects one in every twelve men and one in every two hundred women. Most people with colour-deficiency can see colour of some sort, but greens and reds both take on a brown or muddy tone and are easily confused.

Colour-deficiency is caused by problems with the colour-sensing receptors that form part of the *retina* (the membrane at the back of the eye on which the images we see are formed). These receptors are nerve-endings that respond to light from a specific region of the spectrum and send an appropriate message to the brain. There are three types of colour receptors, all mixed up together and concentrated in the central portion of the retina: the *tritos,* which reacts to blue light; the *deuteros,* which reacts to green; and the *protos,* which reacts to red. All three work together so that the eye can see all colours correctly. Experts once thought that people with colour-deficiency lacked one of these receptors. However, it is now believed that people with colour-deficient vision do have all three types, but one of the receptors is not functioning properly and is distorting the mix of colour data conveyed to the brain.

Up to now colour-deficiency has been impossible to correct with spectacles. But the new opinion about its origin has suggested a fresh approach to the problem. Scientists believe that the malfunctioning receptor is in fact being stimulated by light from a "wrong" part of the spectrum. The response of the receptor has been effectively shifted to a different part of the spectrum, and this is what is causing the distortion in the colour information reaching the brain. Two Hungarian scientists, Dr György Ábrahám and Dr Klara Wenzel, from the Technical University of Budapest, have come up

▲ This is the sun cycle, designed to take the puff out of cycling. Solar panels behind the seat are linked to a lead-acid battery bolted to a carrier above the rear wheel. The battery powers a motor on the front wheel which takes the sun cycle to a maximum speed of 24 kph, with no strain on the rider's legs.

with a process for correcting colour-deficiency by the use of coloured coatings on lenses or contact lenses. The coatings filter light entering the eye in order to counteract the spectral shift in the sensitivity of the faulty receptors. Some people with colour-deficient vision have already received Ábrahám and Wenzel's new filter-coated lenses, and

▶ The wind-up torch that could light the way for many more wind-up inventions. The BayGen company believes that there are 150 gadgets that could be adapted to use wind-up power – including computers and CD players.

hundreds more are expected to benefit from them, and will soon be able to see colours normally.

Wind-up future

A few years ago an engineer and inventor called Trevor Baylis started something of a revolution with his wind-up radio. Now BayGen, the company that manufactures the radio, which can now be bought all over the world, will soon launch a wind-up torch. The torch, known as the Freeplay self-powered lantern, eats up electrical energy at a much faster rate than the radio. Whereas the radio can run for up to an hour on a single winding, the torch uses more energy and will only work for five minutes at a time. But BayGen have found a way around the problem by providing a means of "dumping" the mechanical energy of the spring through the generator into a special electrical energy store of its own patented design. The store can hold enough electrical energy for two hours of use. To store enough energy for 15 minutes of light, all you have to do is fully wind up the torch and dump the energy into the store three times. By dumping energy in this way and using it when you need it, you could have plenty of power to run several types of machine, from radios and laptop computers, to CD players and mobile telephones. Just like a torch, each of these gadgets currently depends on batteries that can run out just as you need them most. With wind-up power as either the main, or the back-up, power source, the gadgets will become far more reliable.

Robots, robots everywhere!

Some people think that robots will outnumber humans in the next century. So many put in an appearance in 1997 that you can almost believe that might be true.

Being a guard in a museum sounds like the perfect job for a robot. In fact, guarding museums is exactly what SR2 has been invented for. SR2 has been programmed with a map of the museum and equipped with sonar. It uses the sonar to detect any changes or intruders in the galleries. The only problem is that it could have trouble running after an intruder, as it can't move as fast as human beings, even when the humans are just walking.

One mechanical marvel unveiled during the year was a robotic waiter that can be trained to take an order, serve food and drink, and then clear up the empty plates and glasses. Another was the "Lawnnibbler", a robot invented by Kevin Hakula and Scott Jantz, two science students at the University of Florida in the United States. This latter machine is the first lawnmower with artificial intelligence. It uses two smart systems, which tell it where it is and how to avoid bumping into things. The trouble

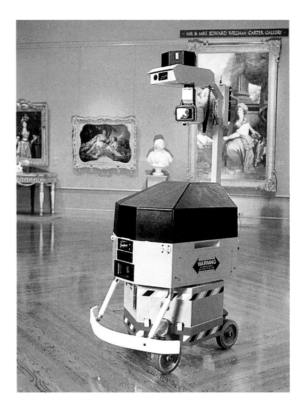

▲ An SR2 robot touring a gallery at the Los Angeles County Museum, California, in the United States. The robot uses video cameras, and infrared and microwave detectors to sense movement, and has temperature, smoke, and humidity sensors.

is, it's a bit small – 60 centimetres high by 60 centimetres deep and just over 30 centimetres wide. It can only cut a strip of grass 15 centimetres wide with its whirling nylon cord. Nevertheless, you will be able to leave it alone to get on with its job, knowing that it will avoid trees, the children's toys, and pets, and will still cope with the rough, hilly parts of the garden.

The year 1997 was a great year for musical robots. Professor Ichiro Kato of Japan trained his robot to read music and play the piano. Japan was also the place to go to see a whole host of *mubots* – musical robots. At the Tokyo Robot Exhibition in November, there were a violin-playing mubot, a cello-playing mubot, and two mubots on recorders. The quartet could play 50 classical and pop tunes.

Archaeology '97
by Martyn Bramwell

Musical cavemen, several new dinosaurs, forgotten cities, and ancient shipwrecks all made the headlines in 1997.

Prehistoric flutes, spears, and chewing gum

The old picture of Neanderthal people as primitive brutes without language or culture may have to be rethought. Scientists in Slovenia have discovered part of a flute made from the thigh bone of a bear. The fragment is 10 centimetres long with two neatly drilled holes on one side and traces of two more at the broken ends. It has been dated between 43,000 and 67,000 years old, which makes it the world's oldest musical instrument by at least 10,000 years. Musicologists believe the original flute was about 38 centimetres long and that it played the same scale used in modern Western music.

In February, the world's oldest throwing spears were unearthed in an opencast coal mine in north-east Germany. The three beautifully made spears are up to 2.3 metres long and just under five centimetres in diameter. They are made from spruce saplings sharpened at the root end into points. Dating back about 400,000 years, they would have been used to hunt deer, elephants, rhinos, and horses. The spears show that humans were skilled hunters much earlier than had been thought.

It seems that Stone Age teenagers (and some adults too, no doubt) were partial to a smoky-flavoured black chewing gum made from birch bark. Samples of the gum have been found in Norway, Sweden, Denmark, and Germany, with teeth marks still clearly visible. It appears the gum was popular from about 7000 BC to 2000 BC, but no one is sure just how it was made. Some of the ingredients contain disinfectant compounds so the gum may have been used to ease stomach aches, sore throats, and toothache.

◀ The discovery of a flute dating back to between 43,000 and 67,000 years ago suggests that Neanderthal man was musical.

More spectacular fossils unearthed

Clay cliffs on the Isle of Wight, England, have yielded a perfectly preserved skeleton of a sleek eight-metre-long flesh-eating dinosaur. The beast had a metre-long head bristling with razor-sharp teeth, puny little forelimbs with sharp claws, massive hind legs on which it ran down its prey, and a long muscular tail which helped the dinosaur keep its balance. The new species, named *Neovenator* (new hunter) is a cousin of the fearsome *Allosaurus* of North America. It roamed the lowland plains of Britain 120 million years ago.

There was great excitement in Australia when palaeontologists found the fossilized skeleton of a 1.8-metre carnivorous amphibian (a meat-eating creature that can live on land or in water). The remains date from the Triassic Period, 220 million years ago. That means it lived about 10 million years earlier than the first dinosaurs. The animal looked rather like an enormous salamander. Its short legs were no good for chasing so it probably hunted by lying in ambush and pouncing on passing fish and other small animals.

In the United States, excavations for a new underground railway, 25 metres under Hollywood Boulevard in Los Angeles, have turned up fossilized remains of mastodons, horses, camels, and bison which roamed the area until the end of the Ice Age about 11,500 years ago. The deepest parts of the site have

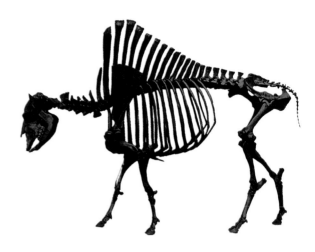

▲ A reproduction of a bison skeleton, one of the creatures which inhabited the Hollywood Boulevard area of Los Angeles, United States, before the Ice Age.

uncovered earlier fossils dating back a million years to when Los Angeles was still covered by a warm sea.

Hidden secrets of the ancient world

Workers digging the foundations for a new museum in Athens, Greece, have uncovered what archaeologists believe is the site of the Lyceum (school) founded by Aristotle in about 335 BC. It is generally regarded as the world's first university. The date is just right, the position is close to where historians believed the school to be, and the layout shows traces of the paths where students would stroll with their teachers as they discussed mathematics, philosophy, and science.

On the northern shores of the Black Sea, British and Russian archaeologists are working on the site of the forgotten Greek city of

▲ An artist's impression of the recently discovered *Neovenator* which roamed Britain 120 million years ago.

▲ Many lives were lost when the *London* sank outside Ilfracombe harbour in Devon, England, 200 years ago.

Phanagoria, founded around 540 BC. Already investigators have found over a thousand graves, filled with jewellery, gold coins of both local and Greco-Roman origin, and beautifully decorated pottery. Part of the city lies underwater due to a rise in the Black Sea water level, but unlike Athens and many other famous sites, Phanagoria has not been built over by a modern city. It covers an area of more than 75 hectares, and will continue to reveal its secrets for many years to come.

London sinking

Up to 60 bodies of shipwrecked slaves are believed buried in Rapparee Cove in Devon, England, where the treasure ship *London* sank 200 years ago. Over the years, several coins thought to be from the ship have been found on the beach, but in February came the exciting discovery of human bones and teeth that had

been thrown onto the beach by a storm. Investigators soon found more bones, and the remains of iron fetters. The 300-ton *London* was chartered by the British Navy to carry supplies to troops fighting in the French Revolutionary Wars. Her captain was a known villain, and was probably heading for Bristol with a cargo of treasure and slaves captured in the Caribbean. He approached the Devon coast in a storm but was too afraid to go into the harbour because the local people were deeply religious and opposed to slavery. Instead he tried to anchor in the bay. It was a big mistake. The ship went down with everyone on board.

Snippets

• There are suspicions that Stonehenge, the prehistoric standing stones in the west of England, may have been built by Bretons from northern France, and not by the ancient Britons. The arrangement of the stones, the carvings on them, and their astronomical alignment, have more in common with French

Queen Anne's Revenge

American archaeologists believe they have found the remains of the ship *Queen Anne's Revenge,* the 18th-century flagship of the English pirate Blackbeard. The wreck was found in the exact spot, a few hundred metres off the shore of North Carolina, where the *Queen Anne's Revenge* came to grief in 1718. Blackbeard, whose real name was Edward Teach, was born in Bristol, England, in 1680. He was a greatly-feared pirate of the high seas who created terror in the early 18th century throughout the Caribbean and along the eastern coast of America.

It was in 1718 that Blackbeard met his fate. Early one morning men from the Royal Navy climbed aboard his ship and attacked the crew. Blackbeard was beheaded and his body thrown overboard. Local legend says the headless corpse swam several times around the ship.

▲ Tutankhamen, pharoah of Egypt from about 1333 BC until his early death in 1323 BC. Was he murdered by his chief adviser?

stone circles than with others in Britain.

• An Egyptologist has claimed that Tutankhamen, the boy pharaoh who died in 1323 BC, probably from a blow to the back of the head, was murdered by his vizier (chief minister). If so, the killer was very clever. The law at the time stated that the vizier could be punished only by the pharaoh!

• Investigations are still going on into claims that archaeological treasures from Iraq are being smuggled to the West and sold by unscrupulous dealers in London.

• An expert on maps and aerial photography has claimed that the fabled city of Atlantis (which the Greek writer Plato said disappeared beneath the waves after an earthquake) is in the middle of a lake in Bolivia, and not in the Mediterranean after all.

• The faces of two Egyptian people who lived nearly 2,000 years ago have been recreated from their skulls using scientific techniques used in criminal investigation to reconstruct the faces of murder and fire victims.

The two heads were modelled in clay from casts of their skulls by Richard Neave, an artist in medicine and life sciences. It wasn't until he had completed the female model that he saw the portrait of the woman he had recreated. The similarity is stunning.

• A beachcomber in Melbourne, Australia, who discovered a coin using a metal detector unwittingly fuelled a long-running argument. The Victoria State Museum identified the coin as a 500-year-old real – good news for the Portuguese historians who claim it as evidence that their navigator ancestors discovered Australia in the 1520s. But a Melbourne numismatist (an expert on coins) believes that the coin is neither Portuguese nor early 16th century, but Spanish and struck around 1580.

• An ancient skull found in Kenya, East Africa, has strengthened claims that early human beings, who looked and behaved like us, were around hundreds of thousands of years earlier than previously thought. Experts believe the skull is around 270,000 years old. It has a full set of teeth and parts of it look very much like a modern human's skull.

▼ The model made from the skull of the Egyptian woman (below) is amazingly similar to her portrait (right).▶

Adventure '97

by Martyn Bramwell

Disabled marathon runners, ocean sailors, and hang-glider pilots are amongst those who made the headlines in 1997. We take a look at some of the most exciting adventure stories of the year.

The man who wouldn't stop running

On 16 April 1997, fellow competitors crowded the finishing line at Tagourite in southern Morocco to cheer home 34-year-old Chris Moon – the most extraordinary runner in the gruelling seven-day Marathon Des Sables. His total time was 47 hours 46 minutes. He finished in 283rd place, out of 343 runners who completed the race. But he was a true winner. He had completed the toughest race in the world just two years after losing his right leg in a land mine explosion.

In 1993, shortly after leaving the army, Chris Moon went to war-torn Cambodia, Southeast Asia, where he spent two years supervising the clearance of up to 30 land mines a day. He then moved on to Mozambique, Africa, to help clear land mines there. But shortly after arriving he walked into a supposedly safe area – and stepped on a mine that the clearance teams had missed. He lost his

▶ Chris Moon, who lost his right hand and leg two years ago in a land mine explosion, endures the searing heat of the Sahara Desert in the 230-kilometre Marathon Des Sables.

right hand and wrist, and his right leg below the knee. Doctors told him he would never run or go hill-walking again. Chris had other ideas.

Within a year, wearing an artificial leg designed for long-distance running, he completed the London Marathon in 5 hours 39 minutes – and raised £50,000 to help land mine victims in developing countries. He then decided to tackle the formidable Marathon Des Sables – a 230-kilometre race across the sand dunes and jagged rocks of the Sahara Desert in Africa. The dunes were up to 180 metres high, and temperatures soared to 40°C by day and plunged close to freezing at night. Competitors had to carry their sleeping bags, food, and snake-bite kits in heavy back-packs – only water was provided along the route. Fifteen runners failed to finish. Dozens more needed treatment for dehydration. Chris finished – blistered, exhausted, but jubilant, having raised another £100,000 for the victims of land mines – this time for the International Red Cross artificial limb programme in Vietnam in Southeast Asia.

Time and Tide proves doubters wrong

Round-the-world yacht racing is a tough business. Changing sails, mending rigging, and holding the boat on course in mountainous seas and freezing gales will

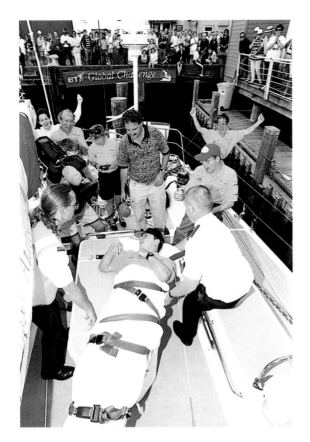

▲ *Time and Tide* crew member Brendan West is carried ashore on a stretcher in Wellington, New Zealand, after he smashed his kneecap in a storm.

push even the strongest crew to the limit. Not surprisingly then, many people assumed that *Time and Tide,* with its crew of disabled sailors, would come in last on each section of the BT Global Challenge – the round-the-world race for amateur sailors. They were proved wrong. On 2 January 1997, *Time and Tide* sailed into Wellington, New Zealand, ahead of *Courtaulds International* and *Heath Insured II,* both with able-bodied crews. But the 12,000-kilometre leg from Rio de Janeiro to Wellington, across the Southern Ocean against the prevailing winds and currents, had taken its toll.

Crewman Brendan West, who lost his left leg in a road accident, was stretchered ashore with a smashed right kneecap, having spent three weeks strapped to his bunk in great pain. John

Rich, who had lost a foot as a result of terrorism in Northern Ireland, was taken to hospital with stomach problems and fever. Most of the rest of the crew were nursing cuts and bruises and aching muscles, but these were all forgotten as a huge crowd cheered the boat into port. Flares were lit, and a mass of red and yellow balloons rose into the sky in welcome.

Brilliant navigation sets a world hang-gliding record

When the women's world hang-gliding champion Judy Leden, and her co-pilot Steve Varden, who has cerebral palsy, arrived in the Kalahari Desert, in Botswana, Africa, they planned to make an attempt on the world

▼ *Time and Tide* under full sail during the BT Global Challenge round-the-world yacht race for amateur sailors which ended in Southampton, England, on 16 July 1997.

tandem altitude record (height record for two people flying "tandem" on a single hang-glider). Unfortunately the weather foiled them. Instead of the bright sunshine and clear skies that they expected, the region had low cloud and ten times the average rainfall for that time of year. The local farmers were delighted – their crops would be successful. The fliers were not – the low cloud base would not allow them any hope of reaching their target. Instead, they decided to go for the tandem "declared goal" record. This is a tricky one. You have to declare a landing site before you set off, so pinpoint navigation is required. They covered 36 kilometres in two hours, and hit their target spot-on. "We didn't think that we had a hope of doing it because it's quite a lot more difficult," said Leden. It was the first time it had been done with a tandem, so it stands as a

◀ Judy Leden and co-pilot Steve Varden set the world "declared goal" record in their tandem hang-glider, after low cloud foiled their attempt to break the world hang-glider tandem altitude record.

new world record. According to Judy, when they landed they just lay on the ground laughing for about five minutes, then burst into tears. She said: "For me it was fantastic but who knows what it means to Steve to break an able-bodied world record and to do it by flying, where he feels so free? Normally he's encased in this wayward and disobedient body but when he flies he's just like anybody else."

France rewards a British hero

On 23 March 1997, British yachtsman Pete Goss sailed into harbour to a hero's welcome at Les Sables d'Olonne in western France. All the town's dignitaries and more than 100,000 people turned out to greet the yellow-hulled 15-metre *Aqua Quorum* as it finished in fifth place in the Vendée Globe single-handed round-the-world race. The boat's time of 126 days and 21 hours was the fastest ever set by a Briton, but that was not the reason for the celebration.

On Christmas Day 1996, in a howling gale in the middle of the Southern Ocean, Goss had picked up a distress signal from another competitor – Frenchman Raphael Dinelli – whose boat had capsized. Goss immediately turned round and battled 200 kilometres against the wind in search of the Frenchman. He found him the next day and radioed the race organizers, "I've just had the best Christmas present ever: Raphael is on board, cold but happy." Soon afterwards, French President Jacques Chirac announced that Goss would receive the coveted Légion d'honneur, France's highest award for bravery. When President

▼ Judy Leden and Steve Varden celebrate their successful flight under the shade of their hang-glider in the Kalahari Desert, Botswana, Africa.

▶ Hero Pete Goss, seen here on his yacht *Aqua Quorum* at the start of the Vendée Globe round-the-world yacht race, was awarded the Légion d'honneur, France's highest award for bravery, by President Chirac in June 1997.

Chirac presented the award on 19 June 1997, he threw his arms around Goss and Dinelli, and called Dinelli's rescue: "a magnificent example of the generosity of spirit and the solidarity of humanity".

▼ Pete Goss pulls Frenchman Raphael Dinelli from his life raft after sailing through 200 kilometres of heavy seas and howling gales to answer his distress call.

It was during this race that British yachtsman Tony Bullimore, from Bristol, had an equally narrow escape. In the same stormy region, Bullimore's boat capsized, and the lone yachtsman spent several days huddled inside the upturned hull of his boat before being rescued by the Australian navy. *See article on pages 58–63.*

Up, up – but not quite away

Businessman Richard Branson loves a

▲ Richard Branson's *Global Challenger* balloon soars into the skies over Marrakesh and the snow-capped Atlas mountains of Morocco. His attempt to circumnavigate the Earth ended 17 hours later, when the balloon was forced to land in Bechar, Algeria.

After months of planning, the *Global Challenger* lifted off at 11.19 a.m. on 9 January 1997 from a military base at Marrakesh, in Morocco. The balloon rose quickly and levelled off at cruising height, but barely seven hours into the flight things went badly wrong. At 5.50 p.m. the balloon suddenly started losing height. The crew had to throw food packets, water bottles, equipment, and fuel overboard to control the descent. The balloon then rose rapidly to 3,600 metres, paused, then plummeted earthwards again. This time the crew tried to jettison one of the six big propane gas tanks fitted to the outside of the capsule. The automatic release catches wouldn't operate. A crash looked inevitable. But disaster was averted when Alex Ritchie climbed out on to the roof of the capsule, wearing a parachute, and tethered only by tank straps. He then managed to release one of the one-tonne tanks manually. The descent slowed, and eventually Lindstrand was able to bring the balloon down to a safe landing near Bechar in Algeria, about 650 kilometres from the take-off site. *Global Challenger*'s mission control centre in London said that the balloon had been falling at an approximate rate of 121 metres a minute when Alex Ritchie bravely took action. They estimate that the balloon was only 20 minutes from a disastrous crash at that point. After landing Richard Branson praised the "unbelievable bravery"

challenge. After crossing the Atlantic and Pacific oceans by balloon, his project for 1997 was an attempt at the first balloon flight around the Earth, accompanied by his pilot on previous trips, Per Lindstrand, and co-pilot Alex Ritchie. They planned to make the 38,600-kilometre journey in about 21 days, riding the jet stream winds at a height of 9,100 metres in a pressurized capsule slung beneath a combined helium and hot-air balloon.

◄ Norwegian explorer Boerge Ousland, the first man to make an unsupported solo crossing of the Antarctic, waves his country's flag four kilometres from the end of his gruelling journey.

The Mystery of Amelia Earhart

The year 1997 marks the 60th anniversary of the disappearance of United States pilot Amelia Earhart (1898–1937), the first woman to fly alone across the Atlantic. After working as an army nurse in Canada during World War I, she learned to fly against the wishes of her family. In 1928 she made history by becoming the first woman to fly across the Atlantic as a passenger. Four years later she made a solo crossing, and in January 1935 she flew alone across the Pacific Ocean, from Hawaii to California. Her career ended tragically in 1937, when her plane vanished in the Pacific, shortly after taking off from New Guinea while she was attempting a round-the-world flight in a twin-engined Lockheed Electra, with Commander Fred Noonan. Amelia Earhart was never seen again, and the circumstances of her disappearance remain unknown.

▲ On 17 March 1997, Linda Finch of San Antonio, Texas (above), attempted a re-creation and completion of Amelia Earhart's ill-fated round-the-world flight, 60 years ago (left). Finch left Oakland International Airport, USA, in one of only two remaining Electras, the original plane flown by Earhart. She completed the trip 73 days later.

that Alex Ritchie had shown. "I truly believe that Alex saved our lives," he said. It's back to the drawing-board for now, but Branson hasn't given up and plans to try again soon!

Trekking to the extremes

In January 1997, Norwegian explorer Boerge Ousland completed the first solo, unsupported crossing of Antarctica on foot. He made the 2,800-kilometre journey in two months, on skis, using a parasail to help him when wind conditions were suitable. With a cumbersome supply sledge weighing 180 kilograms at the start, every little helps!

It was Boerge Ousland's second attempt to cross Antarctica on foot. His first attempt failed when he suffered from frostbite in the extreme cold. This time he managed to beat his main rival, British explorer Sir Ranulph Fiennes, who was forced to give up because of ill health. When Ousland was a few kilometres away from the end of his epic journey, Julian Tangaere, leader at New Zealand's Scott Base, who had been tracking his progress throughout the epic journey, said: "A message has been relayed to us that the first thing he wants is a cup of tea."

Arts '97

In 1997 exhibitions in London, England, celebrated a magical sculpture garden in northern India, and statues so life-like that you would swear that they were real. Helen Alfrey discovered that some artists in 1997 were fascinated and inspired by death, and visited the "performance artist turned dog" in New York. She has also taken a look at how new technology may help to reduce the number of art thefts in the future, and at the destruction of art treasures after an earthquake in Assisi, Italy.

The cement kingdom in India

The Rock Garden of Chandigarh, an extraordinary magic kingdom in northern India, was discovered in 1972 when workers were clearing an area of forest outside the city of Chandigarh. They were amazed when they stumbled upon an enchanted garden with several hectares of terraces, pathways, and waterfalls, inhabited by almost 2,000 life-sized statues of people and magical animals. The statues were decorated with pieces of glass and pottery and glittered in the sunlight.

The story of how the garden was built is almost as fascinating as the place itself. Nek Chand, the creator of the garden, started working on it as a secret hobby in 1958. At that time he was employed as a roads inspector for the new city of Chandigarh which became the capital of the Punjab state in 1947, after India became independent from the United Kingdom. The city was designed by the famous French architect Le Corbusier (1887–1965) who mostly worked in steel and concrete. Chand had no training in art or architecture but he was inspired by Le Corbusier's work. "I didn't dare to speak to him because he was the big boss, but I watched him work at close quarters many times." He taught himself to cast cement so that he could create his kingdom with its population

▲ The thousands of figures in the concrete garden in Chandigarh are decorated with pieces of glass, tiles, and other recycled material that Nek Chand found on the sites of many villages that were demolished to make way for the new city of Chandigarh.

of kings and queens, children, servants, and animals. As a number of village sites were being cleared to make space for the new city he was able to collect and recycle all kinds of junk materials, including broken pottery, old bicycle frames, tools, bits of jewellery, oil drums, and even human hair from local barber shops.

Each day after work Chand would load his junk collection into the basket of his bicycle and ride across town to his secret garden. Sometimes he worked all night, shaping walls, buildings, and statues and decorating them with mosaics made of glass and pottery. "For the first six months I didn't tell anyone, then I brought my wife, Kamla, here to see the hut I had built. She was very interested and at first came out here a lot to help me. I worked four hours minimum every day, and sometimes all night. I would collect old bicycle tyres, and light them to work by."

Today the sculpture kingdom is one of India's most popular tourist attractions with more than 5,000 visitors every day. Chand himself has become internationally famous. In 1997 his work was celebrated in exhibitions in London and Nottingham, England. His garden is no longer a secret but its magic remains as powerful as ever.

▲ Stephen Wiltshire stands in front of one of his recent oil paintings of a busy street scene in the United States.

Child prodigy makes the grade

Chand's work is an example of what is sometimes called *outsider art* because he had no formal training as an artist. *Outsider art* also includes work by children and by people who are mentally disturbed. Ten years ago a television documentary featured the work of another outsider. Stephen Wiltshire, from London, England, was diagnosed as autistic when he was three years old. Autistic children are withdrawn, locked inside their own imaginary worlds, and unable to relate normally to other people. Although Stephen could not communicate with his family and often had fits of screaming, he showed an amazing talent for drawing. The documentary, made when he was 13 years of age, showed the extraordinarily detailed drawing of buildings and places he had seen, sometimes for only very short periods of time, and memorized. His fine drawings of buildings

▶ Stephen Wiltshire's early drawing of the Eiffel Tower in Paris, France, is very different from the large, bold, and colourful oil paintings of street scenes and cars that he produces today.

were published and the money these books made helped to fund his years at art school.

Ten years on, in 1997, Stephen graduated from a three-year painting course in London with an exhibition at his degree-show of his latest preoccupation – oil paintings of street scenes in the United States. The paintings are large, bright, and confident. They show big yellow taxis seen through a car window, skyscrapers, neon signs by night, and the large American cars that are Stephen's passion.

The real thing

In 1997 an exhibition featured the work of US-sculptor Duane Hanson (1925–1996) whose life-sized figures look so real that you almost expect them to walk away from you and get on with their lives. Hanson, a Minnesota farmer's son, made ordinary people the subject of his sculptures. The exhibition included a couple of tourists clutching cameras and souvenirs, a jogger examining his foot with a discarded running shoe lying beside him, and an old lady with a shopping bag. They are exact replicas of ordinary

 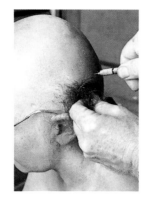

▲ Duane Hanson applies plaster of Paris (above left) on top of a fast-setting mould of silicone rubber onto the leg of the model for his sculpture called *Jogger* (below). Then the artist applies hair to the soft material of the head of the sculpture using a needle (above right). This creates the illusion that the hair is actually growing.

people from the United States doing everyday things.

Hanson went to great lengths to make his figures look life-like. He used real people to make vinyl body casts which he then sprayed with flesh-coloured paint. He gave them glass eyes and wigs, added body hair, and even bruises and blemishes. He dressed them in real clothes with real accessories, carefully chosen to express their taste and identity. The results are breathtakingly realistic. Hanson wanted those seeing his art to be confronted by a stand-in for a person so convincing that they would forget that it wasn't a real person. He often chose working class people such as waitresses, cleaning ladies, and delivery men as his subjects. These are people who work hard and are often exhausted by their lives. Hanson felt that he understood them and said: "I express my feelings of sympathy for the subjects I portray through their weariness and despair."

Body art?

Hanson used real people to make his vinyl body casts but the models he chose were very much alive. Throughout the history of art, artists have also been inspired by death. Leonardo da Vinci (1452–1519) studied the dead bodies of paupers to make sure that he understood how the internal organs, muscles, and bones of the human body worked. In this way he could be sure that his drawings of human figures were anatomically correct. Caravaggio (c. 1571–1610) was thought to have sketched the body of a dead girl in preparation for his painting *Death of the Virgin,* and it is likely that the Dutch painter Rembrandt (1606–1669) studied a dead body for his famous masterpiece *The Anatomy Lesson* in which a group of young men and their teacher are shown examining a corpse. The nineteenth-century French artist Théodore Géricault (1791–1824) is known to have made many visits to hospitals to study corpses in preparation for his painting *The Raft of the Medusa.* This dramatic work shows the aftermath of a shipwreck with a group of people, some dead, others dying, on a make-shift raft in high seas.

The artist's fascination with death is not just a thing of the past. Earlier this year police detectives were called in to investigate the theft of human remains by a British sculptor accused of using them in his work. In a newspaper interview earlier in the year Anthony-Noel Kelly had admitted acquiring parts of human bodies from medical schools and using them to make casts for his work. Although bodies can be donated for medical research it is against the law to use body parts for any other purpose.

Another artist fascinated by the idea of death is currently attracting attention in London. Christine Borland, a Scot, was one of four women artists short-listed for the Turner prize, an annual award for art run by the Tate Gallery in London intended to represent the best of modern British art. Ms Borland has a fascination with death; her work includes arrangements of human bones which she is said to obtain through the post from medical schools.

▼ Sculptor Anthony-Noel Kelly was arrested by detectives after a visitor to an exhibition of his work thought that she recognized the face of a dead relative in one of his sculptures. Kelly had previously admitted using human body parts in his work.

One-dog show

In recent years *performance art,* a form of art which has close links with the theatre, has become popular. The artist becomes a performer

▲ A gallery visitor wearing a protective suit faces "Dog Man" Oleg Kulik who lived as a dog for two weeks, snapping and snarling at people who came too close to him.

the public are transformed into spectators. A bizarre example of performance art could be seen in New York, this spring when Oleg "Dog Man" Kulik spent two weeks locked in a room in an art gallery in the fashionable Soho district of the city pretending to be a dog. Wearing only a leather collar, the Russian artist crawled about the room, ate and drank from a bowl, and communicated by barking, growling, and snarling. The show had the intriguing title *I Bite America and America Bites Me,* a reference to the work of a German performance artist called Joseph Beuys who in 1974 presented a work called *I Love America and America Likes Me.* On that occasion, the artist shared a cage with a coyote. Kulik went one step further. As well as being able to watch the "Dog Man" through the barred windows of his room, more daring visitors were invited to put on a special padded suit and enter his cell. He was not a friendly, loveable pet but an aggressive and ferocious animal. On one occasion television cameras covering the show filmed one unfortunate visitor being chased around the cell.

Not surprisingly the show attracted large numbers of visitors, who might well wonder what Mr Kulik's next exhibition will be, especially as Mr Kulik's previous performances have involved him hanging from a rope as a bird and wearing bull's horns.

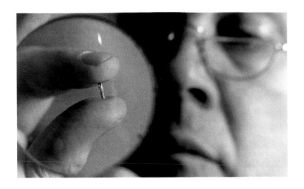

▲ David Webster holds the tiny computer chip that can carry information about a work of art and its owner.

Stop thief!

In 1997 a painting by Picasso worth £700,000 was stolen from a London art gallery in a raid lasting 35 seconds. The pony-tailed thief, armed with a sawn-off shotgun, walked out with the painting *Tête de Femme* (Head of a Woman), painted in 1939, and disappeared in a taxi.

Every year has its crop of stories about major art thefts. Recovering these stolen pictures is a difficult operation. Even when such pictures are found, police often find it difficult to prove who they belong to, especially when they are less well known than a painting by Picasso. Now however, thanks to up-to-date computer technology, the process of returning stolen art works to their owners may become a much simpler one. A computer chip has been developed which can be inserted into a painting, sculpture, or piece of furniture. The chip which is no bigger than a grain of rice and is completely invisible once it is in place, carries information about the item and its owner which can be read with a scanner. It's almost an invisible electronic fingerprint. The man behind the chip, former picture restorer and dealer, David Webster, used technology

developed by a US company in the late 1960s to help identify war casualties in the Vietnam war.

Earthquakes destroy frescoes

In September 1997, two earthquakes in succession hit Assisi's basilica of St Francis in central Italy. The earthquakes killed at least 10 people, destroying a fresco by Giotto di Bondone (c. 1267–1337), and frescoes of New Testament scenes by Giovanni Cimabue (1251–1302). Giotto, a pupil of Cimabue, was one of the greatest Italian painters of the fourteenth century who laid the foundations of the Italian Renaissance. He was one of the first painters to give up painting the human body in a flat one-dimensional manner. Instead he painted rounded, life-like human beings.

The vast basilica, divided into upper and lower churches, and housing the tomb of St Francis of Assisi, was begun in 1228, two years after the death of the saint. Leading artists of the day including Cimabue, Giotto, and Pietro Cavallini (c. 1250–c. 1330), were all believed to have contributed to the decoration of the completed basilica.

▶ This thirteenth-century fresco by Giotto of St Francis and St Claire painted on the vault above the altar of Assisi's St Francis Basilica was cracked after an earthquake struck central Italy. Minutes after this photograph was taken a second quake caused a large part of the vault to collapse, badly damaging the fresco and killing four people.

Architecture '97

It was quite a year for architecture. The longest, the tallest, and the biggest projects ever, entered the record books. William Gould reports on where and how they all happened.

Kuala Lumpur, Malaysia's bustling capital city is no stranger to the skyscraper. But the latest addition to its skyline is breathtaking even by Malaysian standards. The Petronas building is, for the time being at least, the tallest building on Earth. Housing the headquarters of the national petroleum and oil exploration company of Malaysia, its twin towers rise 451.9 metres above the busy streets of the Golden Triangle, Kuala Lumpur's business area. Each tower has 29 high-speed lifts and ten escalators. Computers control the vast amount of energy used in the building, and regulate humidity, temperature, and all other aspects of the environment, to ensure comfortable working conditions.

The design of this ultra-modern 88-storey office building was inspired by the geometric patterns found in traditional Islamic art. In the park area at the base of the towers there stands a beautiful mosque, designed with these same lovely patterns. Moving from the spiritual to more worldly matters, the Petronas complex also has a vast six-level shopping centre connected to the rest of the city by a high-speed light railway system, a huge concert auditorium, and an art gallery. Probably the most hair-raising feature of the Petronas building is the bridge linking the two towers. It connects them at levels 41 and 42, a dizzying 175 metres above street level.

Bridges in the sky

Talking of bridges, 1997 saw the opening of an important new one in Canada, linking Prince

▶ The 88-storey twin towers of the Petronas building in Kuala Lumpur, the capital city of Malaysia, are linked halfway up by a "sky" bridge.

▲ This man-made island is the site of Hong Kong's new international airport. The building project, the most expensive ever, will create the largest building in Hong Kong.

▼ The Confederation Bridge, spanning the eight-mile gap between Prince Edward Island and New Brunswick in Canada, is the world's longest multi-span bridge.

Edward Island with the mainland province of New Brunswick. The Confederation Bridge was opened with much ceremony and public celebration on 31 May and sets another world record – as the longest multi-spanned continuous bridge in the world. Its structure, which is 12.9 kilometres long, is made of reinforced concrete parts cast in steel. The "bridge" is really three in one. The centre piece stretches 11 kilometres over water. Its 44 spans are made up of 175 separate sections, each weighing around 7,500 tonnes. Leading up to it from each side are two approach bridges, one of 14 spans on the New Brunswick side and one of seven spans on the Prince Edward Island side. This spectacular bridge took 33 months to build – hard graft in one of the bitterest climates on the planet. The 44 spans of the main bridge were manoeuvred into position with the help of a heavy duty floating crane called a Svanen.

Hong Kong's new airport

Hong Kong can claim two new records for its state-of-the-art international airport, due to open in April 1998. It is being built at a cost of £4.5 billion, making it the most expensive building project ever. And it stands on the largest artificial island in the world.

Chek Lap Kok airport is to replace Hong Kong's former international airport at Kai Tak. To build the island it stands upon, two small natural islands had to be levelled. The 347 million cubic metres of earth dug out during the levelling was used to fill in the sea around

▶ The Commerzbank headquarters in Frankfurt, Germany, is made out of steel beams, pre-assembled and then hoisted into place and welded together.

▼ The spectacular Tokyo Forum, Japan's new cultural centre, is built largely of glass. It has 11 storeys above ground and three below with an auditorium that can seat 5,000 people.

the islands, making a single island nearly 6.1 kilometres long and 3.3 kilometres wide.

Outdoors inside

The beautiful triangular tower housing the headquarters of the Commerzbank (shown on previous page), one of Germany's leading financial institutions, opened in Frankfurt am Main in May. It took three years to build, and although it would be dwarfed by the Petronas building described at the beginning of the article, at 298.74 metres it is the tallest office building in Europe. But it isn't its height that makes the

building so special; it is the way in which the architects have created offices that workers may well be reluctant to leave each evening.

The Commerzbank building is constructed around an empty core with gaps in its structure to let natural light come flooding into each office.

One of the most pleasing things for the workers in the building is that its 52 floors include nine gardens. They are inside, but because of the clever design, are lit by natural light. The gardens are four tiers high and overflow with greenery and flowers – perfect for picnic lunches, whatever the weather.

Tokyo glass forum

The Tokyo Forum (shown on previous page), which opened in the winter of 1997, is a splendid building made of glass. Glass might seem an odd choice for Japan, a country prone to earthquakes, but the building's designers took no risks. Every likely force that might hit the building has been calculated using

◀▼ The new Guggenheim Museum glimmers on the dockside in Bilbao, northern Spain. It rivals the original Guggenheim Museum in New York (left) and has been acclaimed by some critics as the greatest building of the 20th century.

► An artist's impression of the new "Paris Las Vegas" resort where it is hoped visitors will experience a taste of the charms of the French capital.

computer models during the design. The glass walls are supported independently of the roof, so that if an earthquake were to shake the building, the roof could rock on special joints without bringing the whole structure crashing down.

The Tokyo Forum is Japan's largest cultural and information centre. It is a spectacular sight, rivalling the Sydney Opera House in originality. It has 11 storeys above ground and three below and is divided into three sections. The Great Halls have a 5,000-seat auditorium for concerts, shows, and plays, 34 conference rooms, and an exhibition centre. The Glass Hall is the Forum's graceful entrance hall and assembly area, and the Plaza is a sweeping public area that links the other two sections.

Spanish grandeur

Like it or loathe it, the sight is breathtaking. An enormous silver-blue magical ship sits on the waterfront in Bilbao, northern Spain. It was designed by the controversial Canadian architect Frank Gery and both imitates and rivals the Guggenheim Museum in New York City. The new Guggenheim, clad in blue titanium which gives it its fairy tale appearance, will house large-scale works of modern art.

Waterfront Hall

The Waterfront Hall, a new concert hall and

conference centre in Belfast, Northern Ireland, opened in January. The circular building with its shallow-domed copper-clad roof and imaginative use of glass, is part of a million-pound development alongside the River Lagan, close to the commercial heart of Belfast. It has two auditoriums, the larger one holding over 2,500 people.

The new Number One

June saw the official opening of the new bowl-shaped Number One court at the All England Lawn Tennis Club in Wimbledon, London.

The design of the new 11,500-seat court has taken account of such issues as sight lines and the angle of the sun. The curved circular roof, made of tubular steel and supported on 72 V-shaped steel columns set into a circular concrete ring, covers only half the spectator seats in order to avoid blocking out the daylight.

Paris, Las Vegas style

It could only happen in Las Vegas, where it seems anything goes! Before long visitors will be able to experience some of the charms of Paris while they enjoy the excitement of Las Vegas, the city that never sleeps. A new hotel complex is to be based upon an enormous reproduction of central Paris. Guests will enter through a mock Arc de Triomphe, and pass a fake 50-storey Eiffel Tower, as well as reproductions of the Opera Garnier, a metro station, and the Rue de la Paix. The mayor of Paris (France!) was asked for his comments. "This is homage from the City of Neon to the City of Light" he declared.

Books '97

In the new stories of 1997, home comes in all shapes and sizes, from a palatial hotel to a caravan. Away from home, young people find adventure in all kinds of places, from sixteenth-century Europe to twentieth-century war-torn Bosnia. Sheila Ray presents her personal choice of the year's best books.

Families vary just as much as their homes and settings. Grandmothers are important in Nina Bawden's *Granny the Pag* and Morris Gleitzman's *Water Wings*. Catriona Brooke, known as "Cat", lives with her grandmother, "the Pag", because her parents are travelling actors. When the time comes for them to settle down, her parents want Cat to come and live with them. She much prefers life with the Pag, and most readers will probably sympathize with her. While we wait to see what will happen, we learn more about the Pag, Cat's friends, her parents, and her school.

Pearl in *Water Wings,* desperately wants a grandmother of her own because her real grandparents are dead. The mother of her own mother's new boyfriend sounds as though she

◀ When Catriona Brooke is threatened with having to leave her biker granny "the Pag" to live with her parents, she becomes a Pag too – and a force to be reckoned with.

hand, a cigarette in her mouth, and a skinny boy in tow. She is very different from the grandma in a rocking chair with fluffy slippers on her feet that Pearl has always dreamed about.

Australian Pearl is an only child but Zinny in Sharon Creech's *Chasing Redbird* lives with six brothers and sisters on a farm in Kentucky, in the United States. One summer she begins work on a project – digging out the old trail that used to lead from their town of Bybanks to Cocton 32 kilometres away. Digging the trail enables her to uncover secrets from the past and to solve some of the problems that have been worrying her.

The luxurious surroundings, wonderful food, and warm family life that Natalie Barnes enjoys at the Palace Hotel, where her father is manager, are a magnet for Tulip in Anne Fine's *The Tulip Touch*. Tulip is an abused child and

might make a good grandmother-substitute, but Pearl is disappointed when she meets the elderly woman with a large suitcase in each

◀ When Zinny Taylor finds a long-forgotten trail in the woods near her home, she decides to unearth it stone by stone and discovers the hidden secrets of her Aunt Jessie's life.

▶ Natalie finds Tulip's outrageous behaviour exciting. But as Tulip's games become more and more sinister, Natalie realizes that she is going too far.

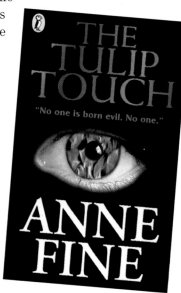

▶ Frankie's Victorian camera reveals the shadows beneath a smile and holds secrets of its own. Is it leading Frankie into danger or telling her what she needs to know?

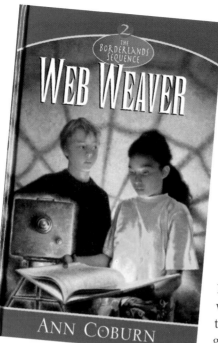

her own home life is very unhappy. Natalie has just started at a new school, and is looking for new friends. She is attracted by Tulip's outrageous behaviour and makes friends with her. Only a major disaster gives Natalie the strength to break free from Tulip's bad influence, although she knows that she will always feel ashamed that she did not help Tulip with her problems. Anne Fine believes that no child is "bad" without a reason.

Magic and mystery

If you enjoy tales of the supernatural and like meeting the same characters again in different books, why not try reading *Web Weaver*, the second adventure in Ann Coburn's *Borderlands Sequence*? Four friends who are all keen photographers, live in a town in the border country between England and Scotland. At first they are all fascinated by the old camera that Frankie buys

◀ Mirabelle the swan has no eggs. Her sister Sophie has seven! Mirabelle and her mate Egbert decide to steal one and so this story of four swans, three children, and an old lady begins.

when the contents of an old house are sold. Cameras are supposed to tell the truth but this camera behaves in a mysterious way, weaving a web of spite and deceit. Can David, Michael, and Anne rescue Frankie from the spell it seems to have cast upon her?

William feels sorry for the swan with no egg to hatch and decides to give her *The Silver Egg,* the last of his Easter eggs, wrapped in silver paper and tied with a green ribbon. His generosity seems to be rewarded when the hatching season arrives, and the swan and her mate swim by with a small fluffy grey cygnet, sparkling silver in the sunlight. William thinks that it is magic, but his brother and sister are not so sure.

Kate Thompson's *Switchers* do have magical powers. From early childhood Kevin and Tess have been able to take on the form and thoughts of creatures of their choice, although they have never met each other. When they do meet as teenagers and Kevin makes a friend of solitary Tess, they need all the powers at their disposal to save the world from the cold and ice that is creeping down from the North Pole. Changing

▶ *Spacebaby* and his friends race to save the Earth. But Silas Stoatwarden has other ideas…

shape as the need arises, Kevin and Tess defeat the mysterious grokes, and another ice age is prevented.

Spacebaby arrives from outer space to save the world from a different disaster – the loss of gravity. Unfortunately, although he has the brains and expertise of a scientific genius, he lands on Earth as a small baby and has to come to terms with nappies and babyfood while directing a complex computer game that will restore the planet to normality.

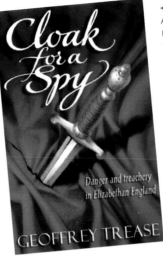

◄ In 1585 as rumours of the Spanish Armada spread through Europe, the mysterious tutor, Stephen Martell, leads Giles Taberdar into a web of intrigue and danger.

Tales set in the past

For over sixty years Geoffrey Trease has been entertaining readers with stories of young people who grow up in the past. When Giles Taberdar in *Cloak for a Spy* sets off for Europe in 1584, he expects to learn a little and enjoy himself a lot. He certainly doesn't expect to find

THE BOOKLIST

Home and School
Angela and Diabola, *Lynne Reid Banks* (E)
Granny the Pag, *Nina Bawden* (M)
The Roman Beanfeast, *Gillian Cross* (M)
The Tulip Touch, *Anne Fine* (M)
Water Wings, *Morris Gleitzman* (M)
The Cabbage Patch War, *Paul Jennings* (E)
The Sandy Bottom Orchestra, *Garrison Keillor and Jenny Lind Nilsson* (M)
Becky Bananas: This is Your Life! *Jean Ure* (M)
The Pete and Mary Kate Stories, *Marin Waddell and Terry Milne* (E)
The Lottie Project, *Jacqueline Wilson* (M)

Magic and the Supernatural
Spacebaby, *Henrietta Branford* (E)
Web Weaver, *Ann Coburn* (M)
Belin's Hill, *Catherine Fisher* (T)

◄ Liza is in trouble but can Rowan help her? Tragedy is lurking in the past – a threat of evil strong enough to send ripples spreading to the present.

Harvey Angell and the Ghost Child, *Diana Hendry* (M)
Robopop, *Emma Laybourn* (E)
Lad, *Robert Leeson* (E)
Hannah's Ghost, *Anne Merrick* (M)
Dark Beneath the Moon, *Christine Purkis* (M)
Harry Potter and the Philosopher's Stone, *Joanne Rowling* (M)

Animals
The Silver Egg, *Vivien Alcock and Ivan Bates* (E)
The Long Patrol: A Tale of Redwall, *Brian Jacques* (M)
Sasha and the Wolfcub, *Ann Jungman* (E)
Sophie's Further Adventures, *Dick King-Smith* (E)
Bug Muldoon and the Garden of Fear, *Paul Shipton* (M)
Switchers, *Kate Thompson* (M)

Away from Home
Paper Faces, *Rachel Anderson* (M)
Chasing Redbird, *Sharon Creech* (T)
No Roof in Bosnia, *Els de Groen* (T)
Spooks Ahoy! *Mary Hooper* (E)
Forever X, *Geraldine McCaughrean* (M)
The Nowhere Girl, *Linda Newbery* (T)

himself drawn into the activities of his tutor – a spy for Sir Francis Walsingham – who needs evidence to prove to Queen Elizabeth I of England that the Spaniards are planning an invasion. Safely home again, Giles sees the beacons warning of the coming of the Spanish Armada and knows he has played a part in making sure

▶ After the end of World War II, Dot is worried by this strange thing called peace. Above all, she is terrified of the return of her father – the man with the paper face.

England is well prepared.

Nearly four hundred years later and another enemy has been defeated. Dot is celebrating the end of World War II in Rachel Anderson's *Paper Faces*. But Dot has a difficult decision to make. Which should she choose? A comfortable life in the country, or city life with her mother and a father who seems a stranger to her after the years he spent in the army. Just in time Dot realizes that home with mum and dad is best: "We have to live where we live," she says.

Cloak for a Spy, *Geoffrey Trease* (T)

Old Favourites
The Felix Trilogy: Go Saddle the Sea, Bridle the Wind, The Teeth of the Gale, *Joan Aiken* (T)
Tell Me About Enid Blyton, *Gillian Baverstock* (E)
The Roald Dahl Treasury, *Roald Dahl* (F)
A Christmas Carol, *Charles Dickens* (F)
True Tilda, *Arthur Quiller-Couch* (M)

Poems and Short Stories
Dibby Dubby Dhu, *George Barker* (F)
The Oxford Treasury of Classic Poems, *Michael Harrison and Stuart Clark, editors* (F)
Stacks of Stories, *Mary Hoffman, editor* (F)

◀ Sasha is always being warned about wolves – they are cruel and dangerous especially when they are hungry. But when he and a little wolfcub get lost in the snow, the two become friends and prove that wolves and humans can live together, without fear... and with fun.

Rebel Rebel, *Gene Kemp, editor* (F)
The Swap and Other Stories, *George Layton* (M)
The Young Oxford Book of Nasty Endings, *Dennis Pepper, editor* (F)

Information Books
Celebration! *Barnabas and Anabel Kindersley* (F)
The World in the Time of Tutankhamun, *Fiona MacDonald* (F)
Celts, *Hazel Mary Martell* (F)
The Greek News, *Anton Powell and Philip Steele* (F)
More Letters to Uncle Albert, *Russell Stannard* (M)
Revolutionaries: Rebels with a Cause, *Paul Thomas* (F)

Key
E = Reading for children under 10
M = Mainstream children's books for 9- to 12-year-olds
T = Teenage novels
F = Books for the whole family to enjoy

Books mentioned in this article were published in the UK in 1997. They may not be available world-wide.

Sadly, wars still rage around the world. *No Roof in Bosnia* by Els de Groen is set in Bosnia during the war that ended in 1995. It tells the story of five teenage friends, drawn from different sections of the war-torn community – Moslem, Croat, Serb, and Romany. At first they hide in the mountains, but they cannot make their home there forever. When the boys are taken to the local Serb camp, the girls know that they must make their own way to the coast and they hope that the boys will find them there. This hope shines through all the hardships. Despite living through the nightmare of the war, they are young and still optimistic about their future.

◄ Five teenage friends from different sections of the war-torn community in Bosnia are drawn together in hope for a better future.

1997 it was turned into a major BBC television serial in the United Kingdom and viewers were able to share the adventures of orphaned Tilda as she rescues Arthur from an orphanage and re-unites him with his family. As the pair travel through the countryside, they are helped and hindered by some colourful characters before they reach the island that Arthur dimly remembers.

Rosemary Sutcliff, who wrote many historical novels, died in 1992 but left the notes and a rough draft for one last story, *Sword Song*. Now her godson has put together this tale of a boy

Writers past and present

Gillian Baverstock, Enid Blyton's daughter, has written the story of her mother's life to celebrate the centenary of the birth of one of the most famous writers of this century. Enid Blyton, born in 1897, began to make up stories when she was quite young and went on to publish over 600 books. In 1997 she is still one of the most popular children's writers. Selections from another popular writer's stories about Matilda, Charlie, James, and other favourite characters appear in *The Roald Dahl Treasury*. In the nineteenth century Charles Dickens was just as popular as Dahl and Blyton are today, and the characters he created such as Oliver Twist and David Copperfield are familiar figures to many people. He also wrote one of the most famous ghost stories ever, *A Christmas Carol*. A lavishly illustrated new edition provides us with pictures showing how people lived in the time of Dickens and how his story has influenced the way we celebrate Christmas today.

Children first enjoyed the story of *True Tilda* by Arthur Quiller-Couch many years ago. In

▼ To celebrate the 100th anniversary of the birth of Enid Blyton, Gillian Baverstock tells the story of her mother's life.

Festivals, carnivals, and feast days from around the world

BRITISH AIRWAYS

BARNABAS AND ANABEL KINDERSLEY
with a foreword by HRH THE DUCHESS OF KENT

DK

▲ Children from more than 25 countries around the world, describe their favourite festivals, carnivals, and feastdays.

banished from his homeland and forced to fend for himself in the harsh world of the Norsemen.

Poems and short stories

Many favourite authors and characters can be found in collections of poems and short stories. *Rebel Rebel* includes the Greek myth of Pandora – the young girl who was so inquisitive that she opened the box that contained all the troubles and miseries of the world. Fortunately she also released the hope that helps most people to cope with life's downside. Alongside Pandora, there are other familiar characters with minds of their own such as Marmalade Atkins from the stories by Andrew Davies and Helen Cresswell's Lizzie Dripping.

The contents of *The Oxford Treasury of Classic Poems* have been enjoyed by many children in the past. Here you can meet *The Highwayman* or *The Owl and the Pussycat* and many other favourite characters. In the final poem, *To Any Reader*, Robert Louis Stevenson reminds us of all that can be seen "through the windows" of a book.

Information please

The small selection of information books listed here are mostly concerned with historical facts but *Celebration!* reminds us of the history behind the traditional celebrations and festivals that remain a part of our lives today. Russell Stannard's *More Letters to Uncle Albert* reflects the need to ask questions about the world around us. Books at home, at school, and in libraries can help with finding the answers.

Award-winning children's books

Caldecott Medal: *US (for illustration)*
Golem, *David Wishiewski*

Carnegie Medal
Junk, *Melvyn Burgess*

Children's Book Award
The Hundred-mile-an-hour Dog, *Jeremy Strong and Nick Sharrat*

Guardian Children's Book Award
Junk, *Melvyn Burgess*

Kathleen Fidler Award
The Falcon's Quest, *John Smirthwaite*

Kate Greenaway Award
The Baby Who Wouldn't Go to Bed, *Helen Cooper*

Newbery Medal: *US*
The True View from Saturday, *E.L. Konigsburg*

Whitbread Literary Award
The Tulip Touch, *Anne Fine*

Music '97
by Sandra Stafford

It was the year when the Spice Girls began to face real opposition, fans remembered Elvis, a tribute to Jimi Hendrix caused a stir, Andrea Bocelli's fanclub mobbed him at every turn, and the bassoon hit the record books. Read on…

▲ Oasis were once again one of the most talked-about bands of the year. Fans queued through the night in the United States and the United Kingdom to buy copies of their latest single and album.

Britpop goes worldwide

It was another successful 12 months for Oasis. Not only did they tour the United States supporting supergroup U2 on their Popmart tour, they also released a long-awaited single "D'you Know What I Mean?" and their third album *Be Here Now* in the United Kingdom. Both sparked off a frenzy of activity around record shops, with fans queuing all night to buy copies. The band appeared live, performing some of their new material, but the tribute band No Way Sis beat them to it by being the first to sing three new Oasis songs at a live gig.

Spice Girls singles topped the charts worldwide and their debut album, *Spice,* is set to become one of the record industry's most successful releases ever. It went straight to the top of the United States album charts, making the Spice Girls the first British band to achieve the Number One position in the United States with a debut album – something that not even the Beatles managed to do.

► The Spice Girls took the world by storm. Their album *Spice* shot to Number One in the United States – making them the first British band to make the top spot with a debut album.

Hip hop/rap

Mary J. Blige suffered at the hands of the Spice Girls when they took the position she held in the United States charts. By way of compensation, the queen of hip hop soul had Top Ten album success in the United Kingdom with *Share My World*. She also featured on rapper Notorious B.I.G.'s album *Life*

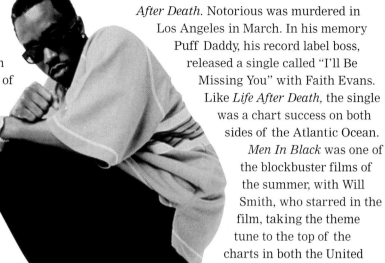

▶ Sean "Puff Daddy" Combs whose Bad Boy Entertainment Group has sold more than 12 million records, was with Notorious B.I.G. on the night of the shooting. His single "I'll Be Missing You" was recorded as a tribute to his friend.

▼ Christopher Wallace, alias Notorious B.I.G., a top rap musician, was murdered in Los Angeles in March. It was the second rap star death in eight months, in what has been dubbed an East-West states "rappers war".

After Death. Notorious was murdered in Los Angeles in March. In his memory Puff Daddy, his record label boss, released a single called "I'll Be Missing You" with Faith Evans. Like *Life After Death*, the single was a chart success on both sides of the Atlantic Ocean.

Men In Black was one of the blockbuster films of the summer, with Will Smith, who starred in the film, taking the theme tune to the top of the charts in both the United Kingdom and the United States.

Around Europe

The United Kingdom won the Eurovision Song Contest for the first time in 16 years with "Love Shine A Light" sung by Katrina and the Waves. The casualty of the 1997 contest was Norway. They scored nil points for the fourth time since the contest began, which is a record in itself!

The San Remo festival, an annual week-long music gathering in Italy, featured the Spice Girls as the star attraction. The weather there was better than at this year's Glastonbury Festival in the United Kingdom when around 90,000 visitors had to plough their way through acres of mud. It's not surprising that the most popular items for sale were Wellington boots. The star attractions, including Kula Shaker, Sting, and Prodigy, made up for the rain.

Rising stars

Look out Spice Girls! Girl bands are emerging all over the world. Pretenders to the Spice Girls' throne include V Alive from Holland and The Angies from Thailand. Meanwhile in Russia the standard at an audition to form a Spice Girls–type band was so high that selecting five girls became a problem. In the end seven were chosen.

Singer Hong Nhung, a sensation in Vietnam, has taken advantage of her country's new approach to pop music. Until this year, Vietnamese artists were only allowed to record traditional songs, but these regulations have been relaxed, which means that the music scene is beginning to change. Nhung is so popular that she often plays four concerts a night, every night of the week.

The English Heritage plaque on the wall of 23 Brook Street in central London where Jimi Hendrix lived. His girlfriend, Cathy Etchingham, led the campaign to have the plaque put up.

ENGLISH HERITAGE
JIMI HENDRIX
1942~1970
Guitarist and Songwriter lived here 1968~1969

and early 1970s, announced that they would be re-forming to release a new album (their first in three decades), and to tour the United Kingdom. They played a handful of live dates throughout March to a lukewarm reception.

Golden oldies

Fans world-wide remembered Elvis on the 20th anniversary of his death, and more than 50,000 visitors paid their respects to the "King" at his mansion, Graceland, in Memphis, Tennessee. Elvis was the first-ever rock'n'roll superstar. Despite that, he is now worth more money dead than alive, mainly because of the business enterprises set up to satisfy his millions of fans.

A massive auction in March called "Beatles for Sale" took place simultaneously at Bonhams, London, and the Tokyo Auction House, Japan. The auction was historic for many reasons. It was the first to sell only Beatles memorabilia. It was also the first to be broadcast live by satellite between the two salesrooms and to millions of viewers via the European Auction Channel TV station. The sale of goods totalled £677,745.

The Rolling Stones embarked on a world tour in September, kicking off in Chicago, Illinois. They are playing large venues as well as small clubs and bars. The last time they performed in very small venues was 30 years ago, before they became really famous. The tour will reach Europe in 1998, where they hope to play in Russia for the first time.

The Monkees, famous for their television series and string of hits during the late 1960s

A touch of heritage

Rock star Jimi Hendrix and classical composer George Frideric Handel have more than one thing in common. They were both acknowledged as geniuses of their generation, and they also used to be next door neighbours – albeit more than 200 years apart.

This year, English Heritage recognized Hendrix as part of Britain's musical culture by placing one of its famous blue plaques on the wall of the house where the guitarist lived for a year. Just a few inches away, a similar plaque commemorates Handel, who came from Germany.

Hendrix was from the United States, but he felt that his music was more accepted in the United Kingdom and decided to make London his home. He stunned audiences worldwide by sometimes playing his electric guitar with his teeth. In 1969 (the year before he died) he played at the United States most famous rock concert ever – Woodstock, New York.

However, not everyone approves of a rock star being acknowledged by the blue plaque. Some people feel that Hendrix's music should not be given the same status as Handel's. Others feel that both men made important contributions to music in general, and therefore that both plaques are justified.

The EMI record label celebrated its 100th

anniversary in 1997. Those who have appeared on its label include a mix of musical artists such as the tenor Caruso, crooner Frank Sinatra, jazz-man Louis Armstrong, Elvis, the Beatles, and the Sex Pistols. A London exhibition celebrating this centenary ran throughout the second half of 1997, giving a full history of the company. Well-known album covers and musical instruments belonging to several of the label's biggest stars were on display plus paintings of Nipper, the dog that appeared on HMV (EMI's trademark) covers. Nipper, much loved in the United Kingdom, was removed from record covers for the Indian market and replaced with a cobra.

Thomas Alva Edison, famous for his invention of the cylinder phonograph, was born 150 years ago in Milan, Ohio, in the United States. The cylinder phonograph, which was patented 120 years ago, endured as a means of recording music until the end of the 1920s. By that time its greatest rival, the flat disc, had firmly replaced it.

The Hungarian composer Béla Bartók made excellent use of the cylinder phonograph when he did the first scientific study of the true folk music of Hungary, Romania, and Slovakia. On his field trip he made sure that he had plenty of waxed cylinders, and his study resulted in about 16,000 recordings.

Plastic pirates

The music industry worldwide lost millions of pounds during the

◄ Andrea Bocelli always dreamed of becoming an opera singer. He has been Number One in the pop charts in Germany, Italy, Switzerland, France, and Belgium, and is set to become one of the largest-selling classical artists of all time.

year because of sales of illegal copies ("pirates") of records, CDs, and cassettes. It is estimated that as many as one in three copies is fake. These copies are made without the approval of the music industry, so the artists and recording companies who should get a percentage of the sales don't receive anything.

Some of the pirated copies are made using increasingly sophisticated equipment, often in specially-built manufacturing units in Eastern Europe, South and Central America, and Asia, and the finished product is often very difficult to detect against a legal version. Other copies are very poor and virtually unplayable.

It is usually only hit recordings that are pirated. Popular targets are the Spice Girls, Michael Jackson, and Oasis. Old favourites by the Beatles and Elvis Presley have also proved to have a good market. The gangs who make and sell these illegal recordings can amass huge amounts of money because their only outlay is the cost of manufacturing. On the other hand, money paid for a legitimate CD pays the artist and songwriter, the manufacturing and distribution costs, as well as a profit margin for the retailer and various other overheads.

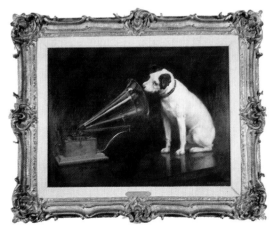

▶ A painting of the famous Jack Russell dog called Nipper, the trademark of the HMV record company, on show at EMI's 100th birthday exhibition.

Pop goes the tenor

Italian singer Andrea Bocelli is an operatic tenor, but he is mobbed like a pop star everywhere he goes. He had phenomenal success in all the European charts, and his single "Time To Say Goodbye" recorded with Sarah Brightman, became the best-selling pop single ever in Germany. His first British album, *Romanza,* went straight to the top of the charts.

When he was 12, Bocelli was blinded in a football accident. Despite that, he copes very well with a hectic schedule of travelling and performing. He uses a braille computer to remind himself of song lyrics when he is in the recording studio.

String section

Violinist Linda Lampenius moved from her home in Finland to a beach-front house in Malibu, California, and changed her name to Linda Brava to fit more easily with her new fans in the United States. Brava is often compared to *Baywatch* star Pamela Anderson. She was even offered a part in the television programme but turned it down. Brava plays all types of music, but was classically trained and takes her classical career very seriously. This means that, despite normally being an adventurous dresser, when she is on stage playing the classics all you will see her in is a long, black dress.

Another violinist, Vanessa-Mae, gave a tour

▲ The Finnish violinist Linda Lampenius was playing the violin with the Helsinki Opera when she caught the eye of record company talent spotters.

▼ British violinist Nigel Kennedy, now known as "Kennedy", is back on the music scene with a new album of Elgar's Violin Concerto. His recording of Vivaldi's "Four Seasons" is the biggest-selling classical record of all time.

of the United Kingdom in 1997. But members of the Bratislav Symphony Orchestra, who she performs with, were refused work permits at the last minute. Bravely, Vanessa-Mae decided to stick to her planned first-half programme, but instead of a full orchestra she used two pianos as her accompaniment: one played by her mother and the other played by the conductor of the absent orchestra.

Nigel Kennedy, who stopped performing classical music on the violin in 1992 to follow a career in pop music, announced his comeback. He became internationally famous with his album of Vivaldi's "Four Seasons", which is the biggest-selling classical record of all time. His new album, for EMI, is a re-recording of Elgar's

▶ Johannes Brahms, the great German composer, died in 1897. It is claimed that the printed scores of his music contain hundreds of mistakes. A project to change them back to the way Brahms wanted them to be, will take about 30 years to complete.

Violin Concerto. The Concerto was Nigel's debut recording, for which he received great critical acclaim. Yehudi Menuhin, whose music school Kennedy attended, took a great personal interest in him as a child. Menuhin also recorded the Concerto in 1932, with Elgar himself conducting.

Key events

Pianist David Helfgott regained public recognition this year, partly due to the film *Shine*, which recorded his traumatic early life, and partly because of the concerts he gave throughout the United States and the United Kingdom. *Shine* won an Oscar in the United States, and David was at the ceremony to play the piano in front of a celebrity-packed audience. David, who is Australian, thrilled his audiences with his performances and often received standing ovations. The critics, however, were not quite so generous

◀ Austria celebrated the 200th anniversary of the birth of the composer Franz Schubert. Almost all of his compositions were performed by the end of the year, including his great Symphony in C major, which Schubert himself never heard.

with their praise.

French pianist Philippe Cassard played all of Debussy's solo piano music at a marathon concert in London in January. The concert lasted more than ten hours, during which time he performed over 80 pieces.

All wind

After six years' work, American bassoonist Daniel Smith has become the only bassoonist in the world to record all of Vivaldi's 37 bassoon concertos. Daniel is the most recorded classical bassoonist in the world, but he also likes to play jazz, as he demonstrated at a festival in Wales in September. Eventually, he would like to play concert programmes that combine jazz and classical items.

Happy anniversary

Austria celebrated the bicentenary of the birth of Franz Schubert with festivals and exhibitions throughout the country. By the end of the year, nearly 1,200 compositions (Schubert's total output) had been heard. A new CD featuring Schubert's final three piano sonatas, played by Andreas Staier, was released. The instrument featured on the CD was made in Vienna (where Schubert was born and died) at the same time as these sonatas were composed.

The year 1997 was also the 100th anniversary of the death of Johannes Brahms. He left behind thousands of compositions. But beware if you play them from printed music. It was discovered that this may still contain the original mistakes made by Brahms' printers when the compositions were typeset from the composer's handwritten manuscripts. It has been reported that Brahms' First Symphony contains some 281 mistakes.

Famous lives

In a year dominated by the death of Diana, Princess of Wales, whose life we celebrate in the article on pages 116–120, Lesley Riley remembers the lives of some talented and influential people who also died in 1997.

THE WORLD AT LARGE

HASTINGS BANDA (1898–1997) was the first president of Malawi (formerly Nyasaland) and for 30 years ruled the country as a dictator. When he was young, after being expelled from school, Banda walked over 1,500 kilometres to South Africa, where he completed his early education and, in 1924, won a scholarship to study medicine in the United States. In 1937 Banda moved to the United Kingdom. From 1945 he became deeply interested in African politics, and his London house became a meeting place for many future African leaders.

From 1953 Banda led Nyasaland's freedom movement, in order to gain independence from Britain. He returned to his country in 1958, and fronted the negotiations with the British government. Independence was granted in 1964, and Banda became prime minister. He became president in 1966, and president-for-life in 1971. His policies made sure that farmers were well paid, and before long Malawi could even afford to export food. Transport, education, and electricity supplies were all dramatically improved. But Banda became unpopular at home for his brutal treatment of political opponents, and in the rest of Africa for keeping up links with white-ruled South Africa. In 1992,

◀ Hastings Banda

Western countries stopped all financial aid to Malawi after government troops killed over 40 pro-democracy demonstrators. In 1994, after the country's first multi-party elections for 33 years, Banda accepted defeat. He finally retired from politics in July 1997.

DIANA, PRINCESS OF WALES (1961–97). *See article on pages 116–120.*

PAMELA HARRIMAN (1920–97), the US-ambassador to France from 1993, led a colourful and often controversial life that was geared to achieving three things: love, money, and power.

Born in Kent, England, she was the eldest daughter of an aristocratic, but not wealthy, family. She was married three times. Her first husband was Randolph Churchill, the son of Britain's wartime prime minister Winston Churchill; then she married the legendary Broadway producer Leland Hayward. Finally, in 1971, she married Averell Harriman, a leading US-diplomat and one of the richest men in America. In between,

◀ Pamela Harriman with France's President Chirac

▲ Mobutu Sese Seko

she had a series of relationships with some of the world's wealthiest and most influential men, including Greek shipping magnate Stavros Niarchos, and French banker Elie de Rothschild.

It was her third marriage that set her firmly on the road to political power. The Harrimans' home in Georgetown, Washington DC, became a meeting place for Democrat politicians and their supporters. Pamela Harriman launched a political action committee, "Democrats for the '80s", and organized grand fund-raising parties at which she collected millions of dollars for the Democratic Party.

She received her reward in 1993 when Democratic president Bill Clinton appointed her US-ambassador to France. She was remarkably successful in the role, helping to ease relations between the United States and France in disagreements over NATO, the Middle East, trade, and the leadership of the United Nations.

MOBUTU SESE SEKO (1930–97) ruled Zaire as a dictator for over 30 years. Born in what was then the Belgian Congo, Mobutu joined the Congolese Nationalist Movement in 1958 and helped to negotiate the country's independence from Belgium. When this was granted in 1960 he was made defence minister. By the end of the year he engineered a coup and declared that the army would rule the country for a year. In fact Mobutu held the real power, imprisoning or hanging opponents and ignoring parliament and the constitution. In 1965 he declared himself president and banned all political parties except his own. In 1971 he changed the name of the country to Zaire.

Zaire's economy slowly collapsed when copper, its main export, lost value in the 1970s. While poverty, disease, and chaos spread among his people, Mobutu amassed a huge fortune by stealing money donated by foreign governments and the earnings from Zaire's mineral resources. He kept himself in power through bribery and a well-trained private army, and by retaining the support of Western governments who welcomed his firm stand against communism. When the Cold War ended, international pressure forced Mobutu to agree to multi-party elections. His delays in bringing reform eventually led to an armed uprising in 1996, and he fled the country in May 1997.

MOTHER TERESA (1910–97) was a Roman Catholic missionary, known all over the world for her care of the poor, the sick, and the dying. The order of nuns she founded in the slums of Calcutta, India, grew into an international network of orphanages, schools, hospices, leprosy clinics, workshops for the unemployed, and hostels for the elderly and the homeless. In recognition of her work she was awarded the Nobel Peace Prize in 1979.

Mother Teresa was born Agnes Gonxha Bojaxhiu, in Skopje, in what is now Macedonia.

◄ Mother Teresa

She was only 12 years of age when she decided to become a nun, inspired by stories she read of missionaries helping the poor in Calcutta. At the age of 18 she joined the Irish Order of Loreto nuns who worked in Bengal, and took the name Teresa in memory of the French saint Thérèse of Lisieux. In Ireland she learned to speak English, and then was sent out to India, where for 17 years she taught at St Mary's, the Loreto convent school in Calcutta, eventually becoming principal there.

It was in 1946, on a train to Darjeeling, India, that Sister Teresa heard what she was convinced was a call from God, telling her to go to live and work among the poorest of the poor. She left the convent two years later, at a time when tens of thousands of refugees from east Bengal filled the streets of Calcutta. Joined by former pupils, she set about helping those who were destitute, feeding the starving, and nursing those who were sick. She set up a home for abandoned children, and a hospice where those who were dying could spend their last hours in comfort and peace.

As word spread about the work of Mother Teresa and the sisters – known as the Missionaries of Charity – donations began to pour in. By the 1960s they had opened new homes in more than 20 cities. Today they operate more than 450 centres in over 100 countries throughout the world.

To those who loved her, Mother Teresa was a living saint; but she was not without her critics. Some condemned her for accepting money from all sources, even from people known to be brutal or corrupt, but Mother Teresa said she had no moral right to refuse anything given for the poor. She was criticized too for not providing pain-killing drugs for her hospice patients; her

◄ Deng Xiaoping in 1920

response was that her mission was not to treat people who were terminally ill, but to help them to die with dignity. The fiercest criticism came from those who objected to her views on contraception and abortion. She called abortion "the greatest evil" – and because of this some people thought she did as much harm as good.

In 1991 Mother Teresa's health was failing and she announced her retirement as Superior of the Missionaries of Charity. But the sisters could not bear the idea of anyone else as their leader, and it was not until March 1997 that they chose someone to replace her.

DENG XIAOPING (1904–97) was China's most powerful leader for 15 years. He was known as a great reformer, a man who vastly improved the lives of the Chinese people. But he will also be remembered for the 1989 massacre in Beijing's Tian'anmen Square, when several hundred students demonstrating for democracy were shot dead by government troops.

The son of a middle-class landowner, Deng grew up in Sichuan province. At the age of 16 he won a scholarship to study in France, and it was here that he joined the Communist Party.

Deng returned to China in 1926, and began organizing peasant armies to help bring about a revolution in the country; by 1930 he had joined forces with Mao Zedong's communist army. When government troops threatened to overwhelm them, Mao led the communists across China to safety in the north. As many as 80,000 people died from the cold and lack of food on the Long March, a journey of 9,500 kilometres that took more than a year.

In 1949 the communists finally seized power

AND ALSO...

John Akii-Bua (1950–97), Ugandan 400-metres hurdles champion.

Sir Isaiah Berlin (1909–97), British philosopher, born in Latvia, who was one of the top political thinkers of the 20th century.

Jeffrey Bernard (1932–97), "Low Life" columnist for British magazine, the *Spectator,* whose wit, colourful life, and legendary drinking were celebrated in Keith Waterhouse's play *Jeffrey Bernard is Unwell.*

Jeanne Calment (1875–1997), French woman who believed that the key to her becoming the world's oldest person at 122 years was her sense of humour.

Denis Compton (1918–97), one of the all-time greats in English cricket, who also played soccer for England.

Dodi Fayed (1955–97), film producer and member of the international jet set, who became a close friend of Diana, Princess of Wales.

Sir James Goldsmith (1933–97), Anglo-French tycoon who founded the Referendum Party in the United Kingdom to fight the introduction of the European single currency.

Chaim Herzog (1918–97), president of Israel from 1983 to 1993, who fought for the expansion of Arab rights.

Michael Kennedy (1958–97), a son of Robert F. Kennedy, died on New Year's Eve in a skiing accident.

"Colonel" Tom Parker (1909–97), Elvis Presley's manager.

Betty Shabazz (1936–97), widow of assassinated civil rights leader, Malcolm X, who carried on his work while bringing up six daughters.

George Thomas (1909–97), Labour Speaker of the British House of Commons, who became one of the best-known politicians of the 1970s and 1980s.

Gumpei Yokoi (1941–97), Nintendo *Gameboy* innovator.

and established the People's Republic of China. Mao was head of the new government, and Deng rose quickly through its ranks, becoming a member of the ruling Politburo in 1955. At first he supported Mao's plans to modernize industry and to reform agriculture, but when the schemes failed disastrously and millions of people died of starvation, Deng and President Lui Shaoqi side-stepped Mao's orders and pushed through reforms of their own, which at least made sure that the people had a supply of food.

During the ten dark years of the Cultural Revolution, when people were urged to become "Red Guards" and denounce anyone who had strayed away from Mao's teachings, Deng was twice stripped of all his powers and sent into exile. But after Mao's death in September 1976,

the Cultural Revolution was over. Deng returned once more to the government.

Deng immediately launched a series of reforms that changed the face of China. He abolished the farming communes, set up by Mao in the 1950s, allowing millions of peasants to grow what they wanted and to sell any surplus crops for the first time. Not only did people now have enough to eat, they could afford to buy such things as televisions and refrigerators. Everyone was encouraged to set up their own business. Deng also invited foreign investment and created special zones to produce goods for export.

For a time, there was more political freedom, too, and people were able to speak more openly than before. Then Deng began to feel threatened by calls for greater democracy and imprisoned anyone suggesting political reforms. By 1989 demonstrations for change were being held in city after city – but these came to an end with the brutal killings in Tian'anmen Square.

Many Western businesses withdrew from China after the massacre, Deng's programme of reforms was slowed down, and Deng himself virtually retired. Then, in 1992, he made a public appeal for the government and people alike to make the most of the country's economic reforms. The result was an economic explosion, and it sealed Deng's reputation as a miracle worker.

As he became older and weaker, Deng Xiaoping faded from public life, but he had already shaped the future of China. *See article on pages 51–56.*

ARTS, MUSIC, AND SCIENCE

THE REV W AWDRY (1911–97) delighted generations of children with his entertaining tales about Thomas the Tank Engine and his friends. Awdry had a lifelong passion for steam trains. His father used to take him to watch them on the railway that passed near their home. He began making up railway stories for his young son Christopher, and his wife sent them to a publisher. *The Three Railway Engines* appeared in 1945, followed in 1946 by *Thomas the Tank Engine.* They were an instant success, and soon Awdry was writing one book a year. In 1965 he gave up his busy life as a parson in order to write full time. He produced 26 titles in all; then, in 1970, his son took over the writing. The books led to several television series and an animated film version, narrated by former Beatle Ringo Starr, as well as a whole range of products from replica model engines to pasta shapes.

JACQUES COUSTEAU (1910–97) was an undersea explorer and film-maker who unlocked the door

◄ The Rev W Awdry

to the secret world of the oceans. With a French engineer, Emile Gagnan, he perfected the aqualung or scuba, portable breathing equipment that enabled divers to move freely underwater for the first time. Through more than 100 films and television documentaries, and some 30 illustrated books, he encouraged millions of people to explore with him the wonders of life in the sea.

Jacques-Yves Cousteau was born near Bordeaux, southwestern France, and was brought up mainly in Paris and New York, where his father worked. He entered the French naval academy when he was 20, intending to train as a naval pilot. But his life changed after he was involved in a serious road accident, in which he broke both arms and several ribs. He took up swimming to strengthen his wasted muscles and at once fell in love with the sea.

For the next 60 years he dedicated himself to learning more about the oceans. He often carried out dangerous experiments in his quest to develop the aqualung so that he could remain under water for long periods. He founded the

▼ Jacques Cousteau

Undersea Research Group, which not only developed diving equipment, but also worked on improving techniques for filming under water. He turned a former mine-sweeper, the *Calypso*, into a floating laboratory, and used it to research and film every aspect of life in the world's oceans, including the frozen waters of Antarctica. Cousteau was head of Monaco's famous Institute of Oceanography for 30 years, during which time he directed an ambitious series of experiments in underwater living. He also campaigned vigorously in defence of the oceans, warning of the damage being done by pollution, nuclear tests, and trawling and dredging on the seabed.

In later years, there was growing criticism of the way Cousteau went about his work; some people thought he was more interested in being a media personality than promoting science. Cousteau responded that he had never claimed to be a scientist, but an impresario – someone who makes things happen. And indeed Cousteau's achievements made it possible for ordinary people, scientists, and technologists to explore the world under the sea.

JOHN DENVER (1943–97) was the world's biggest-selling singer in the mid-1970s. He sold more than a million copies of the single "I'd Rather be a Cowboy", and had Number One hits in 1974–75 with "Annie's Song", "Sunshine on My Shoulders", "Thank God I'm a Country Boy", and "I'm Sorry". Between 1971 and 1982 his recordings were often in the charts.

Denver was born Henry John Deutschendorf, Jr, the son of a US-Air Force colonel. He grew up on military bases across the USA and in Japan. In the early 1960s he dropped out of college, where he was studying architecture, to follow a career in music.

Calling himself John Denver, after his favourite city, he got his first break in 1965, when he beat 250 other applicants in an audition for a folk group called the Chad Mitchell Trio. Denver stayed with them until 1968, when he signed a recording contract as a solo artist. Denver's talent as a songwriter was recognized the following year, when his "Leavin' On A Jet Plane" was recorded by Peter, Paul, and Mary and became a world-wide hit, selling over a million copies.

His move to Aspen, Colorado, in 1972 produced another lasting favourite, "Rocky Mountain High", which was his first hit single in Britain. In the next ten years Denver was to release 15 albums, of which five sold over a million copies. At the same time, his songs gradually moved away from folk music towards a "soft-rock" style. In 1982 Denver appealed directly to a family audience with an album recorded with the tenor Placido Domingo, and he followed that in 1983 with *A Christmas Together,* made with the Muppets.

As his recording career waned in the 1980s, Denver devoted his energy to the causes of saving wildlife and the environment. Several environmental organizations benefited from royalties from his music.

ALLEN GINSBERG (1926–97), the US-poet, was one of the central figures of the Beat Generation of the 1950s. The "Beats" were a group of writers, including Jack Kerouac and William Burroughs, who rejected conventional ways of writing, and respectable middle-class

◀ John Denver

▲ Stephane Grappelli

society.

Ginsberg made his reputation in 1956, with the publication of *Howl,* a long, chaotic poem that became the bible of beatnik culture. Initially banned in the United States for obscenity, it became the best known US-poem of the years after World War II. During the 1960s, the beatniks gave way to the hippies, and Ginsberg became the chief guru of this new drug and protest movement. He travelled widely, and gave countless poetry readings, performing at mass festivals alongside rock musicians such as Bob Dylan. He led rallies against the Vietnam war, nuclear weapons, and censorship. An openly homosexual man himself, he campaigned for gay rights and the legalization of drugs.

For the last 20 years of his life, Ginsberg devoted much of his time to a Buddhist college in Colorado, where he taught poetry.

STEPHANE GRAPPELLI (1908–97), a French violinist, was a towering figure in European jazz. He taught himself to play the violin before he was ten, and showed such talent that he was accepted by the Paris Conservatoire as a pupil. By the age of 15 he was earning a living playing in cinemas and cafés. In 1929 he joined a popular French big band, through which he met the

Belgian guitarist Django Reinhardt. With a bass player and two more guitarists the pair formed the Quintet of the Hot Club of France. The group made a series of the classic jazz records in the 1930s and played with many leading US-jazzmen. Reinhardt and Grappelli played together until 1939. When war broke out that year they were in England, where Grappelli remained until 1946.

Grappelli worked mainly as a dance band leader for many years after that. Then in the early 1970s, at an age when most people would have retired, Grappelli's career began to blossom again. He made several jazz records with the renowned classical violinist Yehudi Menuhin, and others with rising young jazz stars such as Gary Burton and Alan Clare. The recordings he made in the last 20 years of his life were the finest of his career. He recorded his last album at the age of 85.

HELENE HANFF (1916–97), the US-writer, became famous for her book *84 Charing Cross Road,* published in 1971. This was a collection of letters exchanged over a period of 20 years with the staff of Marks & Co, a second-hand bookshop in London. She first wrote to Marks in 1949, asking for out-of-print books. Gradually the

▼ Helene Hanff

letters became filled with news of life in New York and London. She sent food parcels when she learned of the shortages in Britain after World War II; in return, the staff of Marks sent her finely embroidered Irish linen and first editions of her favourite books. The captivating *84 Charing Cross Road* amused and touched many readers. It was filmed as a television play, adapted for the stage, and in 1987, was made into a film starring Anne Bancroft and Anthony Hopkins. All this changed Helene Hanff's life. For many years she had struggled to make a career as a playwright. She had some success writing television scripts, magazine articles, and books, but she felt that she was a failure. The popularity of *84 Charing Cross Road* restored her confidence and her self-esteem. She described her adventures as a visitor to London in *The Duchess of Bloomsbury Street,* 1976, and she made regular broadcasts for BBC radio, which were published as *A Letter from New York* in 1992.

MICHAEL HUTCHENCE (1960–97) was the lead singer and principal songwriter for the Australian rock band INXS. He met his future song-writing partner, Andrew Farriss, at school in Sydney, Australia, when Farriss saved him from a playground fight. They found that they enjoyed the same kinds of music and, in 1977, formed a six-piece band that they called the Farriss Brothers. They began their career by performing at small bars in the countryside, and built such a reputation that they were soon playing 300 nights a year. In 1979 they changed their name to INXS – which stood for "in excess".

Their first Australian hit single was "Just Keep Walking", 1981, for which Hutchence wrote

◀ Willem de Kooning

the lyrics. Their third album, *Shabooh Shoobah,* 1983, made them international stars – one track went to Number One in the United States – but their most successful album was *Kick,* 1987, which sold nine million copies. Much of INXS's appeal was due to Hutchence's good looks and dramatic performances, and these were used to the full in promotional videos of the band. In the 1990s, INXS had fewer and fewer hits. Hutchence moved to London, where he was content to enjoy the wealth his songs had brought him and take occasional film parts.

WILLEM DE KOONING (1904–97) was a founder of the modern art movement known as Abstract Expressionism (a combination of Abstract art and Expressionism), which began in New York in the mid-1940s and dominated art in the United States and Europe for the next 20 years.

De Kooning was born in Rotterdam in The Netherlands. In 1926, he travelled to the United States as a stowaway and settled in New York. He made a living as a decorator and carpenter until, in 1935, he decided to work full-time as an artist. His work went through several phases, ranging from realistic paintings of figures in the 1930s, to abstract landscapes, and pictures that combined living forms and geometric shapes. He won public recognition with his first one-man exhibition, held in 1948, at which he showed large abstract canvases painted in black and white. His most famous work is the series called *Woman I–VI.* Produced in the early 1950s, these paintings caused a sensation because of their alarmingly savage images and aggressive use of colour.

De Kooning continued to paint until 1990,

using mainly primary colours of red, yellow, and blue. But his earlier work is the most popular, and it commands high prices. At a sale in 1989, *Interchange,* painted in 1955, achieved a record price for a living artist of £13 million.

LAURIE LEE (1914–97), the English writer and poet, made his name with the publication of *Cider With Rosie,* in 1959. This evocative novel described Lee's childhood and adolescence in the village of Slad, in Gloucestershire, England. It captured the essence of rural life in a bygone age, and brought the landscape and people vividly to life.

Lee left Slad in the summer of 1934 at the age of 20, and made his way to London. There he worked as a labourer by day, writing poetry by night. In 1935, he went on a walking trip across Spain, earning his keep by playing the violin. He returned to Spain the following year, in the middle of the Civil War, was arrested and threatened with execution as a spy. Lee described his Spanish adventures in two books, *As I Walked Out One Midsummer Morning,* 1969, and *A Moment of War,* 1991.

Back in England, Lee continued to write

◀ Laurie Lee

poetry, and published *The Sun My Monument,* the first of four collections of verse, in 1944. He made little money from his writing, until the publication of *Cider With Rosie.* The book was an instant success. It enabled him to buy a house in the village where he was born, and he lived there for the rest of his life.

ROY LICHTENSTEIN (1923–97) was a leading figure in the 1960s US-Pop Art movement, which was inspired by all aspects of popular culture, such as television, magazines, and advertising. His best-known works resemble huge comic-strip cartoons, complete with speech balloons. He had an instantly recognizable style, with boldly outlined figures and objects in clear, bright colours. He often painted gigantic dots to imitate the process of colour printing used in comics. The most highly regarded of his comic-strip pictures is *Whaam!* which shows a fighter plane being destroyed by another in mid-air.

Lichtenstein studied at the School of Fine Arts at Ohio State University in the United States, then worked as a commercial artist and designer in Cleveland, Ohio. He became a teacher and, in 1960, was appointed assistant professor at Rutgers University in New Jersey. One of his colleagues, the painter Allan Kaprow, saw some of Lichtenstein's early Pop drawings and persuaded him to take them to an art dealer.

The first exhibition of Lichtenstein's Pop Art was held in a New York gallery in 1962 and it caused a sensation. Some critics, however, were not at all enthusiastic: the *New York Times* called him "one of the worst artists in America". In spite of that, Lichtenstein's name was made, and within a couple of years he could afford to dedicate himself to painting full time.

Although best known for his comic-strip paintings, Lichtenstein worked in many styles.

▼ Roy Lichtenstein

AND ALSO...

Sir Rudolf Bing (1902–97), Austrian impresario who managed New York's Metropolitan Opera from 1950 to 1972.

Jeff Buckley (1966–97), singer-songwriter from California, USA, whose remarkable voice attracted a cult following.

William Burroughs (1914–97), US-author, most famous for his novel *The Naked Lunch*.

Hans Eysenck (1916–97), British psychologist best known for his controversial theories on human intelligence.

Elspeth Huxley (1907–97), Kenyan-born writer whose best works were based on her childhood on the family farm in Kenya.

Ronnie Lane (1946–97), British pop singer and songwriter, a founder member of the 1960s pop group, the Small Faces.

Dora Maar (1907–97), French photographer and painter who became Picasso's lover and the model for many of his weeping-woman paintings such as *Dora Maar Seated*.

James Michener (1907–97), US-novelist whose book of short stories was the inspiration for the musical *South Pacific*.

Conlon Nancarrow (1912–97), influential US-composer best known for the exhilarating music he composed for the piano.

Notorious B.I.G. (1973–97), alias Christopher Wallace, a top US-rap artist.

V S Pritchett (1900–97), British author who was a master of short-story writing and a fine literary critic.

Svyatoslav Richter (1915–97), Ukrainian pianist regarded as one of the most outstanding musicians of the century.

Harold Robbins (1916–97), popular US-novelist, whose books have sold millions world-wide.

A L Rowse (1903–97), controversial British historian specializing in the life and times of Queen Elizabeth I of England.

Eugene Shoemaker (1928–97), US-astronomer and co-discoverer of Comet Shoemaker-Levy 9.

Jimmy Witherspoon (1923–97), one of the USA's classic jazz and blues singers whose recording career spanned more than 50 years.

He produced witty versions of pictures by artists such as Cézanne, Picasso, and Monet, and experimented with other materials such as glass, enamelled steel, and ceramics. In 1988 he made a 6-metre-high statue of Christopher Columbus for the city of Genoa, Italy.

SIR GEORG SOLTI (1912–97) was one of the great conductors of modern times. Whether in the concert hall or the opera house, he performed with enormous energy and enthusiasm; and *Time* magazine described him as "the fastest baton in the West". Although he was a stickler for discipline and drove his musicians and singers hard, most acknowledged that he inspired them to give their very best performances. Georg Solti was born in Budapest, Hungary, the son of Jewish Hungarian parents. After studying at the Liszt Academy, he started his musical career as a concert pianist and accompanist, but

◀ Sir Georg Solti

▲ Gianni Versace

later decided he wanted to become a conductor. He joined the Budapest Opera in 1930, and made his conducting debut there at the age of 25, with Mozart's opera *The Marriage of Figaro*.

In the next 60 years he worked with most of the major orchestras in Europe and the United States, and at many of the great opera houses. One of the high points of his career came in 1961 when he was given the job of musical director at the Royal Opera House, Covent Garden in London. Although the first works he produced there were regarded by many as disastrous, in his ten years at Covent Garden the opera house became recognized as the best in the world. The work Solti did as musical director of the Chicago Symphony Orchestra and the London Philharmonic, in the 1970s and 1980s, was also hugely successful.

Solti was just as dynamic, and just as demanding, in the recording studio as he was in the concert hall. Many of the recordings he made, always on the Decca label, set new standards of performance and won numerous international awards. He earned a place in history in 1965 by becoming the first conductor to record the entire cycle of Wagner's *Ring* operas. The project took seven years to complete, but it was soon acknowledged as a classic.

GIANNI VERSACE (1946–97) was one of the most flamboyant and successful fashion designers of the 1980s and 1990s. His clothes were often made of striking combinations of materials – such as silk and leather – in dazzling colours, and were bought by celebrities as diverse as Diana, Princess of Wales; Bruce Springsteen; Elizabeth Taylor; and Elton John.

Born in Reggio, southern Italy, Versace began working for his mother, a dressmaker, when he was 18. From her he learned the essential skills of cutting and stitching clothes. Within a few years he was producing his own designs and selling them to a manufacturer in Milan. He moved to Milan – the centre of the Italian fashion industry – in 1970, to work freelance for several companies. In 1978, he presented his first collection under his own name.

From the start Versace's clothes were unusual. His patterns and colours reflected his insatiable appetite for visual excitement – drawing on sources such as medieval paintings, African tribal art, and Japanese prints. He constantly experimented with materials, once cutting an outfit from clear plastic.

Fashion critics were not impressed at first by what they thought was his vulgar style. Versace responded by designing outfits for opera and ballet, by publishing huge advertisements, and by packing his shows with the superstars who bought his clothes. In 1983 he won Italy's top award for design. By 1996 he was selling clothes, watches, china, and perfume bearing his name throughout the world.

Versace's personal tastes were as extravagant as his designs. He spent millions on artworks and furnishings for his huge houses in Milan, New York, and Miami, and entertained lavishly. Yet he also enjoyed few things better than quietly reading books on art and gardening. And, for all their eye-catching daring, his clothes were always very comfortable to wear.

STAGE AND SCREEN

ROBERT MITCHUM (1917–97), the Hollywood film actor, was considered one of the great stars in the years after the end of World War II. Yet

◄ Robert Mitchum

many people dismissed his work, because he made acting look so effortless that it seemed that he was not acting at all.

Tall and powerfully built, with sleepy, hooded eyes, Mitchum was usually cast as a tough guy. It was an image he did little to discourage off-screen. He drank a great deal of alcohol, often got into fights, and showed little respect for studio bosses or any kind of authority. He made his film debut in 1943, as an extra in a Hopalong Cassidy western. His first starring role was as a tough but sensitive soldier in *The Story of GI Joe,* 1945. After that he was never out of work, and made more than 120 films in all. He gave his finest performances as an evil preacher in *The Night of the Hunter,* 1955, and as Raymond Chandler's private detective Philip Marlowe in the remake of *Farewell, My Lovely,* 1975. Other notable films included *Cape Fear,* 1962, *Ryan's Daughter,* 1970, and *The Friends of Eddie Coyle,* 1973. Although he never won an Oscar, he was honoured by the film industry with a Special Lifetime's Achievement Award in 1992.

JAMES STEWART (1908–97), the US-film actor, was unusually modest and shy for a Hollywood star. He insisted that his distinguished record as a bomber pilot in World War II should not be used in publicity material. He and his wife Gloria were extremely happily married for 45 years. When she died in 1994, he was devastated and became a virtual recluse.

Stewart started acting when he was studying architecture at Princeton University, New Jersey. After graduating he went to New York, where he was spotted by talent scouts on Broadway. He won an Oscar for his part in *The Philadelphia Story,* 1940, which showed his

AND ALSO...

Adriana Caselotti (1916–97), US-singer who was the voice of Snow White in Walt Disney's classic cartoon film.

Samuel Fuller (1911–97), US-film director hailed as an important influence on both French and US cinema.

Stubby Kaye (1918–97), US-song-and-dance man and star of Broadway musicals such as *Guys and Dolls.*

Burgess Meredith (1907–97), popular US-actor best remembered for his role as the arch-villain Penguin in the *Batman* television series in the 1960s.

Tomoyuki Tanaka (1910–97), Japanese film producer and creator of the science fiction monster Godzilla.

Fred Zinnemann (1907–97), Hollywood film director who made some of the best films of the 1950s and 1960s.

natural flair for comedy. His role in *Harvey,* 1950, as a likeable drunk who talks to an imaginary giant rabbit, was one of his own favourites, and he recreated the part on stage several times.

He played tougher, darker characters in westerns such as *Winchester 73,* 1950, and *The Man from Laramie,* 1955, and in four films directed by Alfred Hitchcock, the most chilling of which was *Vertigo,* 1958. His most powerful performance was in *Anatomy of a Murder,* 1959.

► James Stewart

Sport '97

Facts and figures from the world of international sport.

ABBREVIATIONS FOR COUNTRIES

Alg	Algeria	Indo	Indonesia
Arg	Argentina	Ire	Ireland
Aus	Australia	It	Italy
Au	Austria	Jam	Jamaica
Bel	Belarus	Jap	Japan
Bra	Brazil	Kaz	Kazakhstan
Bulg	Bulgaria	Ken	Kenya
Can	Canada	Mex	Mexico
Chin	China	Neth	Netherlands
Col	Colombia	N. Zeal	New Zealand
Cro	Croatia	Nic	Nicaragua
Cu	Cuba	Nor	Norway
Czech	Czech Republic	Phil	Philippines
		Pol	Poland
Den	Denmark	Rom	Romania
Dom Rep	Dominican Republic	Rus	Russia
		SA	South Africa
E. Ger	East Germany	Scot	Scotland
Eng	England	S. Kor	South Korea
Eth	Ethiopia	Spa	Spain
Fin	Finland	Swe	Sweden
Fra	France	Swi	Switzerland
GB	Great Britain	Thai	Thailand
Ger	Germany	Ukr	Ukraine
Ghan	Ghana	US	United States
Grc	Greece	USSR	Soviet Union
Hun	Hungary	Ven	Venezuela

AMERICAN FOOTBALL

Two teams with varied fortunes in the National Football League (NFL) premier event advanced to Super Bowl XXXII, in San Diego – the Denver Broncos and the Green Bay Packers. The Broncos had lost in all four of their previous Super Bowl appearances, while the Packers had won three out of three, including last year's game in New Orleans.

The defending champions, the Packers, were led by quarterback Brett Favre, who was named NFL Most Valuable Player for an unprecedented third time. The Packers won the NFC Central Division and

▼ The Green Bay Packers beat the New England Patriots 35–21 at Super Bowl XXXI, in January 1997.

advanced to the Super Bowl with a comfortable victory over the NFC West Division champion San Francisco 49ers in the NFC championship game.

Denver Broncos lost their AFC West Division crown to Kansas City Chiefs but gained revenge in the second round of the playoffs by beating the Chiefs to advance to the AFC title decider in Pittsburgh. Despite a hostile crowd, the Broncos edged out the Pittsburgh Steelers 24–21 to make it to the Super Bowl.

There was a shift of power in the NFC East Division this season, with the New York Giants breaking the Dallas Cowboys' five-year stranglehold. They won the division but crashed to the Minnesota Vikings in the first round of the playoffs. The Vikings in turn lost to the 49ers in the following round.

Jacksonville Jaguars made the playoffs for the second time in their three-year existence, although they lost the AFC Central Division to the Steelers and their opening playoff clash to the Broncos. Other playoff qualifiers included the AFC East champion New England Patriots and the Miami Dolphins.

National Football League – Final Standings
American Football Conference Division Winners: New England Patriots *(East)*, Pittsburgh Steelers *(Central)*, Kansas City Chiefs *(West)*
National Football Conference Division Winners: New York Giants *(East)*, Green Bay Packers *(Central)*, San Francisco 49ers *(West)*

College Football
Citrus Bowl: Florida 21, Pennsylvania State 6
Cotton Bowl: UCLA 29, Texas A & M 23
Fiesta Bowl: Kansas State 35, Syracuse 18
Heritage Bowl: Southern 34, South Carolina State 28
Orange Bowl: Nebraska 42, Tennessee 17
Peach Bowl: Auburn 21, Clemson 17
Rose Bowl: Michigan 21, Washington State 16
Sugar Bowl: Florida State 31, Ohio State 14

ATHLETICS

Merlene Ottey (Jam) finished third in the 200-metre race at the World Outdoor Championships in Greece. This gave her a record 14th medal in the tournament, at the age of 37. Carl Lewis (US), with 10 medals and next in the list of medal winners, announced his retirement at the end of the season.

A race to find the "world's fastest human" took place between Olympic 100-metre champion Donovan Bailey (Can) and Olympic 200- and 400-metre champion Michael Johnson (US). It was run over 150 metres on a specially constructed track in Toronto. However, the result was indecisive. Part way through Johnson pulled up clutching his left thigh, leaving Bailey to finish alone in 14.99 seconds.

WORLD RECORDS IN THE MAIN TRACK AND FIELD EVENTS

MEN

100 metres*	9.84 sec	Donovan Bailey (Can)	1996
200 metres	19.32 sec	Michael Johnson (US)	1996
400 metres	43.29 sec	Harry Reynolds (US)	1988
800 metres	1 min 41.11 sec	Wilson Kipketer (Den)	1997
1,000 metres	2 min 12.18 sec	Sebastian Coe (GB)	1981
1,500 metres	3 min 27.37 sec	Noureddine Morceli (Alg)	1995
Mile	3 min 44.39 sec	Noureddine Morceli (Alg)	1993
2,000 metres	4 min 47.88 sec	Noureddine Morceli (Alg)	1995
3,000 metres	7 min 20.67 sec	Daniel Komen (Ken)	1996
5,000 metres	12 min 39.74 sec	Daniel Komen (Ken)	1997
10,000 metres	26 min 27.85 sec	Paul Tergat (Ken)	1997
3,000 metres steeplechase	7 min 55.72 sec	Bernard Barmasai (Ken)	1997
110 metres hurdles	12.91 sec	Colin Jackson (GB)	1993
400 metres hurdles	46.78 sec	Kevin Young (US)	1992
Marathon**	2 hr 6 min 50 sec	Belayneh Dinsamo (Eth)	1988
4 x 100 metres relay	37.40 sec	United States	1992
4 x 400 metres relay	2 min 54.29 sec	United States	1993
High jump	2.45 metres	Javier Sotomayor (Cu)	1993
Pole vault	6.14 metres	Sergey Bubka (Ukr)	1994
Long jump	8.95 metres	Mike Powell (US)	1991
Triple jump	18.29 metres	Jonathan Edwards (GB)	1995
Shot	23.12 metres	Randy Barnes (US)	1990
Discus	74.08 metres	Jurgen Schult (E. Ger)	1986
Hammer	86.74 metres	Yuriy Sedykh (USSR)	1986
Javelin	98.48 metres	Jan Zelezny (Czech)	1996
Decathlon	8,891 points	Dan O'Brien (US)	1992

WOMEN

100 metres	10.49 sec	Florence Griffith Joyner (US)	1988
200 metres	21.34 sec	Florence Griffith Joyner (US)	1988
400 metres	47.60 sec	Marita Koch (E. Ger)	1985
800 metres	1 min 53.28 sec	Jarmila Kratochvilova (Czech)	1983
1,000 metres	2 min 28.98 sec	Svetlana Masterkova (Rus)	1996
1,500 metres	3 min 50.46 sec	Qu Yunxia (Chin)	1993
Mile	4 min 12.56 sec	Svetlana Masterkova (Rus)	1996
2,000 metres	5 min 25.36 sec	Sonia O'Sullivan (Ire)	1994
3,000 metres	8 min 6.11 sec	Wang Junxia (Chin)	1993
5,000 metres	14 min 28.09 sec	Jiang Bo (Chin)	1997
10,000 metres	29 min 31.78 sec	Wang Junxia (Chin)	1993
20,000 metres	1 hr 6 min 48.8 sec	Izumi Maki (Jap)	1993
Marathon**	2 hr 21 min 6 sec	Ingrid Kristiansen (Nor)	1985
100 metres hurdles	12.21 sec	Yordanka Donkova (Bulg)	1988
400 metres hurdles	52.61 sec	Kim Batten (US)	1995
4 x 100 metres relay	41.37 sec	East Germany	1985
4 x 400 metres relay	3 min 15.17 sec	USSR	1988
High jump	2.09 metres	Stefka Kostadinova (Bulg)	1987
Pole vault	4.55 metres	Emma George (Aus)	1997
Long jump	7.52 metres	Galina Chistyakova (USSR)	1988
Triple jump	15.50 metres	Inessa Kravets (Ukr)	1995
Shot	22.63 metres	Natalya Lisovskaya (USSR)	1987
Discus	76.80 metres	Gabriele Reinsch (E. Ger)	1988
Hammer	73.10 metres	Olga Kuzenkova (Rus)	1997
Javelin	80.00 metres	Petra Felke (E. Ger)	1988
Heptathlon	7,291 points	Jackie Joyner-Kersee (US)	1988

*   Ben Johnson's 100-metre record of 9.83 seconds was removed from the record books in 1989. So was his later record of 9.79 seconds achieved at the Olympic Games in Seoul.

** Best performance at the marathon distance of 26 miles 385 yards (42.195 km). No official records exist because of the varying severity of courses.

▲ Merlene Ottey (centre) shows her mettle in the World Championships 200-metres semi-finals in Athens.

Haile Gebrselassie (Eth) and Noureddine Morceli (Alg) faced each other over two miles. Morceli, the 1,500-metres, one-mile, and 2,000-metres world record holder, was left trailing. Gebrselassie, the 5,000-metres world record holder, ran the last three laps out on his own, failing by just 1.08 seconds to win the million dollars offered by the race sponsors. He beat the existing world's best time but not the eight-minute barrier. However, in July, he did manage to smash the 10,000-metres world record by almost seven seconds.

Other world records to fall during the year included the 800 metres to Wilson Kipketer. Kipketer is now a Danish national but was born in Kenya. On 22 August, in Brussels, the 5,000-metres and 10,000-metres records were both taken by Kenyan athletes; Daniel Komen took the first and Paul Tergat took the second. Both of these records had only recently been set by Haile Gebrselassie. Another Kenyan, Bernard Barmasai, set a world record in the 3,000-metres steeplechase event, emphasizing African dominance in distance running.

The only women's records to fall in 1997 were the pole vault to Emma George (Aus), the hammer to Olga Kuzenkova (Rus), and the 5,000 metres to Jiang Bo (Chin). The latter was set at the China National Games in Shanghai, where several junior world records were set by Chinese women. As in the case of recent performances by female Chinese swimmers, there was speculation that performance-enhancing drugs were responsible for the outstanding results; many of the athletes were not highly ranked. The Chinese attributed the records to special nutritional supplements and hard training.

AUSTRALIAN RULES FOOTBALL
Adelaide FC won its first title in the Australian Football League (AFL), in the seventh season playing in the league. It defeated St. Kilda in its first grand final appearance to become only the second club outside Victoria to win the title.

League newcomer Port Adelaide fared well in its first season, having replaced Fitzroy, which had merged with Brisbane. Footscray changed its name to the Western Bulldogs.

Australian Football League (AFL) Champions: Adelaide FC

BADMINTON

World Championships (Glasgow, Scotland)
Men's Singles: P. Rasmussen (Den)
Women's Singles: Ye Zhaoying (Chin)
Men's Doubles: Budiato Sigit and Chandra Wijaya (Indo)
Women's Doubles: Gu Jun and Ge Fei (Chin)
Mixed Doubles: Liu Yong and Ge Fei (Chin)
World Mixed Team Championships: China

BASEBALL
The Florida Marlins won the North American World Series, defeating the Cleveland Indians by four games to three. This had only been the Marlins' fifth season in the league, which they had joined in 1993. They beat a record set in 1969 by the New York Mets, who won the World Series in their eighth season. Although the Marlins became world champions, they failed to win their league division, finishing nine games behind the leaders, Atlanta Braves. They only qualified by having the best record of second-placed teams in the National League.

In the American League, the Baltimore Orioles, of the East Division, finished with the best record, winning 98 of their 162 games. They were joined in the playoff for league champion by the other two divisional winners, Cleveland Indians and Seattle Mariners, plus the defending league champions, the New York Yankees. The Yankees were eliminated by the Indians 3–2 after leading 2–1 in a best-of-five series, while the Orioles beat the Mariners 3–1. In

▼ The view from behind the plate at the Dodgers 5–2 win over the Mets in New York's Shea Stadium.

the American League Championship series the Indians overcame the Orioles 4–2.

In the National League playoff for league champion, the Atlanta Braves beat Houston Astros 3–0, and the Florida Marlins triumphed over the San Francisco Giants by a similar margin to set up a rematch between the two East Division qualifiers, the Marlins and the Braves. This time the Marlins, the division's runners-up, came out on top. The Marlins won 4–2 to win the National League title from the defending champions.

The World Series, which is decided on the best of seven matches, went to the deciding game for the first time since 1991. The Marlins won the first game, the Indians won the second, and so on until the score was 3–3. The deciding game, in front of the Marlins' home crowd, went Florida's way.

The sport continued to recover from the damaging players' strike of 1994. Attendance was up and matches between teams from the two leagues created interest. Two new teams joined the leagues, Arizona Diamondbacks (National League West) and Tampa Bay Devil Rays (American League East).

North America
World Series
Florida Marlins beat Cleveland Indians, four
  games to three

▼ Michael Jordan of the Chicago Bulls tries for a basket.

Final Standings
American League: Baltimore Orioles *(East)*, Cleveland
  Indians *(Central)*, Seattle Mariners *(West)*
National League: Atlanta Braves *(East)*, Houston Astros
  (Central), San Francisco Giants *(West)*

BASKETBALL
In 1997 two new women's leagues were set up in the United States with enough promotion from the National Basketball Association (NBA) to move Michael Jordan of the Chicago Bulls from the centre of attention for once. The new leagues, the Women's National Basketball Association (WNBA) and the American Basketball League (ABL), were given a high-profile send off, gaining support from the media, fans, and from college and Olympic stars. Both leagues began with eight teams. The ABL announced a ninth, Long Beach Sting Rays, to play in the following season.

Jordan helped the Chicago Bulls to their fifth NBA triumph in seven years. They overcame Utah Jazz by four games to two in the finals. Jordan also won his fifth "Most Valuable Player" award in the playoffs, but threatened to retire if either coach Phil Jackson or forward Scottie Pippen was allowed to leave the team. Both men were retained and Jordan accepted a $36 million contract to play another season for the Bulls. The loss of Jordan would have been disastrous for the NBA and for Chicago basketball.

United States
NBA Championship: Chicago Bulls
WNBA Championship: Houston Comets
ABL Championship: Columbus Quest
Men's US NCAA Championship: Arizona
Women's US NCAA Championship: Tennessee

NBA Final Standings
Atlantic Division: Miami
Central Division: Chicago
Midwest Division: Utah
Pacific Division: Seattle

International
European Championships (men): Yugoslavia
European Championships (women): Lithuania
Euro Stars: The East
European Cup: Real Madrid (Spa)
European Korac Cup: Aris Salonica (Grc)
Women's European Champions' Cup: Bourges (Fra)
Ronchetti Cup: CSKA Moscow (Rus)

BOWLS (LAWN BOWLS)
World Indoor Singles (men): H. Duff (Scot)
World Indoor Singles (women): N. Shaw (Eng)
British Isles Outdoor Singles (men): J. Henry (Ire)
British Isles Outdoor Singles (women): M. Johnston (Ire)
English Indoor Singles (men): R. Newman (Eng)
English Indoor Singles (women): N. Shaw (Eng)
English Outdoor Singles (men): R. Brittan (Eng)
English Outdoor Singles (women): M. Price (Eng)

BOXING

The world heavyweight championship, generally regarded as the focal point of boxing, brought the sport into disrepute on several occasions during the year, most notably during the much-awaited fight between Mike Tyson (US) and the current World Boxing Association (WBA) title holder, Evander Holyfield (US). Tyson was disqualified for twice biting his opponent, removing part of his ear in the process. He was fined the maximum amount possible – 10 per cent of his fee. The rule was later changed to make it possible to fine offenders 100 per cent of their fee in future.

Elsewhere, Lennox Lewis (GB) reversed a

▼ "Prince" Naseem Hamed floors Kevin Kelley at the Madison Square Garden, New York.

previous knockout defeat against Oliver McCall (US) for the World Boxing Council (WBC) title. The referee stopped the fight because McCall "refused to defend himself" – McCall had stopped throwing punches and was turning his back on his opponent. Lewis's next opponent, Henry Akinwande (GB) was disqualified for "blatant and persistent holding".

The lower weights produced better performances. Oscar de la Hoya (US) retained the WBC super lightweight crown, then moved up a division and captured the welterweight title from Pernell Whitaker (US), giving him 26 undefeated fights. Meanwhile, Roy Jones (US) carelessly lost his WBC light heavyweight title and unbeaten record of 35 fights when he was disqualified for hitting challenger Montel Griffin (US) after flooring him. Jones knocked him out in one round in a rematch five months later. Iko Quartey (Ghan) made a sixth defence of his WBA welterweight title, outpointing Jose Luis Lopez (Mex). Twelve hours later, the score of one of the judges was changed, altering the result to a draw, but this was still enough for Quartey to retain his crown.

In Britain, "Prince" Naseem Hamed reached 28 bouts without defeat at the featherweight level. Many of his opponents had been disposed of swiftly, and it was thought that his ability had not been properly tested. At the end of 1997, he won his debut fight in the United States at Madison Square Garden, New York, against Kevin Kelley (US). Steve Collins (Ire) relinquished his World Boxing Organization (WBO) super middleweight crown when he announced his retirement after 11 years as a professional.

WORLD BOXING CHAMPIONS

Weight	World Boxing Council (WBC)	World Boxing Association (WBA)	International Boxing Federation (IBF)
Heavyweight	L. Lewis (GB)	E. Holyfield (US)	E. Holyfield (US)
Cruiserweight	M. Dominguez (Arg)	F. Tiozzo (Fra)	I. Mayfield (US)
Light Heavyweight	R. Jones (US)	L. Del Valle (US)	W. Guthrie (US)
Super Middleweight	T. Malinga (SA)	F. Lilles (US)	C. Brewer (US)
Middleweight	K. Holmes (US)	J. C. Green (Dom Rep)	B. Hopkins (US)
Super Welterweight	K. Mullings (US)	L. Boudouani (Fra)	Yori Boy Campas (Mex)
Welterweight	O. de la Hoya (US)	I. Quartey (Ghan)	F. Trinidad (US)
Super Lightweight	vacant	K. Rahilou (Fra)	V. Phillips (US)
Lightweight	S. Johnston (US)	O. Nazarov (Rus)	S. Mosley (US)
Super Featherweight	G. Hernandez (US)	Yongsoo Choi (S. Kor)	A. Gatti (Can)
Featherweight	L. Espinoza (Phil)	W. Vazquez (US)	H. Lizzaraga (US)
Super Bantamweight	E. Morales (Mex)	vacant	V. Bungu (SA)
Bantamweight	Joichiro Tatsuyoshi (Jap)	N. Konadu (Ghan)	T. Austin (US)
Super Flyweight	G. Penalosa (Phil)	Satoshi Iida (Thai)	J. Tapia (US)
Flyweight	Chatchai Sasakul (Thai)	J. Bonilla (Ven)	M. Johnson (US)
Light Flyweight	Saman Sorjaturong (Thai)	Pitchnoi Siriwat (Thai)	M. Pastrana (Col)
Straw-weight	R. Lopez (Mex)	R. Alvarez (Nic)	Z. Pethelo (SA)

CRICKET

Australia confirmed its position as the world's strongest Test-playing nation, winning 8 out of 15 Test matches in 1997. Its achievements included victories over South Africa, the West Indies, and a record fifth successive victory in the Ashes series against England. The series with South Africa was the unofficial world championship, which Australia won 2–1. A partnership of 385 by Greg Blewett and Steve Waugh set up an innings win for Australia in the first Test, while Steve Waugh's twin Mark scored 116 in the second Test to guide Australia to a two-wicket victory. The West Indies was still undergoing a rebuilding programme when it was decisively beaten by the Australians. India's discovery of three world-class bowlers held out hope for the future.

The Ashes Series started promisingly for England. They won the first Test by nine wickets with Australia losing eight wickets before lunch on the first day and Nasser Hussain scoring 207 for England. Rain helped England to a draw in the second Test, but Australia won the next three to retain the Ashes. England won the final Test, bowling the visitors out for 104 on the third day to make the result of the series respectable.

In Colombo, Sri Lanka, on a pitch almost perfect for batsmen, Sri Lanka scored 952 for 6 against India in August. Sri Lanka's S.T. Jayasuriya came in sight of Brian Lara's world record 375 but succumbed to nerves and was out on 340. He faced 578 balls in an innings lasting over thirteen hours.

Major Test Series

Australia v West Indies: Australia 3, West Indies 2
South Africa v India: South Africa 2, drawn 1
New Zealand v England: England 2, drawn 1
New Zealand v Sri Lanka: New Zealand 2
South Africa v Australia: South Africa 1, Australia 2
West Indies v India: West Indies 1, drawn 4
Sri Lanka v Pakistan: drawn 2
West Indies v Sri Lanka: West Indies 1, drawn 1
England v Australia: Australia 3, England 2, drawn 1
Sri Lanka v India: drawn 2
Zimbabwe v New Zealand: drawn 2
Pakistan v South Africa: South Africa 1, drawn 2
Australia v New Zealand: Australia 2, drawn 1
Pakistan v West Indies: Pakistan 3
India v Sri Lanka: drawn 3

England

English County Champions: Glamorgan
Benson & Hedges Cup: Surrey
NatWest Trophy: Essex
Sunday League: Warwickshire

Rest of the World

Australia – Sheffield Shield: Queensland
India – Ranji Trophy: Mumbai (Bombay)
New Zealand – Shell Trophy: Canterbury
West Indies – Red Stripe Cup: Barbados

▲ The leaders of the Tour de France fight it out on the Disneyland-to-Paris stage.

CYCLING

The Tour de France was won by 23-year-old Jan Ullrich of Germany, the youngest winner since 1983. In finishing 9 minutes 9 seconds ahead of Frenchman Richard Virenque, he also established the biggest winning margin since 1984. Virenque won the competition for the best mountain climber for the fourth time. France dominated the world track championships, winning six gold medals. Felicia Ballanger won both the women's sprint and 500-metre trial for the third successive year. France set a world record of 44.926 seconds in the three-man Olympic sprint over 750 metres, while Jean-Pierre Van Zyl became the first South African cyclist to win a world championship medal since his country's return to international competition.

The sport's governing body, Union Cycliste Internationale (UCI), continued its fight to eliminate drug-taking by introducing random blood testing in an attempt to cut down the use of a hormone that stimulates the production of oxygen-rich blood cells.

Tour de France: J. Ullrich (Ger)
Tour of Italy: I. Gotti (Italy)
Tour of Spain: A. Zulle (Swi)

World Road Championships (San Sebastian, Spain)
MEN
Individual Road Race: L. Brochard (Fra)
Individual Time Trial: L. Jalabert (Fra)

WOMEN
Individual Road Race: A. Cappellotto (It)
Individual Time Trial: J. Longo-Ciprelli (Fra)

EQUESTRIAN SPORTS

Germany, the host nation, won the team event of the European Show Jumping Championships in Mannheim, in August. This was the first time that

Germany had won the title since 1981. Germany also carried off the individual championship, won by Ludger Beerbaum on Sprehe Ratina. Hugo Simon of Austria, on E.T. FRH, came second. Simon won all three legs of the World Cup in Gothenburg, Sweden, in May. Anky van Grunnsven of The Netherlands won the World Dressage Cup on Gestion Bonfire, but was beaten in the European Championship by Isabell Werth of Germany.

The Badminton Horse Trials Three-Day Event was won by David O'Connor of the United States on Custom Made and the Burghley Horse Trials by the New Zealand rider Mark Todd.

European Show Jumping Championship (team): Germany
European Show Jumping Championship (individual):
   L. Beerbaum (Ger)
European Dressage Championship: I. Werth (Ger)
World Cup (show jumping): H. Simon (Au)
World Cup (dressage): A. van Grunnsven (Neth)

FENCING

World Championships (Cape Town, S. Africa)
Men's Foil: S. Golubitsky (Ukr)
Women's Foil: G. Trillini (It)
Men's Epee: E. Srecki (Fra)
Women's Epee: M. Garcia-Soto (Cu)
Sabre (men): S. Pozdniakov (Rus)

European Championships (Gdansk, Poland)
Men's Foil: A. Krzesinski (Pol)
Women's Foil: M. Weber (Ger)
Men's Epee: G. Boczko (Hun)
Women's Epee: I. Mincza (Hun)
Sabre (men): A. Frossine (Rus)

GOLF

The arrival of the young Californian Eldrick "Tiger" Woods on the golfing scene led to an explosion of interest in the sport. At tournaments in which he played, ticket sales increased by 25 per cent and US television audiences were up by 60 per cent on the closing days. It was predicted that golf was entering a period of unprecedented growth.

Woods' performance in the Masters at Augusta, Georgia, his first major championship, was outstanding. He produced rounds of 70, 66, 65, and 69, giving an overall total of 270,

▶ "Tiger" Woods tees off in the opening round of the US Masters.

18 strokes under par and the lowest in the Masters' history. He finished a record 12 strokes ahead of his nearest rival, Tom Kite. He also won his next competition, the GTE Byron Nelson Classic, and looked like being the first player ever to win all four major tournaments in one season. In the event, he didn't even come close. The US Open went to the South African Ernie Els, the 1994 winner, forcing Scotland's Colin Montgomerie into second place. At the British Open, Sweden's Jesper Parnevik looked promising but was unable to hold the lead; the 25-year-old Texan, Justin Leonard, scored a closing round of 65 to win by three strokes.

The Professional Golfers of America (PGA) championship also had a US first-time winner. Leonard was again prominent, tying for the lead with Davis Love III at seven strokes ahead of the field. However, Love finished much the stronger and completed the tournament five strokes ahead of Leonard, with Jeff Maggert a further two strokes behind.

The Ryder Cup was played in continental Europe for the very first time, at Valderrama in Spain. Europe won by the narrowest of possible margins for the second year running.

US Open: E. Els (SA)
US Women's Open: A. Nicholas (GB)
Masters: E. Woods (US)
PGA: D. Love III (US)
British Open: J. Leonard (US)
British Women's Open: K. Webb (Aus)
World Matchplay: V. Singh (Fiji)
Ryder Cup: Europe
Alfred Dunhill Cup: South Africa

GYMNASTICS

World Championships (Lausanne, Switzerland)
MEN
Team: China
All Round: I. Ivankov (Bel)
Floor: A. Nemov (Rus)
Pommel Horse: V. Belenki (Ger)
   Rings: Y. Chechi (It)
   Vault: S. Fedorchenko (Kaz)
   Parallel Bars: Zhang Jinjing (Chin)
   Horizontal Bar: J. Tanskanen (Fin)

WOMEN
Team: Romania
All Round: S. Chorkina (Rus)
   Floor: G. Gogean (Rom)
   Vault: S. Amanar (Rom)
   Asymmetric Bars: S. Chorkina (Rus)
   Beam: G. Gogean (Rom)

HOCKEY, FIELD
Australia, World Cup holders and Olympic champions, continued to dominate the women's game. In June

they won the Champions' Trophy in Berlin for the fourth successive time, defeating Germany 2–1. However, later in the year Germany beat Australia 3–2 in the men's Champions' Trophy final in Adelaide.

A new annual event, the World Hockey Series, was to have begun in November, but it was decided in September to postpone the launch indefinitely because of lack of sponsorship and the absence of television coverage. An international competition on a European basis had been planned, but only 34 out of 119 International Hockey Federation countries expressed interest. The Netherlands' refusal to take part was a serious blow.

Champions' Trophy (men): Australia 2, Germany 3
Champions' Trophy (women): Germany 1, Australia 2

HOCKEY, ICE

Canada won the 61st World Championship, which was contested by 36 nations and held in Helsinki, Finland. Somewhat bizarrely, the runner-up, Sweden, had beaten the champions three times earlier in the tournament – twice in group matches and once in the opening game of the best-of-three final. Canada won the final by two games to one. The Czech Republic beat Russia 4–3 to take the bronze medal. The 1998 Pool A tournament between the best teams in the world is scheduled to take place in Switzerland. Sixteen teams, rather than 12, as previously, will take part: Belarus, Switzerland, and Japan, plus two qualifiers will join the top 11 teams of 1997.

The Detroit Red Wings won the Stanley Cup for the first time in 42 years, easily overcoming the Philadelphia Flyers. In the best-of-seven-games final, Detroit won the first two games in Philadelphia with identical 4–2 scores and routed the Flyers 6–1 in the third, played in Detroit. They only needed one more win to take the cup, which they gained with a 2–1 victory in front of almost 20,000 fans at the Joe Louis Arena, Detroit. The Flyers' coach, Terry Murray, was fired six days after the defeat. It had only been the Flyers' first appearance in the final since 1974–75. Wings' goalie, Mike Vernon, won the Conn Smythe Trophy as the most valuable player.

Lada Togliatti of Russia beat Modo Domsjo of Sweden 4–3 in the European Cup final, which was held at Oberhausen, Germany. The competition was to be replaced in the following year by an inter-club European league consisting of 20 teams from 12 nations. It is possible that North American teams will participate in the future.

International
Men's World Championships: Canada
Women's World Championships: Canada
European Cup: Lada Togliatti (Rus)

North America
Stanley Cup
Detroit Red Wings beat Philadelphia Flyers, four games to nil

US NHL League Division Champions
Eastern Conference: Philadelphia Flyers
Western Conference: Detroit Red Wings

HORSE RACING

US Horse Racing
Breeders' Cup Classic: Skip Away, M. Smith
Kentucky Derby: Silver Charm, G. Stevens
Belmont Stakes: Touch Gold, C. McCarron
Preakness Stakes: Silver Charm, G. Stevens

British Horse Racing
National Hunt
Cheltenham Gold Cup: Mr Mulligan, T. McCoy
Champion Hurdle: Make A Stand, T. McCoy
Grand National: Lord Gyllene, T. Dobbin

Flat
Derby: Benny The Dip, W. Ryan
Oaks: Reams Of Verse, K. Fallon
1,000 Guineas: Sleepytime, K. Fallon
2,000 Guineas: Entrepreneur, M. Kinane
St Leger: Silver Patriarch, P. Eddery

ICE SKATING

The 1997 World Championships were held in Lausanne, Switzerland. Elvis Stojko of Canada regained the men's title from American runner-up and defending champion, Todd Eldredge. It was Stojko's third triumph in four years. His programme included a combination of quadruple and triple toe-loops, the first time such a combination had been used in a world championship. The women's competition saw the continuing trend towards teenage dominance. Following concerns about the physical and mental demands

◀ Tara Lipinski of the United States picked up the women's title at the World Championships in Lausanne, Switzerland.

placed on younger competitors, a minimum age of 15 was introduced, exempting those who had already competed under that age. The winner was the youngest-ever champion, Tara Lipinski (US), aged just 14 (32 days younger than the 1927 champion, Sonja Henie of Norway). Her compatriot, the defending champion Michelle Kwan, finished a close second.

In a close pairs contest, Germany's Mandy Wotzel and Ingo Steuer took their first pairs title after twice finishing second. They defeated the defending Russians, Marina Yeltsova and Andrey Bushkov. The Russians Oksana Grishuk and Yegevny Platov swept to their fourth successive ice dance success.

The Champions' Series, held for the second time, was again based on results at six venues. It provided a pointer to performances at the later world championships. Stojko outpointed Eldredge and Lipinski defeated Kwan.

Figure skating
World Championships (Lausanne, Switzerland)
Men: E. Stojko (Can)
Women: T. Lipinski (US)
Pairs: M. Wotzel and I. Steuer (Ger)
Dance: O. Grishuk and Y. Platov (Rus)

Speed skating
World Championships (Nagano, Japan)
Men: I. Postma (Neth)
Women: G. Niemann (Ger)

JUDO

World Championships (Paris, France)
MEN
Under 60 kg:	Tadahiro Nomura (Jap)
Under 65 kg:	Hyuk Lim (S. Kor)
Under 71 kg:	Kenzo Nakamura (Jap)
Under 78 kg:	Chul Cho In (S. Kor)
Under 86 kg:	Ki Young (S. Kor)
Under 95 kg:	P. Nastula (Pol)
Over 95 kg:	D. Douillet (Fra)
Open:	R. Kubacki (Pol)

WOMEN
Under 48 kg:	Ryoko Tamura (Jap)
Under 52 kg:	M. Restoux (Fra)
Under 56 kg:	I. Fernandez (Spa)
Under 61 kg:	S. Vanderhende (Fra)
Under 66 kg:	K. Howey (GB)
Under 72 kg:	Noriko Anno (Jap)
Over 72 kg:	C. Cicot (Fra)
Open:	D. Beltran (Cu)

MOTOR RACING
The world championship reached a climax in Australia, with the two main rivals, Michael Schumacher of Germany and Jacques Villeneuve of Canada, in head-to-head confrontation. A real collision effectively decided the outcome of the drivers' championship. The incident was similar to

one three years earlier when Schumacher collided with Britain's Damon Hill. That one was officially described as an accident, although many felt that the German had caused it intentionally to stop his rival from getting ahead.

In the 1997 incident, Schumacher led Villeneuve by one point into the last race. Schumacher appeared to steer into Villeneuve as he attempted to pass. It was seen by millions as another attempt to win at any cost. But this time it failed – Schumacher's car spun off and Villeneuve managed to get home to take third place and enough points to win the championship. Many people called for a massive fine and a ban to be placed on Schumacher. The FIA, the sport's governing body, took away all the points that he had won during the season and stripped him of second place in the championship.

Indianapolis 500: Arie Luyendyk (Neth)
Le Mans: M. Alboreto (It), T. Kristiansen (Den), S. Johansson (Swe)

Formula 1 Grand Prix Winners
Australia (Melbourne): D. Coulthard (GB)
Brazil (Interlagos): J. Villeneuve (Can)
Argentina (Buenos Aires): J. Villeneuve (Can)
San Marino (Imola): H.-H. Frentzen (Ger)
Monaco (Monte Carlo): M. Schumacher (Ger)
Spain (Catalunya): J. Villeneuve (Can)
Canada (Montréal): M. Schumacher (Ger)
France (Magny-Cours): M. Schumacher (Ger)
Britain (Silverstone): J. Villeneuve (Can)
Germany (Hockenheim): G. Berger (Au)
Hungary (Hungaroring): J. Villeneuve (Can)
Belgium (Spa-Francorchamps): M. Schumacher (Ger)
Italy (Monza): D. Coulthard (GB)
Austria (A-1 Ring): J. Villeneuve (Can)
Luxembourg (Nürburgring): J. Villeneuve (Can)
Japan (Suzuka): M. Schumacher (Ger)
Europe (Jerez): M. Hakkinen (Fin)

Formula 1 Drivers' Championship: J. Villeneuve (Can)
Formula 1 Constructors' Championship: Williams-Renault

▼ David Coulthard beats Jean Alesi out of the pits at the Italian Grand Prix.

ROWING

Boat Race (London, England)
Cambridge University

World Championships (Lake Aiguebelette, France)
MEN
Single Sculls: J. Koven (US)
Double Sculls: S. Volkert and A. Hajek (Ger)
Quadruple Sculls: Italy
Coxed Pairs: S. Fentress and J. Irving (US)
Coxless Pairs: M. Androux and J-C. Rolland (Fra)
Coxed Fours: France
Coxless Fours: Great Britain
Eights: United States
Lightweight Single Sculls: K. Nielsen (Den)
Lightweight Double Sculls: T. Kucharski and R. Sycz (Pol)
Lightweight Quadruple Sculls: Italy
Lightweight Pairs: M. Binder and B. Schmidt (Swi)
Lightweight Fours: Denmark
Lightweight Eights: Australia

WOMEN
Single Sculls: E. Khodotovich (Bel)
Double Sculls: E. Meike and K. Boron (Ger)
Quadruple Sculls: Germany
Coxless Pairs: E. Robinson and A. Korn (Can)
Coxless Fours: Great Britain
Eights: Romania
Lightweight Single Sculls: S. Garner (US)
Lightweight Double Sculls: M. Darvill and A. Brand (Ger)
Lightweight Pairs: E. Blair and J. Joyce (Aus)
Lightweight Quadruple Sculls: Germany

RUGBY LEAGUE

On the international scene, Australian teams dominated rugby league. The Brisbane Broncos captured the breakaway Super League Telstra Cup in September, defeating the Cronulla Sharks 26–8. They also triumphed in the World Club Challenge in October, overcoming Hunter Mariners 36–12. The official Australian Rugby League Championship was won by the Newcastle Knights.

Meanwhile, the Australian national side defeated Great Britain in a best-of-three Test series. They won the Anzac Day Test 38–14, but lost the second meeting 20–12. Australia won the deciding test 37–20. France fought out a 30–30 draw with Ireland and scraped a 22–20 victory over Scotland.

GB Rugby League
League Championship: Bradford Bulls
Challenge Cup: St Helens
Premiership: Wigan Warriors

RUGBY UNION

The 1997 New Zealand All Blacks established themselves as the best rugby union side ever, despite the loss of their "Man Mountain" Jonah Lomu for much of the year. South Africa may be officially the world champions, following their

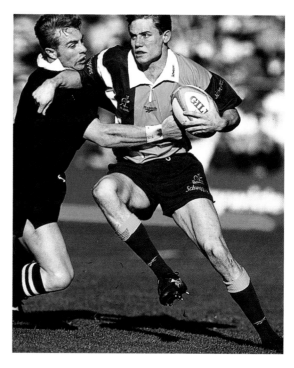

▲ Stephen Larkham (Aus) holds off Justin Marshall (N. Zeal) in the Tri-Nations Championship.

narrow victory over New Zealand in the 1995 tournament, but New Zealand's triumph over South Africa and Australia in the Tri-Nations Championship put them out in front. The coaches of both defeated countries handed in their resignations soon afterwards. For good measure, New Zealand also had the world's most successful club team, the Auckland Blues, who won the Super 12 Championship for the second year in succession.

Many people now feel that only the British Lions – a team made up of the best players from England, Scotland, Wales and Ireland – can seriously challenge the dominance of the Southern Hemisphere nations. The Lions showed their quality in beating South Africa 2–1 in a Test series away from home, Jeremy Guscott's drop goal in the dying minutes of the game in Durban proving decisive.

France won the Five Nations Championship and the Grand Slam, scoring a total of 14 tries. It was confirmed that Italy will enter the competition in two years' time. The sport looked forward to participating in the 1998 Commonwealth Games.

History was made in England when Va'aiga Tuigamala of Samoa became the sport's first £1 million player, moving from Wigan, a rugby league side, to rugby union side Newcastle Falcons.

Five Nations Championship

18 January	Scotland 19, Wales 34 Ireland 15, France 32
1 February	Wales 25, Ireland 26 England 41, Scotland 13
15 February	Ireland 6, England 46 France 27, Wales 22
1 March	Scotland 38, Ireland 10 England 20, France 23
15 March	Wales 13, England 34 France 47, Scotland 20

England
Pilkington Cup: Leicester
County Championship: Cumbria

SAILING
Sydney–Hobart Classic: "Morning Glory", H. Plattner
Admiral's Cup: United States

French Olympic Sail Week
Finn: F. Loof (Swe)
Laser: B. Ainslie (GB)
Soling: Germany
Tornado: Van Teyligen/Dercksen (Neth)
Europe: C. Brouwer (Neth)
470 (women): Taran/Pakholchik (Ukr)
Mistral (men): T. Philp (Fiji)
Mistral (women): A. Sensini (It)

SKIING
Deborah Compagnoni deposed Alberto Tomba as Italy's skiing superstar by winning both the Women's Slalom and Giant Slalom events at the1997 World Championships. Compagnoni was the only racer to gain more than one title at the championships. She has made a commendable comeback from a career fraught with injuries. The Super Giant Slalom title also stayed in Italy, won by Isolde Kostner, who repeated her 1996 success. Norway dominated the men's events, taking three of the five titles. Switzerland took the other two.

Luc Alphand triumphed in the Alpine World Cup series, clinching the overall men's trophy in the final event at Vail, Colorado. He became the first downhill specialist, and the first Frenchman for nearly 30 years, to win the cup. Pernilla Wiberg became the first Swede to take the women's crown, emphasizing the Scandinavians' prominence in Alpine events.

In the year's oddest story, officials of the International Ski Federation re-awarded the women's 1966 Slalom World Championship to France's Marielle Goitschel, 31 years after the event. Why? The winner in 1966, Erika Schinegger, has now become "Erik", after surgery, disqualifying himself.

▲ Deborah Compagnoni won both the World Slalom and Giant Slalom titles in Sestriere, Italy.

Alpine skiing
World Championships (Sestriere, Italy)
MEN
Combined: K. A. Aamodt (Nor)
Downhill: B. Kernen (Swi)
Slalom: T. Stiansen (Nor)
Giant Slalom: M. von Grunigen (Swi)
Super Giant Slalom: A. Skaardal (Nor)

WOMEN
Combined: R. Götschl (Au)
Downhill: H. Lindh (US)
Slalom: D. Compagnoni (It)
Giant Slalom: D. Compagnoni (It)
Super Giant Slalom: I. Kostner (It)

Nations Cup (men): Austria
Nations Cup (women): Germany

Nordic skiing
World Championships (Trondheim, Norway)
MEN
Overall winner: B. Daehlie (Nor)

WOMEN
Overall winner: Y. Vyalbe (Rus)

SNOOKER
Scotland's Stephen Hendry won the Player of the Year award for the seventh time in eight years, but surprisingly lost the final of the World Championship. His conqueror was the former world amateur champion, Ken Doherty, of Ireland, who won the event 18–12. Hendry won two of the top 10 world-ranking events, as did his compatriot John Higgins.

Steve Davis, a former world champion, gave notice that he was back as a force to be reckoned with by taking the Benson & Hedges Masters, his first title for two years. Meanwhile, Welshman Dominic Dale took his first major title, the Grand Prix, despite being ranked only number 54 in the world.

The sport faced problems caused by the British government's proposal to ban the sponsorship of sporting events by tobacco companies. Existing sponsorship contracts would be allowed to run, but new sponsors would have to be found for the future.

World Championship: Ken Doherty (Ire)
European Open: John Higgins (Scot)
British Open: Mark J. Williams (Wales)
Benson & Hedges Masters: Steve Davis (Eng)
Liverpool Victoria UK Championship: Ronnie O'Sullivan (Eng)
Grand Prix: Dominic Dale (Wales)
German Open: John Higgins (Scot)
Regal Welsh: Stephen Hendry (Scot)
International Open: Stephen Hendry (Scot)
Singha & Eagle Cement Thailand Open: Peter Ebdon (Eng)

SOCCER

The qualifying matches of the World Cup, the finals of which are to be held in France in 1998, dominated the international scene. Despite losing to Italy at home, England took the lead in its group because of its better away results. Eight months later, England drew against Italy in Rome, ending Italy's 100 per cent record in home World Cup qualifying games. England won the group and qualified automatically for the finals, but the Italians had to beat Russia in the playoffs to clinch their place in the finals.

Scotland also qualified for their sixth appearance in the finals in seven tournaments, a great feat for a small country. They were the only team to take points away from the winner of their group, Austria. Scotland qualified as the best European runner-up.

Manchester United won its fourth FA premiership title in five years, and looked set to dominate English soccer for the next few years. Bolton Wanderers won Division 1, ensuring an immediate return to the premier league, and Bury won Division 2, guaranteeing its return to the first division, which it last played back in 1969. Wigan Athletic won

▼ Ronaldo scores for Barcelona in the European Cup Winners' Cup final.

Division 3, completing a clean sweep of league division winners from the northwest of England.

Rangers won its ninth consecutive Scottish League championship, equalling the record of its great rivals, Celtic. Rangers also won the Scottish League Cup but were put out of the Scottish Cup by Celtic, who were surprisingly beaten by Division 1 side Falkirk in the semi-finals. Falkirk themselves lost to Kilmarnock 0–1 in the final. This was Kilmarnock's first success since 1929.

England & Wales
FA Cup: Chelsea
League Cup: Leicester City
FA Charity Shield: Manchester United

Football League Championship
FA Premiership: Manchester United
Division 1: Bolton Wanderers
Division 2: Bury
Division 3: Wigan Athletic

Scotland
Scottish Premiership: Rangers
Scottish Cup: Kilmarnock
Scottish League Cup: Rangers

Europe
European Champions' Cup: Borussia Dortmund (Ger)
European Cup-Winners' Cup: Barcelona (Spa)
UEFA Cup: Schalke (Ger)

NATIONAL CHAMPIONS

Nation	League winner	Cup winner
Albania	Flamurtari	Partizani
Argentina	River Plate	
Austria	Austria Salzburg	Sturm Graz
Belarus	MPKC Mozy	Belshina
Belgium	Lierse	Ekeren
Bolivia	Bolivar	
Brazil	Vasco da Gama	
Bulgaria	CSKA Sofia	CSKA Sofia
Chile	Colo Colo	
Colombia*	Deportivo	
Croatia	Croatia Zagreb	Croatia Zagreb
Cyprus	Anorthosis	Apoel
Czech Republic	Sparta Prague	Slavia Prague
Denmark	Brondby	FC Copenhagen
Ecuador	Nacional	
England	Manchester United	Chelsea
France	Monaco	Nice
Germany	Bayern Munich	Stuttgart
Greece	Olympiakos	AEK Athens
Hungary	MTK Budapest	MTK Budapest
Ireland, Rep. of	Derry City	Shelbourne
Israel	Beitar Jerusalem	Hapoel Beersheba
Italy	Juventus	Vicenza
Lithuania	Kareda	Zalgiris
Netherlands	PSV Eindhoven	Roda JC
Northern Ireland	Crusaders	Glenavon
Norway*	Rosenborg	Tromso
Paraguay	Olimpia	
Peru	Alianza	

*1996 information.

Nation	League winner	Cup winner
Poland	Widzew Lodz	Legia Warsaw
Portugal	Porto	Boavista
Romania	Steaua Bucharest	Steaua Bucharest
Russia	Spartak Moscow	Lokomotiv Moscow
Scotland	Rangers	Kilmarnock
Slovakia	Kosice	Slovan Bratislava
Spain	Real Madrid	Barcelona
Sweden	IFK Gothenburg	AIK
Switzerland	Sion	Sion
Turkey	Galatasaray	Kocaeli
Ukraine	Dynamo Kiev	Donetsk
Uruguay	Penarol	
Venezuela	Caracas	
Wales	Barry Town	Barry Town
Yugoslavia	Partizan Belgrade	Red Star Belgrade

*1996 information.
(S. American cup winners not available.)

SQUASH

Men's World Open: R. Eyles (Aus)
Men's World Team Championship: England
Women's World Open: S. Fitz-Gerald (Aus)
Women's World Junior Championship: T. Bailey (Eng)
Women's World Junior Team Championship: England

SWIMMING

1997 was a turbulent year for swimming. It saw a number of world records broken, but these achievements were accompanied by allegations of drug-taking. Ireland's Michelle Smith de Bruin faced such accusations when she won two titles at the European Championships in Seville (Spa). Similar questions had been raised when she won three gold medals at the 1996 Olympics.

The Chinese women's performances caused most controversy. They set two world records and achieved top times for the year in 10 out of a total 13 individual events. Such an improvement in performance had been seen twice before – once in East Germany, in the 1970s, and again in China, in the early 1990s. On both occasions, drugs were later shown to have been involved. The Chinese feats were especially questionable as some swimmers were not ranked among the world's best – indeed, four were not even among the top 150. No swimmer outside the world's top 50 had ever before broken a world record.

Claudia Poll of Costa Rica was voted female World Swimmer of the Year by *Swimming World* magazine. Poll was the first competitor from either Central or South America to be given this award. She broke the world records for 200-metres and 400-metres freestyle events at the Short Course (25-metre pool) World Championships in Gothenburg, Sweden, and produced outstanding performances at the Pacific Championships in Japan.

Denis Pankratov (Rus), winner of two gold medals at the 1996 Olympics, set new records for all three butterfly events – 50 metres, 100 metres, and 200 metres. However, he swam poorly in the Gothenburg and European championships and failed to win a medal in either competition.

European Championships (Seville, Spain)
MEN
50 m Freestyle: A. Popov (Rus)
100 m Freestyle: A. Popov (Rus)
200 m Freestyle: P. Palmer (GB)
400 m Freestyle: E. Brembilla (It)
1500 m Freestyle: E. Brembilla (It)
100 m Backstroke: M. Lopez-Zubero (Spain)
200 m Backstroke: V. Selkov (Rus)
100 m Breaststroke: A. Goukov (Bel)
200 m Breaststroke: A. Goukov (Bel)
100 m Butterfly: L. Frolander (Swe)
200 m Butterfly: F. Eposito (Fra)
200 m Individual Medley: M. Wouda (Neth)
400 m Individual Medley: M. Wouda (Neth)
5 km: A. Akatiev (Rus)
25 km: A. Akatiev (Rus)
4 x 100 m Freestyle: Russia
4 x 200 m Freestyle: Great Britain
4 x 100 m Medley: Russia

WOMEN
50 m Freestyle: N. Mesheryakova (Rus)
100 m Freestyle: S. Voelker (Ger)
200 m Freestyle: M. de Bruin (Ire)
400 m Freestyle: D. Hase (Ger)
800 m Freestyle: K. Kielgass (Ger)
100 m Backstroke: A. Buschschulte (Ger)
200 m Backstroke: C. Rund (Ger)
100 m Breaststroke: A. Kovacs (Hun)
200 m Breaststroke: A. Kovacs (Hun)
100 m Butterfly: M. Jacobsen (Den)

▲ Agnes Kovacs won both women's breaststroke events for Hungary at the European Championships.

200 m Butterfly: M. Pelaez (Spa)
200 m Individual Medley: O. Verevka (Rus)
400 m Individual Medley: M. de Bruin (Ire)
4 x 100 m Freestyle: Germany
4 x 200 m Freestyle: Germany
4 x 100 m Medley: Germany
5 km: P. Buchse (Ger)
25 km: R. Kovacs (Hun)

TABLE TENNIS

World Championships (Manchester, England)
Men's Singles: J.-O. Waldner (Swe)
Women's Singles: Deng Yaping (Chin)
Men's Doubles: Kong Linghui and Liu Guoliang (Chin)
Women's Doubles: Deng Yaping and Yang Ying (Chin)
Mixed Doubles: Liu Guoliang and Wu Na (Chin)
Men's Team: China
Women's Team: China

TENNIS
Both the men's and women's tournaments saw newcomers arriving to compete for the honours. Pete Sampras became only the second man in recent years to finish as the world's top-ranked player five years running. He triumphed on the fast surface of Wimbledon and in the Australian Open but failed to reach the final stages of the other major tournaments. Patrick Rafter of Australia took his first major title at the US Open and it was the first appearance in Grand Slam finals for both Greg Rusedski of Britain and Brazil's Gustavo Kuerten. Rusedski finished runner-up at the US Open and the 20-year-old Kuerten won the French Open, beating three former French Open champions on the way.

The women's competitions saw an astonishing talent emerge from Switzerland, Martina Hingis, the daughter of the former Czech player Melanie Molitor. She stormed through the Australian Open, winning the title without dropping a set, to become the youngest winner of a Grand Slam event this century, at the age of only 16. She fought through to the finals of the other three Grand Slam tournaments, failing only to win the French Open. At Wimbledon she beat Jana Novotna. In the final Novotna won the first set, but Hingis powered back to win the match 2–6, 6–3, 6–3. Hingis's victim in the US Open final was another promising youngster, Venus Williams of the United States. Williams proved no match for Hingis, going down 0–6, 4–6. The French Open also looked a Hingis certainty, but Iva Majoli of Croatia beat her convincingly, 6–4, 6–2, to gain her first major title.

Steffi Graf failed to win a Grand Slam event this year. She lost to South African Amanda Coetzer in the fourth round of the Australian Open and suffered a serious injury when playing Coetzer in the French Open. This prevented her from playing again competitively in 1997.

Davis Cup: Sweden

MEN
Tournament	Winner	Runner-up
Australian Open	P. Sampras (US)	C. Moya (Spa)
Wimbledon	P. Sampras (US)	C. Pioline (Fra)
French Open	G. Kuerten (Bra)	S. Brugera (Spa)
US Open	P. Rafter (Aus)	G. Rusedski (GB)

WOMEN
Tournament	Winner	Runner-up
Australian Open	M. Hingis (Swi)	M. Pierce (Fra)
Wimbledon	M. Hingis (Swi)	J. Novotna (Czech)
French Open	I. Majoli (Cro)	M. Hingis (Swi)
US Open	M. Hingis (Swi)	V. Williams (US)

▼ Martina Hingis of Switzerland won three out of four Grand Slam tournaments.

World events

World events is an A–Z fact file of all the countries of the world, highlighting the important developments in each during 1997.

Income figure is average annual income per adult according to 1995 World Bank figures. Amounts are quoted in US dollars, as exchange rates change.

AFGHANISTAN

Republic in central Asia

Area: 652,225 sq km
Population: 23,738,000
Capital: Kabul
Income: Not available
Life expectancy: 44.0 (men), 43.0 (women)
President: Burhanuddin Rabbani
Prime minister: Gulbuddin Hekmatyar

In July, the UN took steps to try to end the fighting between armed factions in Afghanistan.

The year ended as it began, with two-thirds of the country run by an Islamic fundamentalist group, the Taliban, and the north remaining the focus of fighting. In the middle of the year, opposition forces had allowed the Taliban into the north, but within a few days it drove them out again.

ALBANIA

Republic in the Balkan Peninsula

Area: 28,748 sq km
Population: 3,323,000
Capital: Tiranë
Income: US$670
Life expectancy: 69.3 (men), 69.0 (women)
Presidents: Rexhep Mejdani; Sali Berisha (until 23 July)
Prime ministers: Fatos Nano; Aleksander Meksi (until 2 March); Bashkim Fino (until 24 July)

In February, Albania was plunged into chaos when the "pyramid" investment schemes collapsed, leaving a third of Albanians very poor.

Public order broke down, and people raided military stores and stole weapons. Thousands fled abroad, including some high-ranking government officials. Parliament declared a state of emergency and a new government replaced the cabinet. The UN sent 7,000 European troops to keep order while elections were held. A new government and a new president were elected.

Albania's economy suffered along with its citizens. By July, inflation levels stood at 28 per cent, and the currency had lost a lot of value.

▲ Soldiers look on as Albanian refugees, who had tried to flee to Italy but were refused entry, return to the Albanian port of Durres.

ALGERIA

Republic on the north coast of Africa

Area: 2,381,741 sq km
Population: 29,476,000
Capital: Algiers
Income: US$1,600
Life expectancy: 67.5 (men), 70.3 (women)
President: Liamine Zeroual
Prime minister: Ahmed Ouyahia

The National Democratic Rally, a new political party that supports President Zeroual, won the parliamentary elections in June.

The horrifying massacres in central Algeria – apparently carried out by the Armed Islamic Group – grew worse. In the autumn the government signed a truce with a different Islamic armed group, the Army of Islamic Salvation.

ANDORRA

A "co-principality" in the Pyrenees Mountains between Spain and France

Area: 468 sq km
Population: 64,600
Capital: Andorra la Vella
Income: Not available
Life expectancy: 75.6 (men), 81.7 (women)
Co-princes (joint rulers): the president of France and the bishop of Urgell, Spain
Prime minister: Marc Forné Molné

The ruling Liberal Union party won a comfortable majority in the general election. This was its first absolute majority, so it could rule without forming a coalition with other parties.

ANGOLA

Republic on the west coast of southern Africa

Area: 1,246,700 sq km
Population: 10,624,000
Capital: Luanda
Income: US$410
Life expectancy: 44.9 (men), 48.1 (women)
President: José Eduardo dos Santos
Prime minister: Fernando José França van-Dúnem

In May, government forces attacked northeast territory held by UNITA, the armed group that had fought the government in Angola's recent civil war. UNITA responded vigorously. The UN threatened to impose sanctions on UNITA unless it complied with the peace treaty and disbanded its troops.

The presence of more than 10 million land mines caused thousands of casualties and prevented farmers growing much-needed food.

ANTIGUA AND BARBUDA

Parliamentary democracy in the eastern Caribbean Sea; member of the Commonwealth

Area: 442 sq km
Population: 64,500
Capital: Saint John's
Income: Not available
Life expectancy: 44.9 (men), 48.1 (women)
Monarch: Queen Elizabeth II
Prime minister: Lester Bird

In the local elections, which are held every other year, the Barbuda People's Movement won all five seats that were contested. They now hold all the seats on the Barbuda Council.

ARGENTINA

Federal republic in South America

Area: 2,780,092 sq km
Population: 35,409,000
Capital: Buenos Aires
Income: US$8,030
Life expectancy: 69.6 (men), 76.8 (women)
President: Carlos Saúl Menem

The economy made good progress and grew faster than expected. However, unemployment levels remained high.

Argentina became a non-NATO ally of the United States, improving President Menem's waning popularity.

In June, the justice minister resigned following claims that some cabinet members were corrupt.

ARMENIA

Republic in Transcaucasia

Area: 27,943 sq km
Population: 3,773,000
Capital: Yerevan
Income: US$730
Life expectancy: 67.2 (men), 74.0 (women)
President: Levon Ter-Petrosyan
Prime ministers: Robert Kocharyan; Armen Sarkisyan (until 20 March)

In August, Armenia and Russia signed a treaty on friendship, co-operation, and mutual assistance.

In September, the president accepted a peace plan for Nagorno-Karabakh, a region of Azerbaijan over which Armenia had become involved in conflict. Earlier in the year, the so-called president of Nagorno-Karabakh (the region is not recognized as an independent state) was appointed prime minister of Armenia.

▼ In January, Diana, Princess of Wales, visited Angola, where every day people are killed or maimed by land mines. This man had to have his leg amputated after he stood on an active land mine.

AUSTRALIA

Federal parliamentary democracy; member of the Commonwealth

Area: 7,682,300 sq km
Population: 18,508,000
Capital: Canberra
Income: US$18,720
Life expectancy: 75.4 (men), 81.1 (women)
Monarch: Queen Elizabeth II
Prime minister: John Howard

Australia moved a step closer towards becoming a republic when the government appointed delegates to attend a conference on the issue in February 1998.

Prime Minister John Howard stated that his top priority was the reduction of unemployment, as levels were still high. The government slashed spending in order to reduce the budget deficit. It also cut interest rates several times, hoping to encourage consumer spending, although this proved unsuccessful.

Pauline Hanson's new right-wing One Nation Party made a major impact on Australian politics. Its policies included an end to immigration and to measures that favour Aborigines. After opinion polls showed that some voters had switched their loyalty from the ruling Liberal Party to the One Nation Party, Howard reduced immigration quotas by a fifth.

AUSTRIA

Republic in central Europe; member of the European Union

Area: 83,859 sq km
Population: 8,087,000
Capital: Vienna
Income: US$26,890
Life expectancy: 73.3 (men), 79.7 (women)
President: Thomas Klestil
Chancellors: Viktor Klima; Franz Vranitzky (until 28 January)

In January, Chancellor Franz Vranitzky resigned, after heading the government since 1986. He chose finance minister Viktor Klima to succeed him, who stated that his priority was the reduction of unemployment.

Local election results showed that the extreme right-wing Freedom Party of Austria (FPÖ) was gaining popularity. The FPÖ is opposed to immigration and the European Union, which Austria joined in 1995.

The economy remained sluggish, although increased exports and investment by businesses stimulated some growth. The government made

▲ A reporter from 2UE, a Sydney radio station, trying to speak to Pauline Hanson, whose right-wing One Nation Party, made a huge impact on Australian politics.

severe budget cuts in order to qualify for the single European currency, due to begin in 1999.

BAHAMAS, THE

Parliamentary democracy in the Caribbean Sea; member of the Commonwealth

Area: 13,939 sq km
Population: 287,000
Capital: Nassau
Income: US$11,940
Life expectancy: 67.7 (men), 75.5 (women)
Monarch: Queen Elizabeth II
Prime minister: Hubert Ingraham

The ruling Free National Movement strengthened its majority in the general election.

In July, former prime minister Sir Lynden Pindling withdrew from politics, five months after a committee stated that he been wrong to accept loans from two businessmen when he was in power.

BAHRAIN

Monarchy (emirate) in the Persian Gulf

Area: 694 sq km
Population: 620,000
Capital: Manama
Income: US$7,840
Life expectancy: 71.1 (men), 75.3 (women)
Monarch: Emir Isa ibn Sulman al-Khalifah
Prime minister: Khalifah ibn Sulman al-Khalifah

The Muslim Shi'ite opposition continued to use violence to express their discontent with the policies

of the ruling Sunni Muslim family. They demanded the return of parliament (which was abolished in 1975), economic reforms, and jobs for the unemployed. Currently, 63 per cent of Bahrain's workforce is foreign.

BANGLADESH

Republic in Asia; member of the Commonwealth

Area: 147,570 sq km
Population: 125,340,000
Capital: Dhaka
Income: US$240
Life expectancy: 58.1 (men), 58.2 (women)
President: Shahabuddin Ahmed
Prime minister: Sheikh Hasina Wazed

In August, three opposition parties led a general strike to protest against rises in fuel prices. At least 150 people were injured in clashes between police and protesters. A week later, the Bangladesh Nationalist Party stormed out of parliament in protest at the government's economic policies.

   The country was once again the victim of major natural disasters. Two cyclones hit southeast Bangladesh in 1997, killing 397 people and leaving more than 1.5 million homeless. The same area also suffered flooding, causing further deaths and homelessness.

▼ Bangladeshi people, carrying their belongings on their heads, trudge through a flooded Dhaka street towards a shelter. Their country was plagued by cyclones and floods in 1997.

BARBADOS

Constitutional monarchy in the Caribbean Sea; member of the Commonwealth

Area: 430 sq km
Population: 265,000
Capital: Bridgetown
Income: US$6,560
Life expectancy: 73.6 (men), 78.7 (women)
Monarch: Queen Elizabeth II
Prime minister: Owen Arthur

Tourism – Barbados's main industry – continued to be successful, but larger hotels fared better than smaller ones. In April, the government allocated £9.5 million to help certain smaller hotels that were having financial problems.

BELARUS

Republic in eastern Europe

Area: 207,595 sq km
Population: 10,360,000
Capital: Minsk
Income: US$2,070
Life expectancy: 66.0 (men), 75.7 (women)
President: Alyaksandr Lukashenko
Prime minister: Syarhey Ling

In June, Belarus and Russia signed a treaty of union, although they remained separate countries. Protesters opposed to the union held demonstrations during which several journalists were beaten by militia and 100 people were arrested.

   President Lukashenko made several changes in the law which gave him more power.

   The economy struggled: the exchange rate plummeted, and prices more than doubled in the first quarter of the year.

BELGIUM

Constitutional monarchy in western Europe; member of the European Union

Area: 30,528 sq km
Population: 10,189,000
Capital: Brussels
Income: US$24,710
Life expectancy: 73.0 (men), 79.8 (women)
Monarch: King Albert II
Prime minister: Jean-Luc Dehaene

The closure of two manufacturing businesses put a large number of

▲ A young Belgian boy dressed as a worker, carries a placard saying "What about me? Will I get a job?" during a demonstration against the closure of the Clabecq steel works.

people out of work. The steelmaker Forges de Clabecq, which employed 1,800 workers, was declared bankrupt and shut down. French car manufacturer Renault also closed its factory near Brussels, with the loss of 2,700 jobs.

The child-sex scandal that shocked Belgium in 1996 led to public pressure for reforms in the police force and in legal procedures. The creation of a European Centre for Missing Children, to be based in Belgium, was approved.

BELIZE

Parliamentary democracy on the east coast of Central America; member of the Commonwealth

Area: 22,965 sq km
Population: 228,000
Capital: Belmopan
Income: US$2,630
Life expectancy: 66.0 (men), 70.0 (women)
Monarch: Queen Elizabeth II
Prime minister: Manuel Esquivel

The opposition People's United Party won all the seats in the local elections in March. A general election was scheduled for mid-1998.

Export levels rose for sugar, bananas, and citrus fruit.

BENIN

Republic in West Africa

Area: 112,680 sq km
Population: 5,902,000
Capital: Porto-Novo
Income: US$370
Life expectancy: 50.3 (men), 54.2 (women)
President: Mathieu Kérékou
Prime minister: Adrien Houngbedji

Japan granted Benin £8.8 million to build 65 new schools.

Continuing its policy of liberalizing the economy, the government sold the state-owned company SONICOG, which produces edible oils, butter, and soap.

BHUTAN

Monarchy in Himalayas

Area: 47,000 sq km
Population: 860,000
Capital: Thimphu
Income: US$420
Life expectancy: 51.2 (men), 50.0 (women)
Monarch: King Jigme Singye Wangchuk

King Jigme Singye Wangchuk met with the Nepalese foreign minister, but failed to resolve the problem of the 100,000 Bhutanese refugees who have been sheltering in camps in eastern Nepal since 1990. The refugees, originally from Nepal, left Bhutan when the government declared that all citizens must follow Bhutanese Buddhist practices.

BOLIVIA

Republic in South America

Area: 1,098,581 sq km
Population: 7,767,000
Capital: La Paz
Income: US$800
Life expectancy: 60.9 (men), 65.9 (women)
Presidents: Hugo Banzer Suárez; Gonzalo Sánchez de Lozada Bustamente (until 6 August)

The Nationalist Democratic Action party, led by former dictator Hugo Banzer Suárez, won the general election and formed a coalition government. Despite Banzer's promise to review the privatization programme, the new government continued the process of economic reforms, including privatization and a strict financial policy.

The Organization of American States began an investigation into an incident that occurred in December 1996: 11 people had died in clashes between government troops guarding two gold mines and the miners who worked there.

BOSNIA-HERZEGOVINA

Republic in the western Balkans

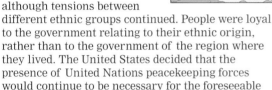

Area: 51,129 sq km
Population: 3,124,000
Capital: Sarajevo
Income: Not available
Life expectancy: 70.5 (men), 75.9 (women)
President: Alija Izetbegovic

Bosnia-Herzegovina enjoyed a second year of relative peace, although tensions between different ethnic groups continued. People were loyal to the government relating to their ethnic origin, rather than to the government of the region where they lived. The United States decided that the presence of United Nations peacekeeping forces would continue to be necessary for the foreseeable future.

The economy was weak, with high unemployment. Most goods still had to be imported. Foreign aid was used to help rebuild houses, bridges, and airports.

▼ Two Bosnian children stroll past a US Army tank in a village near Tuzla. The soldiers are part of the UN peace force positioned there to provide security for the villagers.

BOTSWANA

Republic in southern Africa; member of the Commonwealth

Area: 581,730 sq km
Population: 1,501,000
Capital: Gaborone
Income: US$3,020
Life expectancy: 48.3 (men), 51.7 (women)
President: Sir Ketumile Masire

Botswana's strong economic growth continued. The budget showed that the government's revenue was considerably more than its spending, and introduced a five per cent cut in income tax.

However, unemployment levels stood at one-fifth of the workforce, and the country's workforce was still growing.

BRAZIL

Federal republic in South America

Area: 8,547,504 sq km
Population: 159,691,000
Capital: Brasília
Income: US$3,640
Life expectancy: 56.6 (men), 67.3 (women)
President: Fernando Henrique Cardoso

Parliament passed a bill that allowed President Cardoso to run for another four-year term of office.

The economy made steady growth, and the inflation rate for 1997 was estimated at only five per cent.

BRUNEI

Sultanate on the north coast of Borneo, in southwest Asia; member of the Commonwealth

Area: 5,765 sq km
Population: 308,000
Capital: Bandar Seri Begawan
Income: Not available
Life expectancy: 73.3 (men), 78.1 (women)
Sultan and prime minister: Haji Hassanal Bolkiah Mu'izzaddin Waddaulah

Brunei looked for ways to encourage tourism, because its economy is dependent on natural resources, such as oil, that will eventually run out. This meant relaxing its strict Islamic traditions, which include disapproval of alcohol consumption and unveiled women.

BULGARIA

Republic in southeastern Europe

Area: 110,994 sq km
Population: 8,329,000
Capital: Sofia
Income: US$1,330
Life expectancy: 68.9 (men), 75.3 (women)
Presidents: Petar Stoyanov; Zhelyu Zhelev (until 19 January)
Prime ministers: Ivan Kostov; Georgi Parvanov (until 12 February); Stefan Sofiyanski (until 24 April)

Bulgaria began the year with severe economic problems. The currency was losing value rapidly, and the International Monetary Fund agreed to provide US$167 million (£105 million) if the government set up a currency board to control the exchange rate.

Protesters took to the streets to demand early elections. The former opposition party, the Union of Democratic Forces, won a clear majority in the April general election. The new government promised to speed up economic reforms and to fight crime and corruption.

A currency board was set up in July.

BURKINA FASO

Republic in West Africa

Area: 274,400 sq km
Population: 10,891,000
Capital: Ouagadougou
Income: US$230
Life expectancy: 45.1 (men), 47.0 (women)
President: Blaise Compaoré
Prime minister: Kadré Désiré Ouédraogo

Early in the year, there were anti-government demonstrations and strikes in protest at living and

working conditions. Several students were arrested, but they were soon released.

Burkina Faso agreed to send troops to join peacekeeping forces in Liberia and the Central African Republic.

BURMA (MYANMAR)

Republic in Southeast Asia

Area: 676,577 sq km
Population: 46,822,000
Capital: Rangoon
Income: Not available
Life expectancy: 58.0 (men), 61.0 (women)
Chairman of the State Law and Order Restoration Council: General Than Shwe

The ruling State Law and Order Restoration Council (SLORC) arrested more than 250 supporters of the National League for Democracy (NLD) over the year. However, in response to international criticism of its human rights record, it allowed the NLD to hold its first party conference in seven years.

More than 20,000 people fled to Thailand to escape SLORC's attacks on the Karen National Union, the only ethnic guerrilla group that still refused to hold talks with the government.

BURUNDI

Republic in central Africa

Area: 27,816 sq km
Population: 6,053,000
Capital: Bujumbura
Income: US$160
Life expectancy: 48.7 (men), 50.7 (women)
President: Pierre Buyoya
Prime minister: Pascal-Firmin Ndimira

In January, the army killed 126 Hutu refugees who had been expelled from Tanzania. Burundi's government troops are mainly Tutsi (a tribe who are bitterly opposed to the Hutu tribe). Hutu rebels responded with a series of attacks.

Some 500,000 Burundians were living in refugee camps because the army had driven them from their homes in order to reduce Hutu support in rural areas.

Peace talks were held between the government and Hutu rebel leaders, but no solution was reached.

◄ Karen children, belonging to an ethnic group in Burma who are fighting for independence, are transported by lorry to a refugee camp to protect them from a government crackdown on the Karen people.

CAMBODIA

Constitutional monarchy in Southeast Asia

Area: 181,916 sq km
Population: 10,385,000
Capital: Phnom Penh
Income: US$270
Life expectancy: 51.0 (men), 54.0 (women)
Monarch: King Norodom Sihanouk
Prime ministers: Norodom Ranariddh; Hun Sen (second prime minister)

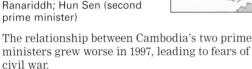

The relationship between Cambodia's two prime ministers grew worse in 1997, leading to fears of civil war.

In July, two days of fighting took place between the forces loyal to each prime minister. Ranariddh then fled the country and Hun Sen ordered his arrest for arms smuggling and conspiracy with the communist group the Khmer Rouge.

In August, the notorious Khmer Rouge leader Pol Pot was sentenced to life imprisonment by a jungle court of his former followers.

▼ A fisherman sorts through his salmon catch in Prince Rupert, British Columbia, Canada. In July, Canadian fishermen blockaded an Alaskan ferry in an argument with the United States over salmon stocks.

CAMEROON

Republic in West Africa; member of the Commonwealth

Area: 475,442 sq km
Population: 14,678,000
Capital: Yaounde
Income: US$650
Life expectancy: 51.9 (men), 54.0 (women)
President: Paul Biya
Prime minister: Peter Mafany Musonge

President Biya's People's Democratic Movement increased its majority in Cameroon's second multiparty general elections.

Relations with Nigeria remained tense. In August, the army was warned to be alert, as Nigeria strengthened its forces at a base near the southern border.

CANADA

Federal parliamentary democracy in North America; member of the Commonwealth

Area: 9,970,610 sq km
Population: 30,287,000
Capital: Ottawa
Income: US$19,380
Life expectancy: 74.7 (men), 81.7 (women)
Monarch: Queen Elizabeth II
Prime minister: Jean Chrétien

The June general elections resulted in a decrease in the Liberal Party's majority. It lost the support of poorer voters because of cuts in health and social welfare spending.

The economy was strong, supported by high consumer spending that showed that Canadians were confident about the future. However, unemployment levels were still fairly high, particularly among young people aged between 15 and 24 years.

Canada and the United States argued over salmon stocks off the northwest coast of North America. In July, Canadian fishermen blockaded an American ferry for three days in the British Columbia port of Prince Rupert, to protest at overfishing by United States fishermen in Alaska.

The Canadian government wrote to the government of Quebec in August, disputing its claim that international law allowed Quebec independence from Canada without Canada's agreement. In February 1998 the Supreme Court of Canada will make a ruling on the issue of Quebec's possible independence.

CAPE VERDE

Republic in the Atlantic Ocean off the west coast of
Africa

Area: 4,033 sq km
Population: 394,000
Capital: Praia
Income: US$960
Life expectancy: 60.7 (men), 64.6
(women)
President: Antonio Mascarenhas
Monteiro
Prime minister: Carlos Veiga

The economy remained stable, although about a
quarter of the workforce was unemployed.

In June, the African Development Bank promised
a loan of US$4.9 million (£3 million) to pay for road
improvements on four of Cape Verde's islands.

CENTRAL AFRICAN REPUBLIC

Republic in equatorial Africa

Area: 622,436 sq km
Population: 3,342,000
Capital: Bangui
Income: US$340
Life expectancy: 46.4 (men), 51.0
(women)
President: Ange-Félix Patassé
Prime ministers: Michel
Gbezera-Bria; Jean-Paul
Ngoupande (until 30 January)

In January, after a year in which three army
mutinies took place, President Patassé and the
leader of the army rebels signed an agreement. But
further violence broke out in May after security
forces killed three rebels, and in June African
peacekeeping forces shelled the capital. At least 100
people died, and thousands fled. Talks began again,
and by August the situation was calmer, with most
army mutineers having returned to their units.

CHAD

Republic in central Africa

Area: 1,284,000 sq km
Population: 7,166,000
Capital: N'Djamena
Income: US$180
Life expectancy: 46.3 (men), 49.3
(women)
President: Lieutenant General
Idriss Déby
Prime ministers: Nassour
Ouaidou Guelendouksia;
Djimasta Koibla (until 16 May)

International human rights groups reported an
increase in human rights abuses in Chad, including

security forces carrying out executions without
trial.

The government signed a peace agreement with
the rebel Armed Forces for a Federal Republic,
allowing the group to become a political party.

CHILE

Republic on south Pacific coast of South America

Area: 756,626 sq km
Population: 14,583,000
Capitals: Santiago; Valparaíso
(site of parliament)
Income: US$4,160
Life expectancy: 72.3 (men), 78.3
(women)
President: Eduardo Frei Ruiz-
Table

Drought damaged corn and
fruit crops, and reduced the production of
electricity. During the summer, heavy rains and
snowstorms forced 800,000 people from their homes.

Coal mines in Lota closed down in April, leaving
1,100 people unemployed. However, production of
copper, Chile's main export, increased by 10 per cent.

CHINA

Republic in Asia

Area: 9,572,900 sq km
Population: 1,222,740,000
Capital: Beijing
Income: US$620
Life expectancy: 69.1 (men), 72.4
(women)
President: Jiang Zemin
Premier: Li Peng

▼ Lorries wait to dump sand and stones into a narrowing
gap of the Yangtze River near Xiaolangdi, China. The river is
being diverted to allow construction of the controversial
Three Gorges Dam, due to be completed in 2009.

In July, tens of thousands of unemployed workers staged protests in the Sichuan region. In Xinjiang, Muslim activists who wanted the region to become independent bombed the capital and assassinated local officials. The authorities kept a tight control on these situations, arresting thousands of people.

Government policy on Tibet remained unchanged: China refused to consider granting full independence to the region.

The president tackled the problem of the nation's 300,000 state enterprises, which were losing money. He suggested that they should become businesses in which people could buy shares, so that the companies would still be owned by the public.

In July, Hong Kong's status changed when the British colony was handed back to China.

The economy prospered. Industrial production rose by 11 per cent, and export levels were high.

In February, Deng Xiaoping, one of China's most important leaders this century, died at the age of 92.

COLOMBIA

Republic in northwest South America

Area: 1,141,568 sq km
Population: 36,200,000
Capital: Santafé de Bogotá, DC
Income: US$1,910
Life expectancy: 69.7 (men), 75.4 (women)
President: Ernesto Samper Pizano

The hostage crisis ended when the Colombia Revolutionary Armed Forces, a guerrilla group, freed 60 soldiers (captured in August 1996) and ten marines (captured in January 1997). However, attacks by terrorist groups increased during the year.

The government was able to show that all the leaders of the Cali drug cartel were either dead or in jail. Even so, the United States refused to add Colombia to its list of countries making progress against drug trafficking, so the threat of economic sanctions remained.

COMOROS

Island republic in the Indian Ocean off the east coast of Africa

Area: 1,862 sq km
Population: 590,000
Capital: Moroni
Income: US$470
Life expectancy: 56.0 (men), 60.6 (women)
President: Mohamed Taki Abdoulkarim
Prime minister: Ahmed Abdou

In August, two of the islands of Comoros – Anjouan and Moheli – declared their independence from the

Comoros. Talks began, sponsored by the Organization of African Unity. Despite this, the government sent 300 troops to Anjouan, but they failed to recapture the island.

CONGO

Republic in central Africa

Area: 342,000 sq km
Population: 2,583,000
Capital: Brazzaville
Income: US$1,784
Life expectancy: 44.2 (men), 47.5 (women)
President: Pascal Lissouba
Prime ministers: Bernard Kolelas; David Charles Ganao (until September 8)

During the first half of the year there was fighting between forces loyal to the president and forces loyal to former head of state Denis Sassou-Nguesso. A truce negotiated in June did not last, but a second truce proved more successful, although outbreaks of violence continued.

CONGO, DEMOCRATIC REPUBLIC OF THE

Republic in central Africa (formerly known as Zaire)

Area: 2,344,858 sq km
Population: 46,674,000
Capital: Kinshasa
Income: US$1,784
Life expectancy: 48.6 (men), 53.4 (women)
Presidents: Laurent Kabila; Mobutu Sese Seko (until 16 May)
Prime ministers: Laurent Kabila; Léon Kengo wa Dondo (until 18 March); Étienne Tshisekedi (until 9 April); Likulia Bolongo (until 16 May)

▼ People in Kisagani, in the Democratic Republic of the Congo, give victory signs as they greet the rebel leader Laurent Kabila at the city's airport.

The uprising in the eastern district of Kivu gathered pace. Government troops were sent to the area in January, but they soon retreated. Rebel forces advanced quickly westwards, and reached the capital in May.

President Mobutu fled to Morocco, where he died, and rebel leader Laurent Kabila became president. Zaire was renamed the Democratic Republic of the Congo.

COSTA RICA

Republic in Central America

Area: 51,100 sq km
Population: 3,468,000
Capital: San José
Income: US$2,610
Life expectancy: 71.9 (men), 77.5 (women)
President: José María Figueres Olsen

The economy performed badly, putting at risk the ruling party's prospects in the elections scheduled for early 1998. Claims that government officials were involved in drug trafficking further damaged the government's reputation. The president's popularity rating was also badly affected by corruption scandals.

CROATIA

Republic in the northwest Balkans

Area: 56,610 sq km
Population: 4,774,000
Capital: Zagreb
Income: US$3,250
Life expectancy: 68.1 (men), 76.5 (women)
President: Franjo Tudjman
Prime minister: Zlatko Matesa

Much effort was put into reintegrating eastern Slavonia, which was returned to Croatia by Serb forces in 1996. Education, transport, and postal and

communications services were reintroduced into the region. However, in September the UN criticized Croatia for its poor handling of the repopulation of eastern Slavonia and other areas of Croatia.

CUBA

Republic in the Greater Antilles of the Caribbean Sea

Area: 110,861 sq km
Population: 11,190,000
Capital: Havana
Income: Not available
Life expectancy: 73.9 (men), 77.6 (women)
President: Fidel Castro Ruz

▼ A Cuban man decorates a poster of Pope John Paul II who is due to visit the country in 1998. In honour of his visit, Roman Catholics in Cuba, which is officially an atheist country, were allowed to celebrate Christmas for the first time in 30 years.

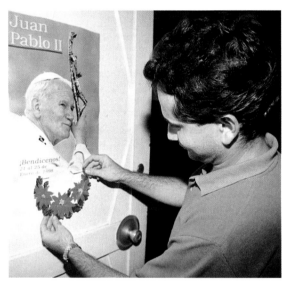

The economy continued to make good progress, helped by a 30 per cent increase in nickel production. However, the US embargo on trade with Cuba cancelled out the economic improvement.

The number of tourists visiting in one year passed the one million mark for the first time, despite several hotel bombings. The government blamed the bombing on Cuban exiles living in the United States.

◄ Croatian soccer supporters show their emotions while watching their team from Zagreb being beaten by the Yugoslav team "Partizan Belgrade". It was the first sports game to be played locally since the countries split in 1991.

CYPRUS

Island republic in the eastern Mediterranean; member of the Commonwealth

Area: 9,251 sq km
Population: 860,000
Capital: Nicosia
Income: Not available
Life expectancy: 74.6 (men), 79.1 (women)
Presidents: Glafcos Clerides (president of Greek Cyprus); Rauf Denktash (president of Turkish Cyprus)

Tension continued between the Turkish and Greek republics of Cyprus. The presidents of the two parts of the country held talks abroad, but failed to resolve their differences. The UN peacekeeping force remained in place.

Work began on equipment to remove the salt from sea water, in order to help overcome the island's shortage of drinking water.

CZECH REPUBLIC

Republic in central Europe

Area: 78,866 sq km
Population: 10,307,000
Capital: Prague
Income: US$3,870
Life expectancy: 68.9 (men), 76.6 (women)
President: Vaclav Havel
Prime minister: Vaclav Klaus

The Czech economy became unstable in the early part of the year and the situation reached crisis point in May when the value of the currency plummeted.

Meanwhile, the country did have foreign policy successes. In July, it was offered membership of NATO and also began membership talks with the European Union.

Also in July, severe flooding killed 47 people and caused considerable damage.

DENMARK

Constitutional monarchy in northern Europe; member of the European Union

Area: 43,094 sq km
Population: 5,284,000
Capital: Copenhagen
Income: US$29,890
Life expectancy: 72.5 (men), 77.8 (women)
Monarch: Queen Margrethe II
Prime minister: Poul Nyrup Rasmussen

The government signed the Amsterdam Treaty, a European Union agreement which included making job creation a formal goal and stepping up co-operation over security issues and foreign affairs. However, it decided to hold a national referendum on the treaty in 1998.

There was hope of an end to the feud between motorcycle gangs that had killed 10 people and wounded 70 across Scandinavia since 1993. In September, gang leaders appeared on television to announce a truce. Even so, Danish laws controlling bikers remained tight.

DJIBOUTI

Republic in northeastern Africa

Area: 23,300 sq km
Population: 622,000
Capital: Djibouti
Income: Not available
Life expectancy: 48.7 (men), 52.0 (women)
President: Hassan Gouled Aptidon
Prime minister: Barkat Gourad Hamadou

In September, 11 Djibouti soldiers were killed in the north of the country. The government suspected Afar rebels who oppose the mainly Issas government. Afar and Issas are the two ethnic groups in Djibouti.

President Aptidon held talks with French president Jacques Chirac, because France was considering withdrawing some of its troops from its former colony, Djibouti. Historically, the French have sided with the Afar people.

▼ A helicopter carrying Czech president Vaclav Havel, flies over the flooded railway station in the city of Olomouc. The president wished to see the destruction caused by heavy floods in the area.

DOMINICA

Island republic in the eastern Caribbean Sea; member of the Commonwealth

Area: 750 sq km
Population: 74,400
Capital: Roseau
Income: US$2,990
Life expectancy: 74.4 (men), 80.2 (women)
President: Crispin Anselm Sorhaindo
Prime minister: Edison James

Opposition politicians voiced strong objections when a British organization, the Commonwealth Development Corporation (CDC), bought Dominica's electricity company. The CDC promised to invest up to £12 million on improving the distribution of electricity and increasing the amount produced.

DOMINICAN REPUBLIC

Republic occupying two-thirds of the Caribbean island of Hispaniola

Area: 48,671 sq km
Population: 7,802,000
Capital: Santo Domingo
Income: US$1,460
Life expectancy: 68.9 (men), 73.1 (women)
President: Leonel Fernández Reyna

Strikes and violent demonstrations were staged to protest rising unemployment, electricity shortages, and price increases. However, the economy performed well.

The government set up investigations into cases of corruption during the previous government's term in office.

ECUADOR

Republic on the west coast of South America

Area: 272,045 sq km
Population: 11,937,000
Capital: Quito
Income: US$1,390
Life expectancy: 67.3 (men), 72.5 (women)
Presidents: Fabián Alarcón Rivera; Abdalá Bucaram Ortíz (until 6 February); Rosalía Arteaga Serrano (until 11 February)

Abdalá Bucaram Ortíz, who was elected president in 1996, became increasingly unpopular. In February, a general strike took place to protest rising prices.

The following day, Congress voted to remove Bucaram from the post of president, and the leader of Congress became president on a temporary basis. A May referendum showed that the public was in favour of the move.

EGYPT

Republic in northeast Africa

Area: 997,739 sq km
Population: 60,896,000
Capital: Cairo
Income: US$790
Life expectancy: 64.7 (men), 67.3 (women)
President: Hosni Mubarak
Prime minister: Kamal al-Janzuri

In February, the People's Assembly approved a further three years of martial law, which began in 1981. Free elections have not been held in Egypt since 1950.

Religious tensions erupted into violence when Islamic terrorists attacked a Coptic (Egyptian Christian) church, killing 10 worshippers. A further 13 people were killed by Islamic fundamentalists in Naj Dawud, a mainly Coptic village.

In November, 58 foreign tourists were killed by Islamic terrorists at a tourist attraction near Luxor. The incident led to the resignation of the interior minister and seemed likely to adversely affect Egypt's booming tourist industry.

▼ An armed policeman guards Queen Hatshepsut's temple in Luxor, Egypt, where 58 tourists were massacred. The temple, built in 1470 BC, is a popular tourist attraction.

EL SALVADOR

Republic on the Pacific coast of Central America

Area: 21,041 sq km
Population: 5,662,000
Capital: San Salvador
Income: US$1,610
Life expectancy: 66.5 (men), 72.5 (women)
President: Armando Calderón Sol

In March, elections were held for some seats in parliament and for mayors. Less than half the electorate voted. The former guerrilla group, the Farabundo Martí National Liberation Front (FMLN) made strong gains. As a result, the opposition parties were able to join together to reverse the law privatizing El Salvador's telecommunications services.

EQUATORIAL GUINEA

Republic on the west coast of Africa

Area: 28,051 sq km
Population: 443,000
Capital: Malabo
Income: US$380
Life expectancy: 50.4 (men), 54.8 (women)
President: Brigadier General Teodoro Obiang Nguema Mbasogo
Prime minister: Angel Serafin Seriche Dougan

Spain urged its former colony, Equatorial Guinea, to speed up the progress towards democracy. A general election was scheduled for 1998, and in July the president stated that he might be willing to share the running of the country with an opposition government.

ERITREA

Republic in northeastern Africa

Area: 121,144 sq km
Population: 3,590,000
Capital: Asmara
Income: Not available
Life expectancy: 48.3 (men), 51.8 (women)
President: Isaias Afwerki

Although there were still no opposition parties – in fact, the sole political party seemed to discourage their formation – political structures were established which showed a clear commitment to democracy.

Eritrea's relationship with neighbouring

▲ A woman in Asmara, Eritrea, casts her vote in the first elections since the country's independence in 1993.

Ethiopia continued to be warm, and relations with Yemen improved. However, relations with The Sudan were tense, as each government accused the other of plotting to overthrow it.

ESTONIA

Republic in northern Europe

Area: 45,227 sq km
Population: 1,463,000
Capital: Tallinn
Income: US$2,860
Life expectancy: 63.9 (men), 75.0 (women)
President: Lennart Meri
Prime minister: Mart Slimann; Tiit Vahi (until 17 March)

The economy continued to progress well, helped by foreign investment.

Estonia's political system was plagued with difficulties. In February, the prime minister resigned following a scandal over privatization of buildings in the capital. In September, the government and the army became engaged in a dispute after 14 soldiers drowned during training.

ETHIOPIA

Republic in northeastern Africa

Area: 1,133,882 sq km
Population: 58,733,000
Capital: Addis Ababa
Income: US$100
Life expectancy: 48.4 (men), 51.6 (women)
President: Negasso Gidada
Prime minister: Meles Zenawi

The economy fared well, especially the agricultural sector, which enjoyed a growth

rate of nearly 15 per cent. However, there were
droughts in some areas.

The government took steps to fight corruption
and this met with international approval. Former
prime minister Tamirat Layne was placed under
house arrest, charged with corruption, and 261
members of the Addis Ababa Administration were
sacked on the grounds of incompetence and
corruption.

FIJI

Island republic in the southern Pacific Ocean;
member of the Commonwealth

Area: 18,272 sq km
Population: 778,000
Capital: Suva
Income: US$2,440
Life expectancy: 70.0 (men), 74.0
(women)
President: Rautu Sir Kamisese
Mara
Prime minister: Sitiveni Rabuka

Parliament approved a new
constitution, and Fiji was then allowed to rejoin the
Commonwealth.

In March Cyclone Gavin hit Fiji, causing 26
deaths and millions of dollars worth of damage.

FINLAND

Republic in northern Europe; member of the
European Union

Area: 338,145 sq km
Population: 5,145,000
Capital: Helsinki
Income: US$20,580
Life expectancy: 72.1(men), 79.5
(women)
President: Martti Ahtisaari
Prime minister: Paavo Lipponen

Unlike its neighbours
Denmark and Sweden, Finland said it would take
part in the third stage of the European Union's
economic and monetary union (EMU). This will
lead to the introduction of a single European
currency.

Unemployment levels remained high, and the
government increased income tax by nearly 10 per
cent.

FRANCE

Republic in western Europe; member of the
European Union

Area: 543,965 sq km
Population: 58,616,000
Capital: Paris
Income: US$24,990
Life expectancy: 72.9 (men), 81.1
(women)
President: Jacques Chirac
Prime ministers: Lionel Jospin;
Alain Juppé (until 3 June)

In April, the political climate changed when Lionel
Jospin's Socialist-led coalition won the general
election. The Green Party won seats in parliament
for the first time, and its leader became environment
minister.

Right-wing president Jacques Chirac now shared
power with a left-wing government, but he soon
made it clear that he intended to be more than a
figurehead. He criticized several government
policies – such as its decision to shut down the
Superphénix nuclear reactor, and to grant an
amnesty to illegal immigrants – but he then
concentrated on foreign affairs.

The economy performed well, but unemployment
levels were over 12 per cent. The government
introduced a job scheme in which it created 350,000
new public-sector posts and asked private businesses
to do the same. It also put pressure on the European
Union to raise the priority of job creation.

◀ Lorry drivers in France brought motorways to a standstill
in their dispute over pay and working conditions.

GABON

Republic in central Africa

Area: 267,667 sq km
Population: 1,190,000
Capital: Libreville
Income: US$3,490
Life expectancy: 53.8 (men), 57.2 (women)
President: Omar Bongo
Prime minister: Paulin Obame-Nguéma

The Gabonese Democratic Party won a resounding victory in the general elections in December 1996. It also won a majority in the new upper house of parliament.

In May, opposition politician Divungui-Di N'Dingue was appointed to the newly created post of vice-president.

President Bongo organized a committee to negotiate peace in neighbouring Congo.

GAMBIA, THE

Republic in West Africa; member of the Commonwealth

Area: 10,689 sq km
Population: 1,248,000
Capital: Banjul
Income: US$320
Life expectancy: 48.7 (men), 45.4 (women)
President: Captain Yahya Jammeh

Nearly three-quarters of the electorate voted in the general elections in January.

▼ Anti-nuclear activists near Dannenberg, Germany, stage a sit-in on a railway line to try to stop a nuclear waste shipment reaching its destination.

The president's Alliance for Patriotic Reorientation and Construction won a clear majority.

In April, the president replaced four regional military governors with civilians, completing the return to civilian rule that he had promised.

GEORGIA

Republic in Transcaucasia

Area: 69,492 sq km
Population: 5,377,000
Capital: Tbilisi
Income: US$440
Life expectancy: 68.5 (men), 76.7 (women)
President: Eduard A. Shevardnadze

Abkhaz and Georgian leaders met to try to bring about an end to the conflict between the two regions.

The government began an anti-corruption drive. In July, the security minister was forced to resign following claims that he had taken part in black-market trading.

Relations with Russia remained tense. In the summer, the Georgian government protested after Russian officials moved a border post further into Georgia.

GERMANY

Republic in central Europe; member of the European Union

Area: 356,978 sq km
Population: 82,143,000
Capital: Bonn
Income: US$27,510
Life expectancy: 73.0 (men), 79.5 (women)
President: Roman Herzog
Chancellor: Helmut Kohl

Germany's economic decline continued, due to several factors, notably the effects of the 1990 unification between East and West Germany (when East Germany was heavily in debt), and the fact that Germany's goods were too expensive to compete with those of foreign companies because of the government's social welfare and industrial policies. In an attempt to become more competitive, the government reduced taxes drastically to encourage investment.

Unemployment levels were high, especially in former East Germany.

The government privatized Deutsche Telekom, the state telephone company, and Lufthansa, the airline.

Several former East German officials stood trial for crimes committed before unification. Some received jail sentences for manslaughter for ordering border guards to shoot East Germans trying to cross the Berlin Wall. More than 750 people were killed in this way during the 28 years of the Wall's existence.

GHANA

Republic in West Africa; member of the Commonwealth

Area: 238,533 sq km
Population: 18,101,000
Capital: Accra
Income: US$390
Life expectancy: 53.3 (men), 57.2 (women)
President: Jerry John Rawlings

Drinks manufacturer Coca-Cola opened a £5.6 million bottling plant in Accra.

In May, exploration companies discovered gold reserves of up to 14,175 kilograms on the Oda river in southwest Ghana.

GREECE

Republic in southeastern Europe; member of the European Union

Area: 131,957 sq km
Population: 10,541,000
Capital: Athens
Income: US$8,210
Life expectancy: 74.6 (men), 79.8 (women)
President: Konstantinos Stephanopoulos
Prime minister: Konstantinos Simitis

Farmers held demonstrations, blocking roads, at the beginning of the year, and strikes were staged by other professions. They were all protesting the government's strict financial measures. However, the prime minister refused to relax his economic policy. Inflation was at its lowest level for 25 years, and economic growth was good, but the trade deficit was large.

Relations with Turkey remained tense, and worsened when the Greek part of Cyprus bought Russian weapons. In July, the prime minister met the Turkish president. They agreed on their commitment to peace, security, and mutual respect.

GRENADA

Parliamentary democracy in the eastern Caribbean Sea; member of the Commonwealth

Area: 344 sq km
Population: 98,400
Capital: Saint George's
Income: US$2,980
Life expectancy: 68.2 (men), 73.2 (women)
Monarch: Queen Elizabeth II
Prime minister: Keith Mitchell

In 1983, relations with nearby Cuba soured when US troops drove out a left-wing group that had staged a coup. In April 1997, the two countries signed an economic co-operation treaty, sealing their return to good relations.

GUATEMALA

Republic in Central America

Area: 108,889 sq km
Population: 11,242,000
Capital: Guatemala City
Income: US$1,340
Life expectancy: 64.7 (men), 69.8 (women)
President: Alvaro Arzú Irigoyen

In December 1996, a peace treaty was signed between the government and the Guatemalan National Revolutionary Unity guerrilla group. In February 1997, the disbanding of the guerrilla forces began, monitored by the UN. About a third of the 30,000 Guatemalan refugees sheltering in neighbouring Mexico returned home.

Now that the civil war was over, the tourist industry boomed.

◄ As the guerrilla forces disbanded, Guatemalan refugees, who fled their country during its civil war, felt safe enough to return.

GUINEA

Republic on the west coast of Africa

Area: 245,857 sq km
Population: 7,405,000
Capital: Conakry
Income: US$550
Life expectancy: 42.3 (men), 46.9 (women)
President: General Lansana Conté
Prime minister: Sidya Touré

Guinea acted as go-between in the conflict between Nigeria and Cameroon concerning the oil-rich Bakassi peninsula. It also sent 1,500 troops to join the West African force trying to restore civilian rule in Sierra Leone.

Preparations continued for the opening of a new gold mine in northeast Guinea.

GUINEA-BISSAU

Republic in West Africa

Area: 36,125 sq km
Population: 1,179,000
Capital: Bissau
Income: US$250
Life expectancy: 46.9 (men), 49.6 (women)
President: João Bernardo Vieira
Prime ministers: Carlos Correia; Manuel Saturnino da Costa (until 5 June)

A political crisis developed when government workers staged demonstrations because they had not been paid. The protests grew into riots, and the army was called in to calm the situation.

GUYANA

Republic in northern South America; member of the Commonwealth

Area: 215,083 sq km
Population: 773,000
Capital: Georgetown
Income: US$590
Life expectancy: 61.1 (men), 67.9 (women)
Presidents: Sam Hinds; Cheddi Jagan (until 6 March)
Prime ministers: Janet Jagan; Sam Hinds (until 17 March)

President Cheddi Jagan, Guyana's most eminent politician in recent history, died in March. His widow, Janet Jagan, was nominated as a candidate in the presidential elections planned for the end of the year.

Until the election, the prime minister held the

▲ Janet Jagan, a presidential candidate in Guyana, shows her symbolically ink-stained finger after voting in Georgetown. Finger-printing was traditionally used during Guyanan elections, although in 1997, ID cards were issued for the first time.

presidential office, and Janet Jagan carried out the prime minister's tasks.

HAITI

Republic occupying one-third of the Caribbean island of Hispaniola

Area: 27,700 sq km
Population: 6,611,000
Capital: Port-au-Prince
Income: US$250
Life expectancy: 47.1 (men), 51.1 (women)
President: René Préval
Prime minister: Rony Smarth

Haiti suffered a year of violence and political uncertainty. Street demonstrations were staged, resulting in 70 deaths, as well as two general strikes. Many believed that the unrest was caused by people within the coalition government.

The main opposition parties boycotted the local and Senate elections, and less than a tenth of the electorate voted. The United States and the UN both expressed deep concern at the running of the senatorial elections.

HONDURAS

Republic in Central America

Area: 112,492 sq km
Population: 5,823,000
Capital: Tegucigalpa
Income: US$600
Life expectancy: 67.5 (men), 72.3 (women)
President: Carlos Roberto Reina Idiaquez

In May, Honduran and Nicaraguan gunboats shot at each other in the Gulf of Fonseca, an area disputed by the two countries.

The two main parties standing in the November general election promised better living standards and action to protect the public from rising crime levels.

Honduras held border talks with El Salvador on marking the border between the two nations.

▼ A municipal worker polishes a statue of Mahatma Gandhi, leader of the Indian nationalist movement, in preparation for the country's 50th anniversary of its independence from Britain.

HUNGARY

Republic in central Europe

Area: 93,030 sq km
Population: 10,157,000
Capital: Budapest
Income: US$4,120
Life expectancy: 64.5 (men), 73.8 (women)
President: Arpad Goncz
Prime minister: Gyula Horn

The economy achieved steady growth, and inflation levels dropped.

In the spring, farmers blocked roads to protest government plans to raise their taxes.

A referendum was held in which the public voted in favour of joining NATO.

ICELAND

Island republic in the north Atlantic Ocean

Area: 102,819 sq km
Population: 271,000
Capital: Reykjavík
Income: US$24,950
Life expectancy: 77.1 (men), 81.0 (women)
President: Ólafur Ragnar Grímsson
Prime minister: Davíd Oddsson

The economy grew, boosted by an increase in production of aluminium.

Iceland's quarrel with Norway and Russia over fishing rights calmed slightly, as catches were down and so Icelandic fishermen made fewer trips into the disputed area.

INDIA

Federal republic in southern Asia; member of the Commonwealth

Area: 3,165,596 sq km
Population: 967,613,000
Capital: New Delhi
Income: US$340
Life expectancy: 58.7 (men), 59.8 (women)
Presidents: Kocheril Raman Narayanan; Shankar Dayal Sharma (until 25 July)
Prime ministers: Inder Kumar Gujral; H. D. Deve Gowda (until 21 April)

Economic growth was good, although export levels were down. The government cut income tax and business tax. The World Bank loaned India $6.7 billion (£4.2 billion) to help with economic reforms.

In the autumn, Indian and Pakistani soldiers shot at each other across the line of control in the

Jammu and Kashmir region.

In September, Mother Teresa died in Calcutta. The Albanian-born nun had devoted her life to caring for the poor. She was given a state funeral.

India celebrated 50 years of independence in 1997.

INDONESIA

Republic in Southeast Asia consisting of over 13,000 islands and islets

Area: 1,919,317 sq km
Population: 199,544,000
Capital: Jakarta
Income: US$980
Life expectancy: 63.3 (men), 67.0 (women)
President: General Suharto

The ruling party won the parliamentary elections with a record 74.4 per cent of the vote. However, the middle class became increasingly critical of the government's lack of political openness.

Forest fires burned out of control, polluting the air for months. In September, the heavy smoke caused a plane crash in which 234 people died.

IRAN

Republic in western Asia

Area: 1,645,258 sq km
Population: 62,305,000
Capital: Tehran
Income: Not available
Life expectancy: 65.8 (men), 68.2 (women)
Presidents: Mohammad Khatami; Ali Akbar Hashemi Rafsanjani (until 8 August)

In May, Mohammad Khatami was elected president with a large majority. He hoped to be able to form political parties and to improve civil rights, and was popular with those opposed to the regime's hardline policies, including many women and young people. However, conservatives holding key posts continued to have influence, and held back Khatami's reforms.

The United States kept sanctions on Iran in place because Iran supported Islamic groups trying to halt the Arab–Israeli peace process.

IRAQ

Republic in western Asia

Area: 435,052 sq km
Population: 22,219,000
Capital: Baghdad
Income: Not available
Life expectancy: 57.3 (men), 60.4 (women)
President: Saddam Hussein

In December 1996, Iraq accepted a UN resolution allowing it to export enough oil to pay for food and medicine, although sanctions remained in place. However, in June the UN threatened Iraq with further sanctions because it was preventing UN officials from searching for documents and weapons in Iraq.

The uneasy ceasefire between two rival Kurdish parties held, despite occasional fighting between them.

In May, 10,000 Turkish troops attacked Turkish Kurds based in northern Iraq.

Iraqi relations with Syria improved and an official border crossing point between the two countries opened.

IRELAND

Island republic west of Great Britain (shares island with Northern Ireland in the northeast); member of the European Union

Area: 70,285 sq km
Population: 3,644,000
Capital: Dublin
Income: US$14,710
Life expectancy: 72.3 (men), 77.9 (women)
Presidents: Mary McAleese; Mary Robinson (until 8 November)
Prime ministers: Bertie Ahern; John Bruton (until 26 June)

◄ Iraqi families inside the presidential palaces in Baghdad, protesting possible attack by the United States. Relations between the two countries became very tense after Iraq refused to allow two US members of a UN team to enter the country.

Five candidates – four of them women – stood in the October presidential elections.

The economy thrived. Ireland had the lowest inflation rate (one per cent) in the European Union in 1997. Even so, the coalition government did not do well enough in the general elections to retain power.

ISRAEL

Republic in the Middle East

Area: 20,320 sq km
Population: 5,652,000
Capital: Jerusalem
Income: US$15,920
Life expectancy: 75.7 (men), 79.5 (women)
President: Ezer Weizman
Prime minister: Benjamin Netanyahu

In January, Israel agreed to withdraw its troops from most of the West Bank town of Hebron. However, from then on, the Middle East peace process went downhill: Palestinians protested when Israel decided to build a Jewish settlement in East Jerusalem on land claimed by the Palestinians. From March onwards, Hamas terrorists opposed to Palestinian negotiations with Israel used suicide bombers to attack Israeli targets. Israel reacted by halting further transfer of land and closing off Palestinian areas.

ITALY

Republic in southern Europe; member of the European Union

Area: 301,323 sq km
Population: 57,511,000
Capital: Rome
Income: US$19,020
Life expectancy: 74.1 (men), 80.5 (women)
President: Oscar Luigi Scalfaro
Prime minister: Romano Prodi

The coalition government cut spending and imposed a one-off "Euro tax" to qualify for the next stage of European economic and monetary union (EMU).

With a view to ending Italy's political instability, the government set up a commission to consider changes to parliament. It favoured a semi-presidential constitution (like the French system) and large-scale transfer of power from central to regional government.

In July the government sent 500 troops into the southern city of Naples after dozens of people were killed in fighting between rival Mafia groups.

Earthquakes struck central Italy in September

▲ A Palestinian voices his outrage as hundreds of peace activists gather at the site where Israel plans to build Jewish homes in East Jerusalem, on land claimed by the Palestinians.

and continued for several weeks, destroying historic buildings and leaving 38,000 homeless.

IVORY COAST

Republic in West Africa

Area: 322,463 sq km
Population: 14,986,000
Capital: Abidjan
Income: US$660
Life expectancy: 50.0 (men), 52.2 (women)
President: Henri Konan Bédié
Prime minister: Daniel Kablan Duncan

Students demonstrated throughout the year. They were protesting long delays in grant payments and poor working and living conditions. In June, talks aimed at resolving their complaints began.

JAMAICA

Parliamentary democracy in the Caribbean Sea; member of the Commonwealth

Area: 10,991 sq km
Population: 2,536,000
Capital: Kingston
Income: US$1,510
Life expectancy: 72.4 (men), 76.8 (women)
Monarch: Queen Elizabeth II
Prime minister: Percival J. Patterson.

The government took steps to help Jamaica's ailing clothing industry by paying part of the running costs of 180 factories.

Jamaica and the United States signed an agreement that included close co-operation in the battle against drug trafficking in the Caribbean.

JAPAN

Constitutional monarchy in the northwestern Pacific Ocean, composed of four main islands

Area: 377,819 sq km
Population: 126,110,000
Capital: Tokyo
Income: US$39,640
Life expectancy: 76.6 (men), 83.0 (women)
Emperor: Akihito
Prime minister: Ryutaro Hashimoto

In the general elections of October 1996, the prime minister's Liberal-Democratic Party (LDP) won the most votes but did not gain an overall majority. In September, the LDP finally achieved a majority when seven independent deputies joined it.

In January, a Russian tanker broke up in the Sea of Japan, polluting the Japanese shoreline with millions of litres of fuel oil.

▼ A worker puts on protective clothing before entering the nuclear power plant near Tokyo, Japan, where, hours before, an explosion had caused a radiation leak.

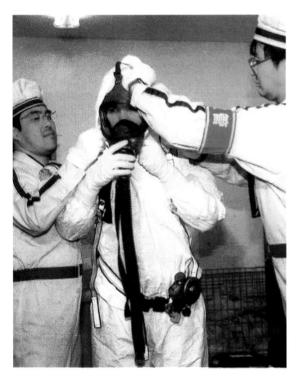

An explosion at a state-owned nuclear power plant in Tokai, near the capital, caused a leakage of radioactive substances. Despite public concerns, officials said there was no threat to the environment.

In the second quarter of the year, the economy suffered its biggest drop for 23 years. Unemployment also remained at a record high, with almost 2.5 million out of work.

Relations with Russia improved. However, a territorial dispute between the two nations continued over four small islands in the southern Kurils, which used to be Japanese but had been occupied by Russia since 1945.

JORDAN

Constitutional monarchy in the Middle East

Area: 89,326 sq km
Population: 4,522,000
Capital: Amman
Income: US$1,510
Life expectancy: 67.7 (men), 71.8 (women)
Monarch: King Hussein I
Prime ministers: Abd as-Salam al-Majali; Abd al-Karim Kabariti (until 19 March)

Relations with the United States and Arab Gulf states improved, and trade with Kuwait resumed after six years. However, relations with Israel got worse, as Israel was unwilling to compromise in the Middle East peace process, in which Jordan was acting as mediator.

The government made progress with privatization in 1997 and introduced measures to attract investment from abroad.

KAZAKHSTAN

Republic in central Asia

Area: 2,724,000 sq km
Population: 16,554,000
Capitals: Aqmola; Almaty (until 10 October)
Income: US$1,330
Life expectancy: 63.2 (men), 72.7 (women)
President: Nursultan Nazarbayev
Prime ministers: Nurlan Balgimbayev; Akezhan Kazhegeldin (until 10 October)

Industrial output increased slightly, and Kazakhstan's economic decline seemed to be at an end. However, in March opposition groups staged a protest against living standards, which were still very low.

Plans went ahead to move Kazakhstan's capital to Aqmola, which was inaugurated in October.

KENYA

Republic in East Africa; member of the
Commonwealth

Area: 582,646 sq km
Population: 28,803,000
Capital: Nairobi
Income: US$280
Life expectancy: 52.3 (men), 55.7
(women)
President: Daniel arap Moi

The president's firm refusal to
reform the constitution
provoked violent protests.

In the summer the International Monetary Fund
stopped its loan programme because the president
was not taking action to curb high-level corruption.

KIRIBATI

Republic in the western Pacific Ocean; member of
the Commonwealth

Area: 811 sq km
Population: 82,400
Capital: Bairiki
Income: Not available
Life expectancy: 62.0 (men), 67.0
(women)
President: Teburoro Tito

In December 1996, President
Tito backed Fiji's call for a
world-wide ban on nuclear testing.

In August, Kiribati signed a treaty of friendship
with nearby Tuvalu.

KOREA, NORTH

Republic in eastern Asia

Area: 122,762 sq km
Population: 24,317,000
Capital: Pyongyang
Income: Not available
Life expectancy: 67.0 (men), 73.3
(women)
President: Kim Jong II
Premiers: Hong Sang Nam; Kang
Song San (until 21 February)

North Korea continued to suffer from famine. In
May, South Korea agreed to send 45,000 tonnes of
food, and the United States supplied $50 million (£31
million) worth of grain.

North and South Korea held official talks for the
first time in three years, and progress was made
towards a permanent treaty to replace the truce that
ended the Korean War in 1953.

KOREA, SOUTH

Republic in eastern Asia

Area: 99,268 sq km
Population: 45,628,000
Capital: Seoul
Income: US$9,700
Life expectancy: 68.0 (men), 76.0
(women)
President: Kim Dae-Jung; Kim
Young Sam (until 18 December)
Prime ministers: Koh Kun; Lee
Soo Sung (until 4 March)

A large steel and construction corporation collapsed
in January, with huge debts. Some members of the
ruling party were accused of taking large sums of
money from the company as payment for arranging
bank loans.

Another scandal erupted in May when the
president's son, Kim Hyun Chul, was arrested for
bribery and avoiding paying tax. Thousands of
students took to the streets to demand the
president's resignation.

In November, the government asked the
International Monetary Fund for help after a
devastating crash in the stock market.

The political arena was dominated by
campaigning for the presidential elections. The
constitution did not allow Kim Young Sam to stand
for re-election.

In March, North and South Korea held peace
talks aimed at formally ending the Korean War.

◀ Riot police in Seoul, South Korea, block the flames of
fire bombs hurled by students at an anti-government rally.
The students were demanding the president's resignation.

KUWAIT

Constitutional monarchy (emirate) on the Persian Gulf

Area: 17,818 sq km
Population: 1,809,000
Capital: Kuwait City
Income: US$17,390
Life expectancy: 74.1 (men), 78.2 (women)
Emir: Sheikh Jabir al-Ahmad al-Jabir as-Sabah
Prime minister: Crown Prince Sheikh Saad al-Abdullah as-Salim as-Sabah

A former oil and finance minister was among those charged with taking large sums of money from a state-owned oil company during the Iraqi occupation of 1990.

Political parties remained illegal, but voluntary groups with political aims were not. In the spring, a group that included several university professors formed a new political organization.

KYRGYZSTAN

Republic in central Asia

Area: 199,900 sq km
Population: 4,595,000
Capital: Bishkek
Income: US$700
Life expectancy: 63.9 (men), 72.6 (women)
President: Askar Akayev
Prime minister: Apas Jumagulov

Industrial growth was stagnant and living standards remained low. The Communist Party asked the government to form a union with Russia, in order to end the economic crisis.

LAOS

Republic in Southeast Asia

Area: 236,800 sq km
Population: 5,117,000
Capital: Vientiane
Income: Not available
Life expectancy: 52.0 (men), 55.0 (women)
President: Nouhak Phoumsavan
Prime minister: General Khamtai Siphandon

In 1997, Laos achieved its long-standing aim of joining the Association of Southeast Asian Nations (ASEAN) and its inter-parliamentary organization.

Laos continued to suffer the effects of the disastrous floods of 1996. The UN supplied 43,000 tonnes of rice, without which many people would have starved.

LATVIA

Republic in northern Europe

Area: 64,610 sq km
Population: 2,472,000
Capital: Riga
Income: US$2,270
Life expectancy: 62.5 (men), 74.3 (women)
President: Guntis Ulmanis
Prime minister: Guntars Krasts; Andris Skele (until 28 July)

Latvian politics were unstable for the first half of the year. Prime minister Andris Skele, who was popular because of the nation's recent economic progress, resigned in January, but was quickly re-elected. However, he was forced to resign again in July when his coalition government collapsed.

Efforts to privatize the economy continued.

LEBANON

Republic in the Middle East

Area: 10,400 sq km
Population: 3,859,000
Capital: Beirut
Income: US$2,660
Life expectancy: 68.1 (men), 71.7 (women)
President: Elias Hrawi
Prime minister: Rafiq al-Hariri

The April 1996 ceasefire between Israel and Hezbollah guerrillas based in

▼ Young Lebanese men burn the Israeli flag at the funerals of four of the six people killed in the bombardment of the southern port city of Sidon by Israel's armed militia.

Lebanon ended in January when Hezbollah forces fired a rocket into northern Israel. In September, Israel and Lebanon began talks aimed at reducing the bloodshed in southern Lebanon.

Sheikh Subhi at-Tufayli, a former secretary-general of Hezbollah, organized protests at the government's policies, including a hunger strike, and non-payment of taxes and electricity and water bills.

LESOTHO

Monarchy in southern Africa; member of the Commonwealth

Area: 30,355 sq km
Population: 2,008,000
Capital: Maseru
Income: US$770
Life expectancy: 50.7 (men), 54.4 (women)
Monarch: King Letsie III
Prime minister: Ntsu Mokhehle

In February, about 100 mounted police captured the police headquarters in the capital in an attempt to have murder charges against eight police officers dropped. Two-thirds of the police force then staged a strike. Government troops recaptured the police headquarters.

Ten police officers were later charged with offences relating to the incident.

LIBERIA

Republic on the west coast of Africa

Area: 97,754 sq km
Population: 2,602,000
Capital: Monrovia
Income: Not available
Life expectancy: 50.0 (men), 53.0 (women)
Head of state: President Charles Taylor; Chairman of the Council of State Ruth Perry (until 2 August)

The 1996 peace agreement that ended the civil war continued to hold, and the armed factions laid down their arms and disbanded.

Charles Taylor and his National Patriotic Front of Liberia Party won the presidential and parliamentary elections. With no public funds and £1.9 billion of debts, they faced a difficult task.

▼ Liberians queue to cast their votes during the presidential election that marked the end of the civil war.

LIBYA

Country in north Africa

Area: 1,757,000 sq km
Population: 5,648,000
Capital: Tripoli
Income: Not available
Life expectancy: 62.1 (men), 60.8 (women)
Head of state: Colonel Muammar al-Qaddafi
Premier: Abd al-Majid al-Qa'ud

Libya refused to allow the two Libyans accused of planting a bomb on a US airliner in 1988 to be tried in Scotland. Consequently, the United States insisted that the trade and air traffic embargo on Libya remained in place. Even so, economic growth was steady, due to revenue from oil exports.

In January, eight Libyans were executed for spying with equipment supplied by the US Central Intelligence Agency (CIA).

▲ Lithuanians wait to receive their voting papers in Vilnius during the presidential election in December.

LIECHTENSTEIN

Constitutional monarchy in central Europe

Area: 160 sq km
Population: 31,300
Capital: Vaduz
Income: Not available
Life expectancy: 66.5 (men), 79.5 (women)
Sovereign prince: Hans Adam II
Prime minister: Mario Frick

In February, the Progressive Citizens' Party left its coalition partner, the Fatherland Union, and formed an opposition group in parliament. It was the end of a political era, as their alliance had been in power for almost 60 years.

LITHUANIA

Republic in northern Europe

Area: 65,301 sq km
Population: 3,706,000
Capital: Vilnius
Income: US$1,930
Life expectancy: 64.9 (men), 76.0 (women)
President: Algirdas Brazauskas
Prime minister: Gediminas Vagnorius

The new coalition government introduced reforms that succeeded in attracting investment from abroad. The annual rate of inflation dropped to nine per cent.

In October, President Brazauskas signed a border treaty with Russian president Boris Yeltsin.

LUXEMBOURG

Constitutional monarchy in western Europe; member of the European Union

Area: 2,586 sq km
Population: 420,000
Capital: Luxembourg
Income: US$41,210
Life expectancy: 66.5 (men), 79.5 (women)
Head of state: Grand Duke Jean
Prime minister: Jean-Claude Juncker

In January, a Luxembourg television firm merged with a German media group. The new company controlled 19 television stations and 23 radio stations in Europe.

The economy continued to prosper, especially the financial and banking sectors.

MACEDONIA

Republic in the central Balkans

Area: 25,713 sq km
Population: 1,984,000
Capital: Skopje
Income: US$860
Life expectancy: 70.1 (men), 74.4 (women)
President: Kiro Gligorov
Prime minister: Branko Crvenkovski

Ethnic tensions flared. A law was passed that allowed ethnic minorities to use their national symbols in certain circumstances, but not to fly their flags from public buildings. The following day, three ethnic Albanians died in clashes with police in Gostivar, a mainly Albanian town.

In September, the UN Commission on Human Rights said that Macedonia had improved its human rights record.

MADAGASCAR

Island republic in the Indian Ocean off the southeast coast of Africa

Area: 587,041 sq km
Population: 14,062,000
Capital: Antananarivo
Income: US$230
Life expectancy: 50.8 (men), 52.9 (women)
Presidents: Didier Ratsiraka; Norbert Ratsirahonana (acting president until 31 January)
Prime ministers: Pascal Rakotomavo; Norbert Ratsirahonana (until 21 February)

Didier Ratsiraka won the presidential elections in December 1996. The former military leader had ruled Madagascar for 16 years until 1991.

Locusts caused major damage to crops.

MALAWI

Republic in East Africa; member of the Commonwealth

Area: 118,484 sq km
Population: 9,609,000
Capital: Lilongwe
Income: US$170
Life expectancy: 40.3 (men), 41.1 (women)
President: Bakili Muluzi

Malawi's economic outlook improved, although nearly two-thirds of the population were still living below the breadline. The tea industry suffered from a drop in world prices.

Donors from abroad offered loans and grants of £200 million.

MALAYSIA

Federal constitutional monarchy made up of the 11 states of the Peninsular Malaya, plus Sabah and Sarawak in Southeast Asia; member of the Commonwealth

Area: 329,733 sq km
Population: 21,767,000
Capital: Kuala Lumpur
Income: US$3,890
Life expectancy: 69.9 (men), 74.3 (women)
Paramount ruler: Tuanku Ja'afar ibni al-Marhum Tuanku Abdul Rahman
Prime minister: Dato Seri Mahathir bin Mohammad

The government and representatives of the Islamic religion argued over several religious rulings, such as bans on beauty contests and body-building competitions.

In the summer the currency crisis in neighbouring Thailand caused Malaysian currency and stock-market values to plunge. In October, the government presented an "austerity" budget aimed at recovery.

Malaysia was badly affected by heavy smoke from forest fires in nearby Indonesia. In September, a ten-day state of emergency was declared in Sarawak because of the smog.

◀ Malaysian fire-fighters use a crane to spray a mist of water in a bid to reduce the smog in Kuala Lumpur, the Malaysian capital. The smog was caused by forest fires in nearby Indonesia.

MALDIVES

Republic in the Indian Ocean; member of the Commonwealth

Area: 298 sq km
Population: 267,000
Capital: Male
Income: US$990
Life expectancy: 65.7 (men), 63.3 (women)
President: Maumoon Abdul Gayoom

Research showed that the Indian Ocean around the Maldives has risen slightly, perhaps due to global warming. The president appealed to the international community for help, concerned that the islands might eventually disappear.

The economy achieved steady growth.

MALI

Republic in West Africa

▲ Stephane Peterhansel of France speeds past bemused Malians during the third stage of the 19th Paris-to-Dakar motorcycle rally.

Area: 1,248,574 sq km
Population: 9,945,000
Capital: Bamako
Income: US$2,410
Life expectancy: 51.9 (men), 55.1 (women)
President: Alpha Oumar Konaré
Prime minister: Ibrahima Boubacar Keita

Results of the first round of the general elections were declared invalid after protests over vote fraud. Opposition parties boycotted the presidential elections, as well as the rescheduled general elections. Turnout was low, but President Konaré and the ruling party were both re-elected with a large majority.

A record cotton harvest – a major Malian export – was expected in 1997.

MALTA

Island republic in the Mediterranean Sea

Area: 316 sq km
Population: 375,000
Capital: Valletta
Income: Not available
Life expectancy: 74.9 (men), 79.1 (women)
President: Ugo Mifsud Bonnici
Prime minister: Alfred Sant

The new Labour Party government withdrew Malta from the NATO Partnership for Peace programme and halted its application to join the European Union.

MARSHALL ISLANDS

Republic in the central Pacific Ocean

Area: 181 sq km
Population: 60,300
Capital: Majuro
Income: Not available
Life expectancy: 61.9 (men), 65.0 (women)
President: Imata Kabua

Scientists reported that Bikini atoll, an area where nuclear tests were carried out in the 1940s and 1950s, could be inhabited again if some soil was removed and the remaining earth treated.

MAURITANIA

Republic in West Africa

Area: 1,030,700 sq km
Population: 2,411,000
Capital: Nouakchott
Income: US$460
Life expectancy: 51.9 (men), 55.1 (women)
President: Colonel Maaouya Ould Sidi Ahmad Taya
Prime minister: Cheikh Afia Ould Mohamed Khouna

Relations between the government and opposition parties worsened. In January, several opposition leaders were arrested and held on conspiracy charges for several weeks.

In April, the opposition staged a protest at sharp rises in living costs. It later decided to boycott the presidential elections.

MAURITIUS

Republic in the Indian Ocean; member of the Commonwealth

Area: 2,040 sq km
Population: 1,143,000
Capital: Port Louis
Income: US$3,380
Life expectancy: 68.3 (men), 75.0 (women)
President: Cassam Uteem
Prime minister: Navin Ramgoolam

The ruling coalition collapsed after Prime Minister Ramgoolam (leader of the Mauritian Labour Party) sacked Deputy Prime Minister Berenger (leader of the Mauritian Militant Movement [MMM]). This provoked the resignation of seven MMM cabinet members.

MEXICO

Federal republic in North America

Area: 1,958,201 sq km
Population: 92,711,000
Capital: Mexico City
Income: US$3,320
Life expectancy: 66.5 (men), 73.1 (women)
President: Ernesto Zedillo Ponce de Leon

Despite Mexico's economic recovery, the ruling party failed to win an overall majority in the parliamentary election. Opposition parties vowed to join together to block the government's policies. The economy remained healthy, helped by strong

▼ Thousands of frightened Mayan Indians flee their isolated south Mexican villages after paramilitary groups massacred 45 people in one village. Amid fears that their village might be attacked, the Mayans sought refuge in nearby towns.

performances from the manufacturing and building industries. The number of unemployed people slowly decreased through the year.

MICRONESIA, FEDERATED STATES OF

Republic in the western Pacific Ocean

Area: 701 sq km
Population: 107,000
Capital: Palikir
Income: Not available
Life expectancy: 72.0 (men), 72.0 (women)
President: Jacob Nena (acting); Bailey Olter (until December)

President Bailey Olter suffered a stroke and Vice-President Jacob Nena took over as acting president.

Typhoon Fern hit Micronesia, causing widespread damage to buildings and crops.

MOLDOVA

Republic in the northeastern Balkans

Area: 33,700 sq km
Population: 4,372,000
Capital: Chisinau
Income: US$920
Life expectancy: 63.5 (men), 71.5 (women)
President: Petru Lucinschi; Mircea Snegur (until 15 January)
Prime minister: Ion Ciubic; Andrei Sangheli (until 16 January)

New president Petru Lucinschi struggled to introduce reforms, owing to lack of support in parliament. However, his supporters formed a new political party to field candidates in the general elections planned for March 1998.

The economy was generally weak. In November, the International Monetary Fund and the World Bank decided to hold back further loan instalments because of Moldova's large budget deficit.

MONGOLIA

Republic in Asia

Area: 1,566,500 sq km
Population: 2,373,000
Capital: Ulaanbaatar
Income: US$310
Life expectancy: 60.0 (men), 63.5 (women)
Presidents: Natsagiyn Bagabandi; Punsalmaagiyn Ochirbat (until 20 June)
Prime minister: Mendsayhany Enhsayhan

The government's progress in economic reforms resulted in an increase in poverty and unemployment. Voters showed their discontent by rejecting the ruling party's candidate in the presidential elections.

▲ Some of the 450 competitors in the dromedary racing show in La'youan, south Morocco.

MOROCCO

Constitutional monarchy in northwest Africa

Area: 458,730 sq km
Population: 27,225,000
Capital: Rabat
Income: US$1,110
Life expectancy: 64.8 (men), 68.5 (women)
Monarch: King Hassan II
Prime minister: Abd al-Latif Filali

The new two-chamber parliamentary system took effect in 1997. The upper house was elected by regional politicians and professional groups, and not by the public.

MOZAMBIQUE

Republic on the southeast coast of Africa; member of the Commonwealth

Area: 812,379 sq km
Population: 18,165,000
Capital: Maputo
Income: US$80
Life expectancy: 45.5 (men), 48.4 (women)
President: Joaquim Chissano
Prime minister: Pascoal Mocumbi

Flooding, caused by heavy rains, forced thousands of people to flee to neighbouring Malawi, and also held up the process of clearing mines. However, the rain boosted cereal grain crops, thus reducing Mozambique's dependence on emergency food aid.

NAMIBIA

Republic on the coast of southwest Africa; member of the Commonwealth

Area: 825,118 sq km
Population: 1,727,000
Capital: Windhoek
Income: US$2,000
Life expectancy: 54.7 (men), 59.9 (women)
President: Sam Nujoma
Prime minister: Hage Geingob

The government refused to allow a South African commission to investigate human rights abuses carried out during Namibia's long guerrilla war. It was also criticized for not doing enough to stop the spread of AIDS.

The severe drought finally came to an end.

NAURU

Island republic in the Pacific Ocean; member of the Commonwealth

Area: 21.2 sq km
Population: 10,400
Capital: Yaren
Income: Not available
Life expectancy: 64.0 (men), 69.0 (women)
Presidents: Kinza Clodumar; Kennan Adeang (until 8 February)

The economy was weak, owing to a drop in world phosphate prices and the poor performance of investments.

In February, Kinza Clodumar was elected Nauru's fifth president in four months.

NEPAL

Constitutional monarchy between India and China

Area: 147,181 sq km
Population: 21,424,000
Capital: Kathmandu
Income: US$200
Life expectancy: 57.6 (men), 57.1 (women)
Monarch: King Birendra Bir Bikram Shah Dev
Prime ministers: Surya Bahadur Thapa; Sher Bahadur Deuba (until 6 March); Lokendra Bahadur Chand (until 4 October)

In March, King Birendra sacked the prime minister and appointed a new one. The new administration, Nepal's fifth coalition government in seven years, introduced measures to liberalize the economy before collapsing after a vote of no confidence.

▲ Crowds cheer the skaters in the 15th Elfstedentocht (Eleven cities) skating tour in The Netherlands. Henk Angenent, leading, won the race, completing the 200-kilometre marathon over ice in 6 hours 49 minutes and 18 seconds.

NETHERLANDS, THE

Constitutional monarchy in northwestern Europe; member of the European Union

Area: 41,526 sq km
Population: 15,619,000
Capital: Amsterdam
Income: US$24,000
Life expectancy: 74.0 (men), 80.0 (women)
Monarch: Queen Beatrix
Prime minister: Wim Kok

Relations with China soured when the Chinese government cancelled a visit from a Dutch trade mission. The minister heading it had supported a European Union resolution condemning China's record on human rights.

In January, 16,000 people competed in the Elfstedentocht, an ice-skating race with a 200-kilometre route through 11 cities. It had not been held for 10 years because the weather had not been suitable.

NEW ZEALAND

Parliamentary democracy in the southern Pacific Ocean; member of the Commonwealth

Area: 270,534 sq km
Population: 3,653,000
Capital: Wellington
Income: US$14,340
Life expectancy: 73.4 (men), 79.1 (women)
Monarch: Queen Elizabeth II
Prime minister: Jennifer Shipley; Jim Bolger (until 17 November)

Both partners in the coalition government lost popularity because the public felt they had no clear policies. Under pressure from his own party, Jim Bolger resigned and was replaced by Jennifer Shipley, who became New Zealand's first woman prime minister.

In September the government returned an area of forest land to a Maori tribe on North Island. It had been taken from the tribe in the 1850s.

NICARAGUA

Republic in Central America

Area: 131,812 sq km
Population: 4,632,000
Capital: Managua
Income: US$380
Life expectancy: 65.8 (men), 70.6 (women)
Presidents: Arnoldo Alemán; Violeta Barrios de Chamorro (until 10 January)

New president Arnoldo Alemán promised to create 500,000 jobs and improve government honesty. Tourism was earmarked for expansion, including the building of nine new hotels.

The government and the Sandinistas reached agreement on compensation for property taken by the Sandinista government, leaving 1,293 foreign claims outstanding.

NIGER

Republic in West Africa

Area: 1,267,000 sq km
Population: 9,389,000
Capital: Niamey
Income: US$220
Life expectancy: 46.9 (men), 50.2 (women)
President: General Ibrahim Baré Maïnassara
Prime minister: Amadou Boubacar Cissé

In January, protesters demanding the full restoration of democracy clashed with police in the capital. A few days later, three opposition leaders were arrested, but after two weeks of violent demonstrations they were released.

The Democratic Renewal Front, the only Tuareg rebel group that had not signed the 1995 peace treaty, finally agreed to do so.

NIGERIA

Republic in West Africa, on the Gulf of Guinea; member of the Commonwealth

Area: 923,768 sq km
Population: 103,460,000
Capital: Abuja
Income: US$240
Life expectancy: 50.8 (men), 54.0 (women)
Chairman of the Provisional Ruling Council: General Sani Abacha

In February, voters were registered. This was the first stage of a gradual return to civilian rule, aimed towards the eventual transfer of power to a civilian president in October 1998.

However, hopes for a peaceful process of political change were marred by bombings. The government accused an opposition party, led by Nobel Prize-winning writer Wole Soyinka, of carrying out the attacks.

NORWAY

Constitutional monarchy in northern Europe

Area: 323,758 sq km
Population: 4,405,000
Capital: Oslo
Income: US$31,250
Life expectancy: 74.2 (men), 80.3 (women)
Monarch: King Harald V
Prime ministers: Kjell Magne Bondevik; Thorbjørn Jagland (until 13 October)

Solid economic growth continued. The number of jobs increased, reducing the unemployment rate to under four per cent.

Norway signed a contract to supply liquefied natural gas to Italy for the next 25 years.

After the general elections the Labour Party was replaced by a centre coalition government.

◄ Nicaraguan university students, armed with home-made mortars, control the lobby of Managua's airport, on 15 July 1997. The students were protesting cuts in government funding.

OMAN

Sultanate in southeast Arabia

Area: 309,500 sq km
Population: 2,265,000
Capital: Muscat
Income: US$4,820
Life expectancy: 68.9 (men), 73.3
(women)
Sultan and prime minister:
Qabus ibn Sa'id

Oman became the first Arab
country to set up diplomatic and trade links with
Israel. However, it changed its policy in March
because new Israeli settlements were being built in
East Jerusalem.

In May, Oman and Yemen signed maps marking
the border between the two countries. The
government also reached agreements with Iran on
sharing natural gas deposits and establishing closer
trade relations.

▼ Dancers perform before portraits of Mohammed Ali
Jinnah, the founder and first governor-general of Pakistan,
and his sister Fatimah, during celebrations to mark 50
years of independence.

PAKISTAN

Federal republic in Central Asia; member of the
Commonwealth

Area: 796,095 sq km
Population: 136,183,000
Capital: Islamabad
Income: US$460
Life expectancy: 62.9 (men), 65.0
(women)
Presidents: Wasim Sajjad
(acting); Farooq Ahmed Leghari
(until 3 December)
Prime ministers: Mohammed Nawaz Sharif; Malik
Meraj Khalid (acting) (until 17 February)

In the February general elections, Benazir Bhutto's
ruling party was resoundingly defeated by the
Pakistan Muslim League. The new government
introduced measures to reduce the powers of the
president and restrict the political role of the army.

The dispute between India and Pakistan over
Kashmir continued and minor border clashes
occurred in the region.

The economy was weak, although the
agricultural sector performed well.

PALAU

Republic in the western Pacific Ocean, made up of a
640-kilometre-long chain of islands

Area: 488 sq km
Population: 17,000
Provisional capital: Koror (a
permanent capital is to be
established on Babelthuap)
Income: Not available
Life expectancy: 69.1 (men), 73.0
(women)
President: Kuniwo Nakamura

Diplomatic relations were
established with the Philippines, and the
government promised that Palau's 5,000 Filipino
workers would be treated fairly.

Plans were under way to set up Palau's first
university.

PANAMA

Republic in Central America

Area: 75,517 sq km
Population: 2,719,000
Capital: Panama City
Income: US$2,750
Life expectancy: 71.8 (men), 76.4
(women)
President: Ernesto Pérez
Balladares

The government approved an

▲ A family in Papua New Guinea paddle across the Fly River near the town of Kiunga, in the Western Province. The river, the largest in the country, is normally over 11 metres deep. The drought has reduced its depth to just 0.2 metres.

independent Panama Canal Authority, in preparation for the handover of the canal from the United States to Panama in 1999. A conference was also held to discuss details of the canal's management.

PAPUA NEW GUINEA

Parliamentary democracy in the southwest Pacific Ocean

Area: 462,840 sq km
Population: 4,400,000
Capital: Port Moresby
Income: Not available
Life expectancy: 57.0 (men), 58.0 (women)
Monarch: Queen Elizabeth II
Prime ministers: Bill Skate; Sir Julius Chan (until 27 March); John Giheno (acting) (until 2 June); Sir Julius Chan (until 22 July)

Fighting continued on the island of Bougainville between government troops and guerrillas seeking independence. In August, new prime minister Bill Skate vowed to seek a peaceful end to the conflict in Bougainville.

Drought and harsh frosts led to severe food shortages in the highlands, where water levels were extremely low.

PARAGUAY

Republic in central South America

Area: 406,752 sq km
Population: 5,089,000
Capital: Asunción
Income: US$1,690
Life expectancy: 67.5 (men), 72.0 (women)
President: Juan Carlos Wasmosy

The government closed three banks after investors withdrew so much money that the banks did not have enough funds to continue trading. The government was then responsible for paying back the banks' remaining investors, which weakened the economy.

PERU

Republic on the west coast of South America

Area: 1,285,216 sq km
Population: 24,371,000
Capital: Lima
Income: US$2,310
Life expectancy: 65.9 (men), 70.9 (women)
President: Alberto Fujimori

The hostage crisis that began in December 1996 ended in April when the army stormed the Japanese embassy. Two soldiers and all 14 Túpac Amaru rebels were killed. The 72 remaining hostages were released.

El Niño – a disruption of the weather pattern that occurs every few years, warming the eastern tropical Pacific – badly affected fish catches and caused a severe drought. This meant that the economy continued its downward trend of the past two years.

PHILIPPINES

Republic of about 7,100 islands in the western Pacific Ocean, in Southeast Asia

Area: 300,076 sq km
Population: 71,570,000
Capital: Manila
Income: US$1,050
Life expectancy: 66.6 (men), 70.2 (women)
President: Fidel V. Ramos

Economic growth declined, partly due to a drought which affected rice crops, and partly due to the currency crisis in Southeast Asia, which caused the Filipino peso to lose value.

A splinter group of Islamic extremists continued

▲ People in central Wroclaw, Poland, pull buckets of drinking water and food up to their apartments, as flood waters cascade through their lower windows.

to carry out guerrilla attacks in the southern islands, despite the 1996 treaty between the government and the Moro National Liberation Front.

POLAND

Republic in eastern Europe

Area: 312,685 sq km
Population: 38,731,000
Capital: Warsaw
Income: US$2,790
Life expectancy: 66.7 (men), 75.7 (women)
President: Aleksander Kwasniewski
Prime ministers: Jerzy Buzek; Wlodzimierz Cimoszewicz (until 31 October)

Poland's political climate changed when a coalition of right-wing parties defeated the former communist alliance in the September general elections.

In July, two flood waves swept north along the Oder River in western Poland, killing 50 people, leaving 40,000 homeless, and destroying 160 bridges and 1,500 kilometres of road.

PORTUGAL

Republic in southwest Europe; member of the European Union

Area: 92,135 sq km
Population: 9,943,000
Capital: Lisbon
Income: US$9,740
Life expectancy: 70.8 (men), 78.0 (women)
President: Jorge Sampaio
Prime minister: António Guterres

Economic growth was strong. The government increased spending on health care and education. It seemed likely that Portugal would qualify to take part in the European Union's economic and monetary union (EMU), due to begin in January 1999.

The government wanted to hand over more powers to regional government, but the opposition strongly objected to this proposal.

QATAR

Monarchy (emirate) on the west coast of the Persian Gulf

Area: 11,346 sq km
Population: 561,000
Capital: Doha
Income: US$11,600
Life expectancy: 70.0 (men), 75.4 (women)
Emir: Sheikh Hamad ibn Khalifah ath-Thani
Prime minister: Sheikh Adbullah ibn Khalifah ath-Thani

The dispute between Qatar and Bahrain over control of several islands in the Persian Gulf moved towards a settlement when both countries agreed to allow the International Court of Justice to rule on the matter.

Qatar suspended ties with Israel after the Arab League decided to restart the Arab boycott of Israel.

ROMANIA

Republic on the Balkan Peninsula in southeastern Europe

Area: 237,500 sq km
Population: 22,572,000
Capital: Bucharest
Income: Not available
Life expectancy: 72.0 (men), 72.0 (women)
President: Emil Constantinescu
Prime minister: Victor Ciorbea

The new government wanted

to introduce major economic and social changes. However, disagreements within the coalition slowed the pace of reform. The government resorted to using decrees in order to pass laws more quickly, although many people regarded this practice as undemocratic.

RUSSIA

Federal republic occupying eastern and northeastern Europe and all of northern Asia

Area: 17,075,400 sq km
Population: 147,231,000
Capital: Moscow
Income: US$2,240
Life expectancy: 58.0 (men), 71.5 (women)
President: Boris Yeltsin
Prime minister: Viktor Chernomyrdin

President Yeltsin re-entered the political arena in March following eight months absence due to ill health. He immediately appointed new ministers to reform Russia's complicated tax system, reduce spending on welfare, and reassert central government's power over regional governments.

The breakaway republic of Chechnya insisted that it was an independent state, while the Russian government still regarded it as part of the Russian Federation. Yeltsin and the Chechnyan president Aslan Maskhadov signed a peace treaty, but Chechnya slipped into anarchy and was ruled by local warlords.

The inflation rate dropped, helping to stabilize the economy. For the first time in eight years, the

▼ A Hutu refugee with her 14-day-old baby arrives in Kigali, Rwanda. They were among thousands of refugees airlifted by the UN out of camps in Zaire, where they lived in appalling conditions.

economy did not decline, although it did not grow either. Private foreign investment increased, reducing Russia's reliance on aid from organizations such as the International Monetary Fund.

In May, Yeltsin signed an agreement with NATO that granted Russia some influence – but no vote – regarding decisions made by the NATO alliance.

Russia and Ukraine agreed on a friendship treaty under which Russia recognized Ukraine's independence and which ended their five-year dispute over the division of the Black Sea fleet.

Relations with other countries in the Commonwealth of Independent States remained tense. Most of them resented Russian dominance of the group.

RWANDA

Republic in Central Africa

Area: 26,338 sq km
Population: 6,853,000
Capital: Kigali
Income: US$180
Life expectancy: 40.8 (men), 43.4 (women)
President: Pasteur Bizimungu
Prime minister: Pierre Celestin Rwigema

In March, about 420 people from the Tutsi tribe were killed on the border between Rwanda and Zaire (now the Democratic Republic of the Congo). It seemed likely that extremists from the Hutu tribe were responsible. The governments of Zaire and Tanzania took steps to persuade Rwandan refugees to return home and more than a million did so. Some 90,000 people remained in Rwandan prisons awaiting trial for crimes against humanity during the 1994 civil war. There was a food shortage caused by a poor harvest, combined with the influx of refugees.

SAINT KITTS AND NEVIS

Island parliamentary democracy in the eastern Caribbean Sea; member of the Commonwealth

Area: 269 sq km
Population: 39,400
Capital: Basseterre
Income: US$5,170
Life expectancy: 63.0 (men), 69.0 (women)
Monarch: Queen Elizabeth II
Prime minister: Denzil Douglas

In October, the Nevis parliament voted to seek separation from St Kitts. A referendum on the issue was scheduled for 1998.

A bumper sugar crop – the largest for more than ten years – was harvested.

SAINT LUCIA

Parliamentary democracy in the eastern Caribbean Sea; member of the Commonwealth

Area: 617 sq km
Population: 144,000
Capital: Castries
Income: US$3,370
Life expectancy: 67.0 (men), 72.0 (women)
Monarch: Queen Elizabeth II
Prime ministers: Kenny Anthony; Vaughan Lewis (until 24 May)

The ruling United Workers' Party (UWP), which had been in power for 30 of the last 33 years, was badly defeated in the general elections, winning only one of the 17 seats.

SAINT VINCENT AND THE GRENADINES

Island parliamentary democracy in the eastern Caribbean Sea; member of the Commonwealth

Area: 389 sq km
Population: 113,000
Capital: Kingstown
Income: US$2,280
Life expectancy: 71.0 (men), 74.0 (women)
Monarch: Queen Elizabeth II
Prime minister: Sir James Fitz-Allen Mitchell

A couple from the United States were tried for the murder of a St Vincent boat-taxi operator. They were freed on the grounds

▼ Hundreds of pilgrims died at a campsite near Makkah, Saudi Arabia, in a stampede to escape a huge fire that engulfed thousands of tents.

of insufficient evidence. The US media angered the government by accusing the nation's legal system of inefficiency.

SAMOA (PREVIOUSLY WESTERN SAMOA)

Constitutional monarchy in the southern Pacific Ocean; member of the Commonwealth

Area: 2,831 sq km
Population: 169,000
Capital: Apia
Income: US$1,120
Life expectancy: 67.0 (men), 71.0 (women)
Head of state: Malietoa Tanumafili II
Prime minister: Tofilau Eti Alesana

Parliament voted in favour of changing the nation's name from Western Samoa to Samoa.

In November, opposition leaders organized a demonstration to demand the government's resignation.

SÃO TOMÉ AND PRÍNCIPE

Island republic off the west coast of Africa, on the Gulf of Guinea

Area: 1,001 sq km
Population: 137,000
Capital: São Tomé
Income: US$350
Life expectancy: 61.8 (men), 65.6 (women)
President: Miguel Trovoada
Prime minister: Raul Bragança Neto

The economy continued to depend on foreign aid. Sixty per cent of the year's finances came from international grants, most of them from the European Union.

SAUDI ARABIA

Monarchy occupying four-fifths of the Arabian peninsula

Area: 2,240,000 sq km
Population: 18,426,000
Capital: Riyadh
Income: US$7,040
Life expectancy: 69.9 (men), 73.4 (women)
King and prime minister: Fahd

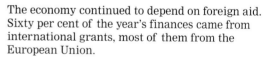

A fire spread through camps full of people taking part in the annual pilgrimage to Makkah, causing more than 300 deaths.

Two British nurses were found guilty of killing

an Australian nurse. One was sentenced to death by beheading, but this sentence was later waived in return for money paid to the victim's family in Australia.

SENEGAL

Republic in West Africa

Area: 196,712 sq km
Population: 8,532,000
Capital: Dakar
Income: US$600
Life expectancy: 50.3 (men), 52.3 (women)
President: Abdou Diouf
Prime minister: Habib Thiam

After a fairly peaceful period, fighting broke out in March between government troops and the Movement of Democratic Forces of Casamance, a group seeking independence for the region of Casamance. Violence then continued throughout the year, forcing thousands to flee to neighbouring Guinea-Bissau.

SEYCHELLES

Island republic in the Indian Ocean; member of the Commonwealth

Area: 455 sq km
Population: 77,300
Capital: Victoria
Income: US$487
Life expectancy: 66.0 (men), 73.0 (women)
President: France-Albert René

Seychelles was no longer dependent on foreign aid. However, it received some money from the European Development Fund to finance projects such as the enlargement of a water treatment plant.

SIERRA LEONE

Republic in West Africa; member of the Commonwealth

Area: 71,740 sq km
Population: 4,424,000
Capital: Freetown
Income: Not available
Life expectancy: 36.0 (men), 39.1 (women)
Government leader: Major Johnny Paul Koroma (from 17 June); President Ahmad Tejan Kabbah (until 25 May)

In May, junior army officers staged a coup. President Kabbah fled abroad. Major Johnny Koroma declared himself head of state, and later set up a military

ruling council. The international community condemned the coup: Nigeria and Guinea sent troops to try to restore Kabbah to power, but this proved unsuccessful.

SINGAPORE

Island republic at the southern end of the Malay Peninsula; member of the Commonwealth

Area: 646 sq km
Population: 3,104,000
Capital: Singapore
Income: Not available
Life expectancy: 75.1 (men), 79.5 (women)
President: Ong Teng Cheong
Prime minister: Goh Chok Tong

The ruling party won the general elections with an overwhelming majority.

The Asian currency crisis hit the economy hard. The Singapore dollar – one of the strongest currencies in Southeast Asia – plummeted in value between June and September. However, Singapore was better equipped to cope with the problem than its neighbours because it had no foreign debt.

SLOVAKIA

Republic in central Europe

Area: 49,035 sq km
Population: 5,372,000
Capital: Bratislava
Income: US$2,950
Life expectancy: 66.6 (men), 75.4 (women)
President: Michal Kovac
Prime minister: Vladimir Meciar

In May, over 90 per cent of the

▼ After the coup in Sierra Leone, a bodyguard of one of the coup leaders stands watch outside the defence ministry in Freetown. He is armed with rocket-propelled grenades.

electorate boycotted a referendum on NATO membership because the government had removed from the ballot a question on the voting system used in presidential elections.

The economy was weakened by an increase in government spending and a growing trade deficit.

SLOVENIA

Republic in the northwestern Balkans

Area: 20,256 sq km
Population: 1,955,000
Capital: Ljubljana
Income: US$8,200
Life expectancy: 69.2 (men), 77.8 (women)
President: Milan Kucan
Prime minister: Janez Drnovsek

General elections were held in November 1996, but no party won a majority. Lengthy talks followed, and a coalition government was finally approved in February.

In July, the government agreed to introduce the reforms needed to qualify for full membership of the European Union, and negotiations began.

SOLOMON ISLANDS

Island parliamentary democracy in the western Pacific Ocean; member of the Commonwealth

Area: 28,370 sq km
Population: 411,000
Capital: Honiara
Income: Not available
Life expectancy: 69.0 (men), 74.0 (women)
Monarch: Queen Elizabeth II
Prime ministers: Bartholomew Ulufa'alu; Solomon Mamaloni (until 27 August)

▼ A member of one of the many Somalian militia groups stands guard over food aid being unloaded from a boat on a flooded river near Bardera.

In May, the government admitted that the economy had been badly managed in the past. The country has large debts and is behind on interest payments.

The economic outlook improved with the establishment of a new gold-mining venture on Guadalcanal, the largest of the Solomon Islands.

SOMALIA

Republic in northeast Africa

Area: 637,000 sq km
Population: 6,870,000
Capital: Mogadishu
Income: Not available
Life expectancy: 47.4 (men), 50.6 (women)
Head of state: Somalia had no functioning government in 1997

The self-declared Republic of Somaliland carried on relatively peacefully, although it did not achieve international recognition. The rest of the country continued to be torn apart by fighting between different groups. Talks resulted in a peace treaty between two of the main groups, but fighting continued in several regions.

There were severe food shortages because of the poor rains of 1996. These difficulties were made worse by severe flooding in many parts of the country towards the end of 1997.

SOUTH AFRICA

Republic occupying the southern tip of Africa; member of the Commonwealth

Area: 1,219,090 sq km
Population: 42,446,000
Capital: Pretoria
Income: US$3,160
Life expectancy: 62.3 (men), 68.3 (women)
President: Nelson Mandela

In February, President Mandela outlined his aims of reducing the budget deficit and increasing exports. He also pointed out the government's successes: between 1994 and 1997 more than a million homes were given access to clean piped water; furthermore, 322,000 houses had been built or were under construction. The nation's healthcare and education systems had also improved.

Crime levels continued to be a major cause for concern. An average of 52 murders were committed every day.

In December, Mandela stepped down as president of the ruling African National Congress (ANC). He was replaced by Thabo Mbeki, who will probably become president when Mandela retires.

SPAIN

Constitutional monarchy in southwest Europe;
member of the European Union
Area: 505,990 sq km
Population: 39,323,000
Capital: Madrid
Income: US$13,580
Life expectancy: 74.9 (men), 81.8
(women)
Monarch: King Juan Carlos I
Prime minister: José María
Aznar López

Euskadi Ta Askatasuna (ETA), a guerrilla group
seeking independence for the Basque people, stepped
up its campaign of violence. After the kidnapping
and murder of a politician from the ruling party,
millions of citizens took to the streets to condemn
ETA for the attack.

Relations with Cuba got worse because the Spanish
government advised tourists not to visit Cuba.

SRI LANKA

Island republic in the Indian Ocean off the
southwest coast of India;
member of the Commonwealth

Area: 65,610 sq km
Population: 18,663,000
Capital: Colombo
Income: US$700
Life expectancy: 70.9 (men), 75.9
(women)
President: Chandrika
Kumaratunga
Prime minister: Sirimavo Bandaranaike

The Liberation Tigers of Tamil Eelam (LTTE)
continued to fight for an independent homeland for
Sri Lanka's two million Tamils. It attacked several
army bases, resulting in huge loss of life on both
sides. Government forces responded with a massive
operation, capturing two towns.

In October, an LTTE bomb in the capital killed 18
people. The two sides could not agree on a basis for
talks.

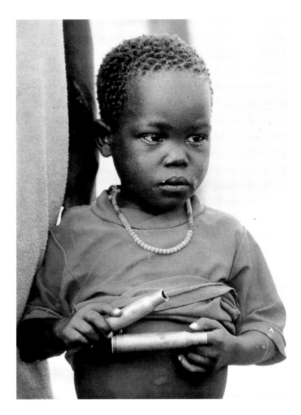

▲ A southern Sudanese child who has fled the war raging
in his home region, holding machine-gun cartridges that he
uses as toys.

In January, rebel National Democratic Alliance
forces captured two Sudanese towns near the
Ethiopian border.

The government and six small southern rebel
groups signed a peace agreement in April. It stated
that a referendum on independence for the south
will be held in 2001.

The United Nations appealed to the international
community for financial help for the 4.2 million
Sudanese citizens affected by the civil war, many of
whom were homeless.

SUDAN, THE

Republic in northeast Africa

Area: 2,503,890 sq km
Population: 32,594,000
Capital: Khartoum
Income: Not available
Life expectancy: 53.6 (men), 56.4
(women)
President and prime minister:
Lieutenant General Omar
Hassan Ahmad al-Bashir

SURINAME

Republic in northern South America

Area: 163,820 sq km
Population: 424,000
Capital: Paramaribo
Income: US$880
Life expectancy: 67.2 (men), 72.4
(women)
President: Jules Wijdenbosch

In April, The Netherlands
decided to prosecute Dési

Bouterse, former military dictator of Suriname and president of the main party in the coalition government. He was accused of trafficking in cocaine. President Wijdenbosch responded by appointing Bouterse to a post that gave him a diplomatic passport.

SWAZILAND

Monarchy in southern Africa; member of the Commonwealth

Area: 17,364 sq km
Population: 1,032,000
Capital: Mbabane
Income: US$1,170
Life expectancy: 57.7 (men), 62.3 (women)
Monarch: King Mswati III
Prime minister: Sibusiso Barnabas Dlamini

King Mswati III had asked for proposed constitutional changes to be submitted to the new constitutional review committee, but many people were frustrated by the slow pace of reform. Opposition groups called for an end to the country's absolute monarchy and the creation of a multiparty democracy.

SWEDEN

Constitutional monarchy in northern Europe

Area: 449,964 sq km
Population: 8,858,000
Capital: Stockholm
Income: US$23,750
Life expectancy: 75.3 (men), 80.8 (women)
Monarch: King Carl XVI Gustaf
Prime minister: Göran Persson

After six years of effort, the government finally achieved economic stability. However, the measures used to attain that goal, such as cuts in welfare budgets, were unpopular with the public.

Although Sweden qualified to join the European Union's (EU) economic and monetary union, the government decided not to take part. This reflected public concern over the issue.

In accordance with the result of a 1980 referendum, the ruling party took steps to begin shutting down Sweden's 12 nuclear reactors, which provided half of the nation's electricity. Industry, trade unions, and opposition parties raised strong objections to the decision.

SWITZERLAND

Federal republic in west central Europe

Area: 41,285 sq km
Population: 7,116,000
Capital: Bern
Income: US$40,630
Life expectancy: 75.1 (men), 81.6 (women)
President: Arnold Koller

At the beginning of the year, the economic outlook was bleak: economic growth was close to zero and the unemployment level had risen steeply. The national debt was high, and the government's measures to reduce spending included imposing public-sector pay cuts.

The government continued negotiations on joining the European Economic Area, a first step towards membership of the European Union.

In September, an armed gang stole 53 million Swiss francs (£23 million) from a Zurich post office. However, by mid-October, 17 people had been arrested and nearly half the money recovered.

SYRIA

Republic in the Middle East

Area: 185,180 sq km
Population: 15,009,000
Capital: Damascus
Income: US$1,120
Life expectancy: 66.7 (men), 71.2 (women)
President: General Hafez al-Assad
Prime minister: Mahmoud Zuabi

Mindful of the improved relationship between Israel and Turkey, Syria took steps to strengthen ties with Iraq, Iran, and Saudi Arabia. A Syrian trade delegation visited Iraq in May to discuss supplying it with food and medicine in exchange for oil. The

◀ More than 13,000 skiers take off in the Vasaloppet ski marathon in Salen, Switzerland. Russian-born Mikhail Botvinov, competing for Austria, won the race.

border between the two countries reopened in June. It had been closed for 15 years.

In June, Syria hosted a meeting of eight Arab countries to discuss the creation of an Arab common market.

TAIWAN

Republic off the coast of China, made up of the islands of Taiwan, Quemoy, and over 80 others

Area: 36,179 sq km
Population: 21,616,000
Capital: Taipei
Income: Not available
Life expectancy: 71.8 (men), 77.7 (women)
President: Lee Teng-hui
Prime ministers: Vincent Siew (from 1 September); Lien Chan (until 21 August)

The government rejected China's view that Taiwan should again become part of China while retaining its own political system.

After the daughter of a television entertainer was kidnapped and murdered, protesters took to the streets to criticize the government for its failure to enforce law and order.

TAJIKISTAN

Republic in Central Asia

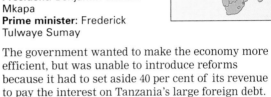

Area: 143,100 sq km
Population: 6,054,000
Capital: Dushanbe
Income: US$340
Life expectancy: 64.2 (men), 70.2 (women)
President: Imomali Rakhmonov
Prime minister: Yahyo Azimov

In June, Tajikistan's civil war ended with the signing of a peace accord between the government and the United Tajik Opposition, an alliance of groups that had been fighting

government forces since 1992.

However, the bloodshed did not end, as small groups of fighters excluded from the peace talks continued to attack both government and opposition forces.

TANZANIA

Republic in East Africa; member of the Commonwealth

Area: 945,090 sq km
Population: 29,461,000
Capital: Dar es Salaam
Income: US$120
Life expectancy: 50.0 (men), 52.8 (women)
President: Benjamin William Mkapa
Prime minister: Frederick Tulwaye Sumay

The government wanted to make the economy more efficient, but was unable to introduce reforms because it had to set aside 40 per cent of its revenue to pay the interest on Tanzania's large foreign debt. To make matters worse, the country was hit by its severest drought for 40 years.

In April, President Mkapa met the Ugandan and Kenyan presidents to discuss setting up an East African common market.

THAILAND

Constitutional monarchy in Southeast Asia

Area: 513,115 sq km
Population: 60,602,000
Capital: Bangkok
Income: US$2,740
Life expectancy: 66.3 (men), 72.3 (women)
Monarch: King Bhumibol Adulyadej
Prime ministers: Chuan Leekpai; Chavalit Yongchaiyudh (until 6 November)

Thailand suffered a severe financial crisis in 1997, sparking social unrest. Production levels dropped and exports declined. The Thai currency (the baht) was put under intense pressure from international currency speculators. At first, the central bank propped up the baht, at huge cost, but eventually it had to abandon this approach. From then on, the baht lost value steadily. The economy was in crisis and the International Monetary Fund stepped in with a financial aid package.

◀ A petrol station attendant updates the price of petrol in Bangkok, Thailand. Prices were increased to raise government revenue to repay a large loan from the International Monetary Fund.

TOGO

Republic in West Africa

Area: 56,785 sq km
Population: 4,736,000
Capital: Lomé
Income: US$310
Life expectancy: 48.8 (men), 51.5 (women)
President: General Gnassingbé Eyadéma
Prime minister: Klutse Kwassi

The European Union agreed to give Togo financial help with healthcare, education, and road-building projects.

Cocoa and coffee exports tripled.

TONGA

Constitutional monarchy in the southwest Pacific Ocean; member of the Commonwealth

Area: 750 sq km
Population: 97,600
Capital: Nuku'alofa
Income: Not available
Life expectancy: 69.0 (men), 74.0 (women)
Monarch: King Taufa'ahau Tupou IV
Prime minister: Baron Vaea

Three journalists linked with the organization seeking democracy were jailed by parliament for publishing details of charges against a government minister before his trial began. They were later released.

TRINIDAD AND TOBAGO

Island republic in the eastern Caribbean Sea; member of the Commonwealth

Area: 5,128 sq km
Population: 1,276,000
Capital: Port of Spain
Income: US$3,770
Life expectancy: 71.5 (men), 76.2 (women)
Presidents: Arthur Napoleon Raymond Robinson; Noor Mohammed Hassanali (until 19 March)
Prime minister: Basdeo Panday

The coalition government's majority increased when two members of the opposition joined it.

▶ Muslims protest the closure of Islamic schools in Istanbul, Turkey. As part of a plan aimed at curbing Islamic extremism, the government will also ban the wearing of traditional Islamic clothing in public.

In February, Arthur Napoleon Raymond Robinson was elected president, succeeding Noor Mohammed Hassanali, who retired.

TUNISIA

Republic on the north coast of Africa

Area: 164,150 sq km
Population: 9,245,000
Capital: Tunis
Income: US$1,820
Life expectancy: 68.4 (men), 70.7 (women)
President: General Zine al-Abidine Ben Ali
Prime minister: Hamed Karoui

European concern about Tunisia's human rights record led to the release from house arrest of former opposition politician Mohamed Mouada.

The International Monetary Fund asked the government to speed up economic reform and reduce unemployment, which stood at 15 per cent.

TURKEY

Republic in southeast Europe and Asia Minor

Area: 779,452 sq km
Population: 63,528,000
Capital: Ankara
Income: US$2,780
Life expectancy: 66.5 (men), 71.7 (women)
President: Suleyman Demirel
Prime ministers: Mesut Yilmaz; Necmettin Erbakan (until 12 July)

The Islamic coalition government's power struggle with the army-backed opposition – which was against religion playing a part in politics – dominated Turkish politics.

In February, army leaders demanded the introduction of eight years of compulsory non-religious education. Erbakan's hesitation over the

issue led to deputies leaving the coalition. With his majority diminished, Erbakan was forced to resign. In August, the military's education proposal became law.

TURKMENISTAN

Republic in Central Asia

Area: 488,100 sq km
Population: 4,695,000
Capital: Ashgabat
Income: US$920
Life expectancy: 61.2 (men), 68.0 (women)
President: Saparmurad Niyazov

The economy was weakened because other countries in the Commonwealth of Independent States were receiving Turkmen gas but not paying for it.

Turkmenistan and Azerbaijan argued over which of them owned oil deposits in the Caspian Sea.

TUVALU

Island constitutional monarchy in the western Pacific Ocean; member of the Commonwealth

Area: 25.6 sq km
Population: 10,300
Capital: Funafuti
Income: Not available
Life expectancy: 67.2 (men), 64.0 (women)
Monarch: Queen Elizabeth II
Prime minister: Bikenibeu Paeniu

The economy depended on foreign aid and money from Tuvaluans living abroad. The government continued to seek work overseas for its citizens.

UGANDA

Republic in East Africa; member of the Commonwealth

Area: 241,038 sq km
Population: 20,605,000
Capital: Kampala
Income: US$240
Life expectancy: 40.4 (men), 42.3 (women)
President: Yoweri Museveni
Prime minister: Kintu Musoke

Uganda's progress with economic reform meant that it qualified for financial help under a World Bank scheme.

Drought hit the east of the country and by June half the population was suffering from famine.

UKRAINE

Republic in eastern Europe

Area: 603,700 sq km
Population: 50,668,000
Capital: Kiev
Income: US$1,630
Life expectancy: 63.6 (men), 74.0 (women)
President: Leonid Kuchma
Prime minister: Valery Pustovoytenko; Pavlo Lazarenko (until 2 July)

In February, the president launched Operation Clean Hands, a programme aimed at stamping out corruption, and in July he sacked the prime minister after criticizing him for not dealing with corruption.

The economic decline continued, despite generous aid from the International Monetary Fund. Crime rates remained high. Unemployment rose and many workers were owed wages. However, foreign investment increased considerably.

UNITED ARAB EMIRATES

Union of seven emirates (Abu Dhabi, Ajman, Dubai, Fujairah, Ras al-Khaimah, Sharjah, and Umm al-Qaiwain) on the eastern Arabian Peninsula

Area: 83,600 sq km
Population: 2,580,000
Capital: Abu Dhabi
Income: US$17,400
Life expectancy: 73.9 (men), 76.5 (women)
President: Sheikh Zaid ibn Sultan an-Nahayan
Prime minister: Sheikh Maktum ibn Rashid al-Maktum

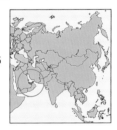

The economy went from strength to strength, and the United Arab Emirates donated large sums of

▼ At a market in central Kiev, in the Ukraine, local people buy cheap second-hand clothes.

money for distribution by organizations such as the International Monetary Fund.

Although the government made efforts to reduce the number of foreign residents, four-fifths of the workforce was foreign.

UNITED KINGDOM

Constitutional monarchy in northwestern Europe; member of the Commonwealth; member of the European Union

Area: 244,110 sq km
Population: 58,919,000
Capital: London
Income: US$18,700
Life expectancy: 74.4 (men), 79.7 (women)
Monarch: Queen Elizabeth II
Prime ministers: Tony Blair; John Major (until 2 May).

In May, the Labour Party won a landslide victory in the general election, after 18 years in opposition.

The Irish Republican Army renewed their ceasefire in July, thereby qualifying to take part in talks on the future of Northern Ireland, which

▼ Britain's prime minister, Tony Blair (centre), who was elected in May, poses with female Labour members of parliament. There are 102 women in the Labour government, the largest number ever.

began in September.

On 1 July, the United Kingdom handed Hong Kong (a former British colony on the south coast of China) back to China.

At the end of August, Diana, Princess of Wales, was killed in a car crash in Paris, France. A remarkable outpouring of public grief followed: millions of bouquets of flowers were laid outside Kensington Palace and Buckingham Palace, in London, and crowds queued for hours on end to write messages in books of condolence.

In September, referendums were held in Scotland and Wales; both voted in favour of establishing their own political assemblies – Scotland by 74 per cent, and Wales by a narrow margin of 50.3 per cent.

The economy achieved steady growth, and in December the unemployment rate reached its lowest figure since 1980.

UNITED STATES

A federal republic of 50 states in North America

Area: 9,363,364 sq km
Population: 267,839,000
Capital: Washington, DC
Income: US$26,980
Life expectancy: 72.6 (men), 78.9 (women)
President: Bill Clinton

The economy achieved outstanding growth, enabling the government to reduce taxes. Unemployment dropped to its lowest level in 25 years. Despite fears that the boom would increase inflation, it remained low. Crime rates – a major concern in cities – declined steadily.

The media raised doubts about some of the people who financed President Clinton's 1996 election campaign. The issue was put before a Senate committee, which concluded that donations from some Chinese businessmen were part of a plan by the Chinese government to exert influence on US politics.

In November the Chinese president, Jiang Zhemin, visited the United States, the first visit by a Chinese head of state for 12 years. He agreed that China would stop giving Iran nuclear aid in return for the United States selling nuclear reactors to China.

A crisis arose when Iraq refused to let UN weapons inspectors continue their task unless six Americans were removed from the team. President Hussein of Iraq also threatened to shoot down US spy planes flying over sensitive Iraqi regions. Clinton strengthened the US military presence in countries surrounding Iraq, and Hussein backtracked and allowed UN inspectors to carry on their search.

▲ Oklahoma City police chaplain, Jack Poe, comforts two young girls in front of the fence surrounding the Oklahoma bomb site in the United States. They had just heard that a Denver jury had sentenced Timothy McVeigh to death for his role in the 1995 bombing.

URUGUAY

Republic in eastern South America

Area: 176,215 sq km
Population: 3,185,000
Capital: Montevideo
Income: US$5,170
Life expectancy: 69.6 (men), 76.1 (women)
President: Julio María Sanguinetti

The economy fared well, with growth of nearly five per cent, and a drop in inflation and unemployment levels. The tourist industry prospered at the beginning of the year, but was later hampered by an increase in violent crime in the capital.

UZBEKISTAN

Republic in Central Asia

Area: 447,400 sq km
Population: 23,664,000
Capital: Tashkent
Income: US$970
Life expectancy: 64.3 (men), 70.7 (women)
President: Islam Karimov
Prime minister: Otkir Sultonov

A car factory set up as a joint Uzbek–South Korean company flourished, and an oil refinery was established, reducing the nation's dependence on imported energy.

In July, Uzbekistan closed its southern border after a nearby Afghan town was captured by the Taliban, the Islamic fundamentalist group which was in control of most of Afghanistan.

VANUATU

Republic in the southwest Pacific Ocean

Area: 12,190 sq km
Population: 176,000
Capital: Vila
Income: US$1,200
Life expectancy: 65.0 (men), 69.0 (women)
President: Jean-Marie Lehe
Prime minister: Serge Vohor

The government tried to reduce spending by privatizing state-owned companies and introducing reforms in the public service.

In January, the president visited China to sign a trade agreement.

VIETNAM

Republic in Southeast Asia

Area: 331,041 sq km
Population: 75,124,000
Capital: Hanoi
Income: US$240
Life expectancy: 64.9 (men), 69.6 (women)
Presidents: Tran Duc Luong; Le Duc Anh (until 17 September)
Prime ministers: Phan Van Khai; Vo Van Kiet (until 25 September)

In May, farmers in the north staged protests about high taxes and official corruption.

As expected, the ruling Communist Party won a large majority in the general elections. A new president and prime minister were appointed.

In November, more than 500 people died and thousands more went missing when Typhoon Linda struck.

VENEZUELA

Republic in northern South America

Area: 912,050 sq km
Population: 22,777,000
Capital: Caracas
Income: US$3,020
Life expectancy: 70.0 (men), 75.7 (women)
President: Rafael Caldera

At the beginning of the year, doctors, university professors, and government workers went on strike, demanding more pay. The government yielded and granted them large rises.

Political divisions and a lack of support in parliament made it difficult for the president to introduce reforms.

Venezuela's economic outlook improved, although the inflation rate was high.

YEMEN

Republic in the southwestern Arabian Peninsula

Area: 555,000 sq km
Population: 16,496,000
Capital: San'a
Income: US$260
Life expectancy: 57.4 (men), 58.4 (women)
President: Major General Ali Abdallah Salih
Prime ministers: Faraj Said ibn Ghanem; 'Abd al-Aziz 'Abd al-Ghani (until 15 May)

Yemen and Eritrea agreed to let a court in The Netherlands settle their dispute over Greater Hanish Island. Relations with Saudi Arabia also improved and further talks were held on marking the border between the two countries.

Foreign donor organizations expressed approval of the government's economic programme, which included spending cuts and privatization.

YUGOSLAVIA

Federal republic in the northern and central Balkans, made up of the republics of Serbia and Montenegro

Area: 102,173 sq km
Population: 10,632,000
Capital: Belgrade
Income: Not available
Life expectancy: 69.8 (men), 75.3 (women)
President: Slobodan Milosevic; Zoran Lilic (until 23 July)
Prime minister: Radoje Kontic

The economy remained weak, largely due to international trade sanctions imposed during the Bosnian war, and the nation's failure to attract foreign investment.

In July, powerful politician Slobodan Milosevic – who was president of Serbia, but was not permitted by the constitution to stand for re-election – became president of Yugoslavia.

The situation in Kosovo, a mainly Albanian region of Yugoslavia that wants to become an independent state, continued to be volatile, despite a 1996 agreement with Serbia.

ZAMBIA

Republic in central southern Africa; member of the Commonwealth

Area: 752,614 sq km
Population: 9,350,000
Capital: Lusaka
Income: US$400
Life expectancy: 42.2 (men), 43.7 (women)
President: Frederick Chiluba

The government continued to carry out reforms, thus ensuring that Zambia qualified for financial aid from abroad. However, the strict economic policy made poverty in rural areas worse.

Tensions rose in August when police fired on an opposition rally, injuring former president Kenneth Kaunda. In October an attempted military coup failed and Kaunda was arrested in connection with this on Christmas Day. He went on hunger strike in protest.

ZIMBABWE

Republic in southern Africa

Area: 390,757 sq km
Population: 11,423,000
Capital: Harare
Income: US$540
Life expectancy: 47.6 (men), 49.4 (women)
President: Robert Mugabe

In July, the government granted public-sector workers a 30 per cent pay rise, in response to strikes.

During a visit to the United Kingdom in October, President Mugabe asked the UK government for money to provide white farmers with compensation for their land, which Mugabe wants to return to black Zimbabweans. This was refused.

◀ A Yugoslav woman holds a toy sword and axe during a demonstration against President Slobodan Milosevic and his government.

WORLD POPULATION TABLE: 1997 ESTIMATES

Afghanistan	23,738,000	Germany	82,143,000	Oman	2,265,000
Albania	3,323,000	Ghana	18,101,000	Pakistan	136,183,000
Algeria	29,476,000	Greece	10,541,000	Palau	17,000
Andorra	64,600	Grenada	98,400	Panama	2,719,000
Angola	10,624,000	Guatemala	11,242,000	Papua New Guinea	4,400,000
Antigua and Barbuda	64,500	Guinea	7,405,000	Paraguay	5,089,000
Argentina	35,409,000	Guinea-Bissau	1,179,000	Peru	24,371,000
Armenia	3,773,000	Guyana	773,000	Philippines	71,570,000
Australia	18,508,000	Haiti	6,611,000	Poland	38,731,000
Austria	8,087,000	Honduras	5,823,000	Portugal	9,943,000
Bahamas, The	287,000	Hungary	10,157,000	Qatar	561,000
Bahrain	620,000	Iceland	271,000	Romania	22,572,000
Bangladesh	125,340,000	India	967,613,000	Russia	147,231,000
Barbados	265,000	Indonesia	199,544,000	Rwanda	6,853,000
Belarus	10,360,000	Iran	62,305,000	Saint Kitts and Nevis	39,400
Belgium	10,189,000	Iraq	22,219,000	Saint Lucia	144,000
Belize	228,000	Ireland	3,644,000	Saint Vincent and the	113,000
Benin	5,902,000	Israel	5,652,000	Grenadines	
Bhutan	860,000	Italy	57,511,000	Samoa	169,000
Bolivia	7,767,000	Ivory Coast	14,986,000	São Tomé and Príncipe	137,000
Bosnia-Herzegovina	3,124,000	Jamaica	2,536,000	Saudi Arabia	18,426,000
Botswana	1,501,000	Japan	126,110,000	Senegal	8,532,000
Brazil	159,691,000	Jordan	4,522,000	Seychelles	77,300
Brunei	308,000	Kazakhstan	16,554,000	Sierra Leone	4,424,000
Bulgaria	8,329,000	Kenya	28,803,000	Singapore	3,104,000
Burkina Faso	10,891,000	Kiribati	82,400	Slovakia	5,372,000
Burma (Myanmar)	46,822,000	Korea, North	24,317,000	Slovenia	1,955,000
Burundi	6,053,000	Korea, South	45,628,000	Solomon Islands	411,000
Cambodia	10,385,000	Kuwait	1,809,000	Somalia	6,870,000
Cameroon	14,678,000	Kyrgyzstan	4,595,000	South Africa	42,446,000
Canada	30,287,000	Laos	5,117,000	Spain	39,323,000
Cape Verde	394,000	Latvia	2,472,000	Sri Lanka	18,663,000
Central African	3,342,000	Lebanon	3,859,000	Sudan, The	32,594,000
Republic		Lesotho	2,008,000	Suriname	424,000
Chad	7,166,000	Liberia	2,602,000	Swaziland	1,032,000
Chile	14,583,000	Libya	5,648,000	Sweden	8,863,000
China	1,222,740,000	Liechtenstein	31,300	Switzerland	7,116,000
Colombia	36,200,000	Lithuania	3,706,000	Syria	15,009,000
Comoros	590,000	Luxembourg	420,000	Taiwan	21,616,000
Congo	2,583,000	Macedonia	1,984,000	Tajikistan	6,054,000
Congo, Democratic	46,674,000	Madagascar	14,062,000	Tanzania	29,461,000
Republic of the		Malawi	9,609,000	Thailand	60,602,000
Costa Rica	3,468,000	Malaysia	21,767,000	Togo	4,736,000
Croatia	4,774,000	Maldives	267,000	Tonga	97,600
Cuba	11,190,000	Mali	9,945,000	Trinidad and Tobago	1,276,000
Cyprus	860,000	Malta	375,000	Tunisia	9,245,000
Czech Republic	10,307,000	Marshall Islands	60,300	Turkey	63,528,000
Denmark	5,284,000	Mauritania	2,411,000	Turkmenistan	4,695,000
Djibouti	622,000	Mauritius	1,143,000	Tuvalu	10,300
Dominica	74,400	Mexico	92,711,000	Uganda	20,605,000
Dominican Republic	7,802,000	Micronesia	107,000	Ukraine	50,668,000
Ecuador	11,937,000	Moldova	4,372,000	United Arab	2,580,000
Egypt	60,896,000	Mongolia	2,373,000	Emirates	
El Salvador	5,662,000	Morocco	27,225,000	United Kingdom	58,919,000
Equatorial Guinea	443,000	Mozambique	18,165,000	United States	267,839,000
Eritrea	3,590,000	Namibia	1,727,000	Uruguay	3,185,000
Estonia	1,463,000	Nauru	10,400	Uzbekistan	23,664,000
Ethiopia	58,733,000	Nepal	21,424,000	Vanuatu	176,000
Fiji	778,000	Netherlands, The	15,619,000	Vietnam	75,124,000
Finland	5,145,000	New Zealand	3,653,000	Venezuela	22,777,000
France	58,616,000	Nicaragua	4,632,000	Yemen	16,496,000
Gabon	1,190,000	Niger	9,389,000	Yugoslavia	10,632,000
Gambia, The	1,248,000	Nigeria	103,460,000	Zambia	9,350,000
Georgia	5,377,000	Norway	4,405,000	Zimbabwe	11,423,000

INDEX

The main events of 1997 in every country in the world are given in *World events*, pages 190–236.

Answers to back cover questions about front cover pictures

Q. *Who won an enormous election victory?*
A. Top left: Tony Blair and the British Labour Party on 1 May 1997. *See page 14.*

Q. *How did the sound barrier get broken?*
A. Top right: *Thrust*, a supersonic car, travelled faster than the speed of sound in the Nevada desert in October 1997.
   See article on page 90.

Q. *Why was an astronaut clinging to the side of a spacecraft?*
A. Bottom left: to repair the *Hubble Space Telescope* in February 1997. *See page 42.*

Q. *When did three US presidents try to help young people?*
A. Middle right: at the Presidents' Summit for America's Future in April 1997 (you can see the date on President Bush's
   sweat-shirt!). *See article on page 30.*

PICTURE CREDITS

t = top, b = bottom, l = left, r = right, c = centre, fc = front cover, bc = back cover

ILLUSTRATORS

Andy Farmer 133; John Flower 44t, 78t; Ken Hooks 132b; Linden Artists: Richard Hook 131/fc; Pete Serjeant 109b/bc.

PHOTOGRAPHS

Allsport 176-81 and 183-89 all pictures, Agence Vandystadt 139b; Courtesy, Andersen Press 114bl; Apex Tim Cliff 146t; Ardea Eric Lindgren 121b; Associated Press 5, 6, 7l&r, 8t, 9, 12bl&r, 14, 15t, 16t, 18t, 20t&b/bc, 21, 25t&b, 26, 27t, 29t&b, 30/fc, 40b, 42t, 67t, 68t, 69, 78b/bc, 81t, 82b, 87t, 89, 97b, 102, 107, 108t&b, 109t, 110t&b, 122, 125t, 140b/fc, 141r, 146b, 164b, 172b, 182, 190, 191, 193, 195-98, 200t, 201, 203, 204, 206-9, 211, 212, 214, 215, 217-19, 221-26, 229-34, 236, NASA 18b, Xinhua 166; Narelle Autio 136; Courtesy, Baygen 129b; BBC 115b, 127; Courtesy, BMG Entertainment 159t&b; Courtesy, Bodley Head/Red Fox 153t, 154b; The British Museum 135t/fc; British Telecommunications plc 137t&b; Tony Bullimore/Jacques Vappillon 58t, 59; Courtesy, Cable Communications Association 100t; Courtesy, California Institute of Technology 36b; Camera Press 163t&b, 164t, 165t, 169, 171, 174, Charles Hopkinson 172t, Anna Malni 111bl, Richard Open 72t, Soren Rud 93, S. Smyth 173; Courtesy, Casio 98t; Courtesy, Children's Express 31b; Colorific Greg Girard/Contact 87b; Courtesy, Creation Records Jill Furmanovsky 158t; Thomas Dallal 86t; Courtesy, Dorling Kindersley 157; Dragon News & Picture Agency 129t; Elite Premier Wayne Plant 96; Courtesy, EMI Classics 162b, Records 161b; Courtesy, English Heritage 160; Courtesy, Evans 156b; Mary Evans Picture Library 134b, 141l; Courtesy, FINCA International Inc 74b, 76b, 77; Courtesy, Foster-Miller Inc 125b; Courtesy, A K Geim, University of Nijmegen 124t; Courtesy, Grameen Bank, Bangladesh 74t; Courtesy, Harper Collins 153br, 155b; Courtesy, Hilton Group 151; Hulton Getty Print 80t; Courtesy, IBM 38, Zurich Research Laboratory 35bl, 37b; INS News Agency 97t; Kent News 121t; Courtesy, Judy Leden 138b; Courtesy, Macmillan 152bl, 154t; Magnum Photos Ltd Ian Berry 80b, Alex Majoli 48t, Martin Parr 45b, Gilles Peress 31b, 32t; John Maizels Raw Vision 142; Courtesy, Models 1 Craig McDean 94b; National Maritime Museum 79b; Network Haviv/SABA 32bl&br; News Team International 115t; NHPA Christopher Ratier 126b; Courtesy, Oxford University Press 155b; Panos Pictures 54, Jean Leo Dugast 112, Zed Nelson 73t, Sandrine Rousseau 55b, Paul Smith 72b, Sean Sprague 73t, Chris Stowers 53, 111t; Peter Payne 143t; Courtesy, Philips Music Group 161t; Popperfoto, 15b, 22b, 28, 36t, 40t, 42b, 51b, 58b, 60t, 61t&b, 62t&b, 63t&b, 116b, 117t, 210, 213, AFP 132t, 199, Reuters fc, bc, 3, 4, 5, 8b, 10t&b, 11, 13, 16b, 17, 19, 22t, 23, 24, 27b, 47t&b, 55t, 56, 71, 76t, 90, 91t/fc&b, 105, 108c, 150b, 192, 194, 200b, 202, 205, 216, 220, 227, 235; PPL J McDonough 139t; Press Association AFP124b; Courtesy, Puffin 152t&br; Quadrant Picture Library 126t; Courtesy, Results Education 73b; Rex Features fc, 4-5, 51t, 52, 64t, 75b, 79t, 81b, 82t, 84t, 88, 92t&b, 95t&b, 100b, 101t&b, 104t&b, 113t&b, 114r, 116t, 117b, 118t&b, 119, 120t&b, 143b, 145b, 148b, 158b, 162t, 168t&b, 170t&b, SIPA 34t&b, 65t, 85b, 111br, 165b, 175l&r; Roslin Institute 64b, 66, 67b, 68b; Courtesy, Saatchi Gallery 144 all pictures; SABA Shepard Sherbell 31t; Science Photo Library 86b, 128, 130, Alex Bartel 15b, Tony Craddock 123b, P. Dumas 39t, Manfed Kage 37t, Kairos/Latin Stock 35br, James King-Holmes 70t&c, Bud Leuhausen 123t, Bill Longcore 85b, Will & Dent McIntyre 98b, NASA fc, 41, 43t&b, North Carolina State University 35t, David Parker 99, W.A. Ritchie/Roslin Institute 70b; Mike and Judy Smith 44b, 45t, 46 all pictures, 48b, 49, 50t&b; Courtesy, Spindlewood 156t; Frank Spooner Pictures 83, J. L. Bulcao/Liaison 150t, Kurita Kaku 149b, Mohamed Lounes 149t, Gilly Saussier 148t; Courtesy, Professor Fraser Stoddart 39; John Stoddart 94t; Justin Sutcliffe 145t; Craig Swan 228; Sygma A. Balaguer 106, S. Compoint 147/bc; Times Newspapers Ltd Andre Camara 135b, Peter Nicholls 140t/bc, Simon Walker 57; Christine Titterington 138t; Courtesy, Walker Books 153bl; Courtesy, Web TV 103.